S0-AFX-849

Visible Histories: Women and Environments in a Post-War British City

Visible Histories

Women and Environments in a Post-War British City

SUZANNE MACKENZIE

McGill-Queen's University Press
Montreal and Kingston, London, Buffalo

© McGill-Queen's University Press 1989
ISBN 0-7735-0712-4

Legal deposit first quarter 1990
Bibliothèque nationale du Québec

Printed in Canada on acid-free paper

Canadian Cataloguing in Publication Data

Mackenzie, Suzanne, 1950–
 Visible histories, mobile geographies: women and
 environments in a post-war British city
 Includes index.
 Bibliography: p.
 ISBN 0-7735-0712-4
 1. Women – Great Britain – Social conditions –
 Case studies. 2. Women – England – Brighton –
 Social conditions. 3. Human ecology – England –
 Brighton. 4. Brighton (England) – Social
 conditions. I. Title.
 HQ1600.B74M33 1989
 305.4'2'0942256   C89-090147-3

This book has been published with the help of a
grant from the Canadian Federation for the Humanities, using funds provided by the Social Sciences and
Humanities Research Council of Canada.

*For Alan and for all the others who believe
we do create our own futures*

Contents

Tables

Illustrative Material

Preface

The joy and the difficulty of writing recent social history and geography are that its makers are living to read it. The joy is in the intersection of the readers' and writers' lives, the number of times one can stop and say "yes, that happens" or "no, it wasn't like that." This intersection allows us to put ourselves, very immediately, in context and to add details of our own daily experience: the rooms we sit in as we read and write, the families we will eat dinner with in an hour, the jobs we will go to tomorrow.

The difficulty is that there is almost too much richness, too many connections, too much feeling. As we read and write, we have to enter into, live out and, take responsibility for the ideas we are absorbing. We have to carry them into our daily lives and connect them to our own environments and our own goals.

Sometimes this joyful and difficult immediacy allows us to dismiss the significance of our own creation of history and geography, as if the thousands of details that make up our lives and thereby our histories and geographies are less important than things that happened long ago and far away, things that – *because* they happened long ago and far away – can be put into a few telling words, encapsulated in concepts and theory, given a resonance that lends them significance.

This is especially true of the history and geography of people who are women. Because so much of what women do is concerned with the reproduction of human life in a market-based society, the specific and essential events and places they create are often taken for granted, seen as natural, and rendered invisible in the social record. So much of what women have created is seen to be over or finished rather than achieved.

For example, in the late 1980s, we read and hear that feminism is dead, that we are living in a post-feminist era. Perhaps this is because women have created so much, so effectively, and in such immediate ways that their achievements have become common sense; they have merged into the fabric of daily life and we have forgotten that it was ever different. As this book documents, women have accomplished so much to change the ways we live our day-to-day lives that it is possible, and essential, to move on to new issues. Women have moved from the simple but immensely difficult beginning stages of making their public presence felt – a stage which resurfaced in the 1960s and 1970s and created a good deal of noise and publicity – to the more complex process of changing the fundamental structures of life to meet their needs, to consolidating some gains, even to enjoying some of the fruits of their efforts.

This book argues that women and men constantly create history and geography. They do so incrementally, in their day-to-day activities. In this process, changes in the activities carried out by women and men, and changes in the social environment through which they effect these changes, are interwoven. It is difficult to explore one set of changes without encountering the other. Change is created in and through the environment, and the environment holds it, freezes it, and allows us to recognize change and to see its implications.

In the late 1980s the process is becoming, as it was in the late 1960s and early 1970s, increasingly public and increasingly contested; it is involving more and more people in the attempt to extend non-restrictive gender relations and in the attempt to create more rigid ones. This is taking place in a period of economic and social restructuring that is altering not only people's lives and work but also the nature of places where they live and work.

Now, as ever, it is important to recapture our history and geography – and ourselves in our history and geography – to see how we have rebuilt ourselves and the places we live and work, and how we can move on. This attempt to make visible the actions which made up a specific history and geography, which created and changed a time and place, is what motivates this book. It attempts to give the actions of ordinary women and men, living ordinary lives, the significance they deserve.

Not surprisingly, the writing of this book has been both joyful and difficult. The research and writing has spanned many years of my life. It began as a D.Phil thesis at the University of Sussex. I have revisited it on a number of occasions, in a number of settings to add new ideas and bring new perspectives to bear on it. It is impossible to name all the people who were part of this process. The body of the work and the bibliography acknowledges many of them. The following names a few.

I said some years ago that Andrew Sayer was a supervisor, colleague, and friend worth crossing the Atlantic for, and that I was only beginning to realize the importance of what I learned from him. I know now I shall continue to learn from him, often with a sense of recognition, sometimes with a sense of surprise. It was Peter Goheen who first told me that writing history and geography would never get any easier but who made it clear, by example, that it was worthwhile. People in a variety of places not only helped me understand history and geography, but figured importantly in my history and my increasingly extensive geography: in England, Sophie Bowlby, Jo Foord, the Olivers, Di Perrons, and Monica Willis; in British Columbia, the Mackenzies, Margaret Tessman, and Wendy Hurst; in Toronto, Bruce Becker and Katharine Willson; in Kingston, John Holmes, Katrina Hendrickx, Evelyn Peters, Becki Ross, and Bob Stock; and in Ottawa, Fiona Mackenzie and Iain Wallace, as well as members of the geography departments at Queen's and Carleton. I would like to thank Peter Goheen and Joan McGilvray of McGill-Queen's University Press; Joan Irving, whose copy editing was actually fun to work with; and Chris Earl, who created the maps. Above all, I wish to acknowledge the many women and men who are characters in this book, as well as my friends and colleagues, Roberta Hamilton, Fran Klodawsky, Audrey Kobayashi, Sally Mackenzie, Alan Nash, Katy Oliver, and Damaris Rose, who, among others, demonstrated just how collective academic work should be, and with whom I am still, gratefully, living and learning.

Visible Histories

1 / Changing Women, Changing Environments

In the decades since the end of World War II, the British welfare state has been created, criticized, and cut back; an apparently limitless economic boom has metamorphosized into "recession" and then "deindustrialization"; the face and function of cities has altered, often beyond recognition or recall; and two generations of women and men have come to maturity, living lives that both resemble and contradict the lives their parents and grandparents lived. In short, people have made history and geography. They have transformed the places where they live and work and altered the activities that make up life and work. They have also changed the nature of what it means to be a woman or a man in society. This book talks about this process, about how, in one city – Brighton, in East Sussex – in one period – the decades between the war and the early 1980s – the activities of women changed the conditions and the content of their lives and the nature of their city.

Throughout this period women's lives, their organizations, and their self-definitions had been conditioned by the fact that the primary job of most women was that of being a mother and housewife. Yet women changed the nature of maternity and domestic work in fundamental ways. Through extending control over their fertility, they limited and shortened the time they spent bearing and nursing children. By the early 1960s this activity took up only 6–7 percent of women's adult lives. [1] Women had severed the association between maternity and a life of full-time work. They had also changed the form of the families in which they lived and worked. No longer were their lives ruled by an "immutable" and "biologically natural" cycle.

Being a housewife had also altered radically. The work involved, the physical place in which it went on, the resources called upon, had all been altered – by smaller families, by the growth of state services to the family and community, and by the expansion of consumer commodities into the home. In the early 1980s, domestic labour was still time-consuming and demanding. But much of the energy that women had spent carrying water up flights of stairs and tending open fires in crowded, pest-ridden rooms in the interwar period was now spent travelling between shops, council housing offices, community centres, and doctor's offices in a more geographically extensive city. The social invisibility and the geographic isolation of the housewives' role was being tempered as these women spilled into the community.

For more and more women, being a housewife had come to include contributing financially to family resources through wage work. Between 1951 and 1971, the British labour force increased by 2.5 million; 2.2 million of these new workers were women.[2] In the early 1960s, combining wage work with unpaid domestic work became a routine feature of many women's lives and the lives of their families; the practice also became entrenched in the wage-labour sphere. Women's lives, organizations, and self-definitions had become conditioned by a dual role. Their primary job as housewife and mother was combined, for a majority of women for most of their adult lives, with a wage-earning job.

Women had thus fundamentally altered biological reproduction, domestic-community work, and wage work – the three areas which made up the fabric of their lives. And as they did so, they altered two of the fundamental institutions which structured their lives: the gender category "woman" and the social environments in which they lived and worked.

For both women and men, although perhaps more noticeably for women, daily life is structured by a set of social understandings – rules about what a woman or a man is and about what she or he should be doing. These rules are so embedded in daily life that they often go unnoticed, except when we overstep their boundaries and do things which are new, or "inappropriate." It is then that we begin to discover how pervasive the boundaries of gender are, how much they structure the wheres and the wherebys of our lives. Daily life is structured by a built environment, a complex set of resources created by past generations of women and men and by our own generation. We move around this, utilize it, alter it, again, often unconsciously, until we overstep its boundaries – until we need things which are not there, find we must travel too far to obtain what we need, or find that the environment gets in our way. Instead of being passive and unexamined, the environment becomes evident and obtrusive, something we must try to alter. And we attempt to alter it using what is already there, using the resources it provides us. These two kinds of "overstepping" often occur together. When the work that women and men do changes significantly, they come up against the restrictions of obsolete gender understandings and obsolete environments. Consciously or inadvertently, their new activities result in changing definitions of gender and in new environments, including new cities, which more closely reflect and reinforce new forms of activity.

Stepping over these dual boundaries has been a feature of life in Brighton for the past forty years. Women altered the nature of maternity and marriage, and of domestic-community and wage work, by changing the way they did these things, by reorganizing the places where they did them, and by reordering the understanding of what was necessary and appropriate for women to do. Many of the changes that contributed to this were unintentional and, apparently, disconnected. They were rarely recognized as politically or socially significant. But in combination they created an altered social reality – one shot through with new opportunities and new conflicts.

This book is a history of some of these changes and some of the women and men who created them. Although it looks back across the post-war period, and even beyond that, it is primarily made up of the words and memories of women in Brighton in the early 1980s.

The early 1980s were something of a watershed. Margaret Thatcher's government had just been elected. Despite increasing cutbacks in social services and a philosophy of "rolling back the state," many people still assumed that the painfully constructed and massively flawed welfare state of the post-war period was workable and should be maintained. But the recession was taking hold of many people's lives; men and women were losing their jobs. Assumptions about the majority of men having secure, life-time jobs were beginning to change, and questions about women's "right to work" for wages were being raised. But restructuring and deindustrialization were not yet household words.[3]

This is therefore a story which freezes that period of time when Britain as a whole, and Brighton – on the southeastern fringes of Britain – were poised for a series of massive social changes. It is also primarily a story told from the point of view of women, that numerical majority of the population whose lives and histories have been largely invisible until recently. The possibility of making them visible is, in part, an outcome of a renewed women's movement.

Itself part of the altered social reality women have created, the women's movement is making explicit the connections among, and the importance of, the varied activities that are incrementally changing cities and the lives of people living in them. The women's movement and the body of feminist analysis which has emerged from it have provided some semblance of a coherent politics and theory making women, as a social group, and women's activities more socially visible. This movement and analysis have assembled the multitude of myths, actions, ideals, and struggles which constitute the gender category "woman" and define women as social actors. It has connected the largely invisible and apparently disparate problems facing women – as wage workers, domestic-community workers, state and retail clients, mothers, sexual beings – and socially located them as *women's* issues. It has named the politically discounted and divergent actions and organizations of women as *women's* organizations. And, as the limitations of legal and formal solutions to these problems became increasingly evident, it redefined issues and organizations as *social* issues and organizations.[4]

The rediscovery of forgotten classics by earlier feminists,[5] and ongoing explorations into history and anthropology, have determined that the patterns of activity by women and men, and the constitituents of sexuality, are historically constructed, reinforced, and changed. The form women's activities take, and thus the constitution and change of the gender category woman, is embedded in social process. Changing this position requires an alteration in all the social relations of life and work. Understanding changes in women's lives in the past involves re-examining the whole social fabric. Feminists have attempted to discover the social origin of women's oppression and to identify how it is reproduced and can be altered. Such work is essentially a study of how sexual differences become translated into and reproduced as gender relations and differences.

Sex categories are those defined by biological differences in reproductive organs and biological capacities. At the most fundamental level, the sex category "woman" is defined as a human being with the capacity for reproduction of her kind, and the sex category "man" as a human being lacking this capacity but able to impregnate a woman. Gender categories are social constructions. They are definitions of the social capabilities and appropriate activities of men and women and of the nature of femininity and masculinity.[6]

The division between sex and gender is not rigid. Many aspects of biological sexuality are socially influenced. Certainly gender categories can be and are occupied by people of either sex; the link between sex and social activity can be broken down.[7]

A growing number of feminists have suggested that the translation of sex into gender can, in the simplest terms, be understood "in terms of the relations of production and reproduction at various moments in history."[8] This perspective derives from and builds upon Frederick Engels' statement that "the determining factor in history is, in the last resort, the production and reproduction of immediate life. But this itself is of a two-fold character."[9] The maintenance of any society requires two kinds of work: the work of producing "the means of subsistence, of food, clothing and shelter and the tools requisite therefore" and the "production of human beings themselves." Social life in any period is "conditioned by both forms of production." And history can be seen as the interrelated development of the process of production and the process of reproducing people.[10]

The latter, the reproduction of people, is a complex social process involving much more than the act of giving birth. It involves generational reproduction – the bearing and socialization of children – and the daily renewal of people's capacities: the provision of food, rest, recreation, tension management, and sexual activity, as well as the maintenance of the milieu in which these take place. The process of reproducing people thus involves both biological and social maintenance.

According to this perspective women, whether or not they are mothers, have been historically defined as central to reproductive work. The relations between production and reproduction have altered, thereby changing women's social position. The kind of activity necessary to produce goods and services in society – whether in a gathering-and-hunting or an industrial society – and the organization of these activities determine the content of women's work (just as they do men's). But the content of women's work also includes the activities of reproduction. These activities, which may make up the greatest proportion of their work, mediate women's participation in production. Similarly, the institutions in which production and reproduction go on – whether a private family setting or a "public" place, in co-operation with others or alone – and most especially the extent to which the two sets of activities are integrated in women's lives, will determine women's social and environmental position, their social and geographic mobility (where they can and where they must go), and their status in the community. So, while women have consistently had primary responsibility for the reproduction of people, the social meaning of this work, the social position attributed to it and attainable through it, has varied with the organization of production and reproduction. Though some form of production and reproduction is necessary to ensure the survival of any society, the way these activities are organized and the way they are related to one another has varied over history. As they varied, so did men's and women's activities, gender categories, and the social environment.

WOMEN AND ENVIRONMENTS

In pre-industrial Britain, the family was the basic social unit – the primary unit for producing social goods and services, as well as for reproducing people. Although there was a distinct gender division of labour, women and men had both productive and reproductive roles; these were spatially and temporally integrated within the family's living and working place. Nearly everyone lived and worked in family units. For most parents, there was no separate time for education or childcare; teaching and supervising children were part of producing goods or maintaining the household. Most cities were small, made up of a series of home workshops and a few special-purpose areas, primarily churches and markets. Production, which was mainly for local markets, was regulated by the size and needs of the immediate population. Individual productivity was relatively low; almost everyone, regardless of age or sex, worked, and, more often than not, people worked in the same building in which they ate and slept. This unity of all aspects of life meant that gender relations were often immediately oppressive. It also meant that women's activities were visible socially and thus given more importance. There is considerable evidence that women in pre-industrial society were, in many respects, less restricted than those in early industrial society.[11]

The establishment of industrial, capitalist relations of production and reproduction presupposed the disintegration of this direct unity of production and reproduction.[12] Production moved out of the home into workshops, factories, and offices. There was a separate time for productive work and generally a separate place for such work, though the activities of caring for children and adults remained in the home. From its local orientation, which was restricted by the needs and resources of the family unit, production began to respond to global demands. It did so in cities that were increasingly large and increasingly crowded.

People's lives had fundamentally altered. Family members moved outside the family core to become part of a wage-labour system. They left home to go work in a separate place, for a specified time determined by someone else, generally producing things they did not need and did not own. For this they received a wage that they used to buy necessities produced by someone else. These they took back to a distinct living space to be pooled with those purchased by other family members, in order that they could renew themselves and be ready for work again the next day.

In the early industrial period, individual productivity was still relatively low, as were wages, so that everyone in the family had a wage job of some kind. But by the late nineteenth century, due to increases in productivity – the result of increasingly sophisticated machinery and a greatly rationized economic infrastructure – the majority of people no longer needed to be directly involved in production. First children and then women were gradually restricted and discouraged from productive work. Childhood became a distinct phase of life, one with a specific responsibility: to absorb sufficient education to make the child a useful future worker. Gender roles also became more distinct. The housewife became the feminine ideal, and the reality, for a growing number of women. Her role also carried specific responsibilities: biological reproduction and domestic-community work in the now separate home and residential neighbourhood. Men, in many families, were defined as the sole breadwinner, the legal and political head of the family.

These divergent roles were reflected and reinforced in an increasingly complex and separated city. In it areas for "work" – generally central industrial-commercial districts – were separated from areas for "life" – suburban residential districts where the home was complemented by a range of schools, shops, and services to assist the family, especially the housewife, in reproducing the work force. The home and its neighbourhood had become separate places, places associated with "living" and with the whole complex of things that was not productive work. Home and neighbourhood were places for bearing and educating children, for rest and recreation, for cooking and eating meals and changing clothes, and for expressing emotion and sexuality. All of these activities, which were separated from the public business of making a living, were seen as personal and private activities. And because women were there, in the home and community, making it work, they became associated with these activities. Women were viewed as naturally suited for this private life – as nurturant, emotional, sexual, and, often, weak.

The separation of productive aspects of life, called "work," from re- productive aspects of life, called "life," thus led, over time, to the creation of several more associated dichotomies: the separation of economy from social life or family; of producing from consuming; of workplace from home; of market rationality and scientific logic from emotion and irrationality; of the political from the personal; of women from men. People talked about "where they worked" as distinct from "where they lived," as if wage work were somehow not part of life, or as if no work went on in the home.

This complex separation of work from life also had some strong normative connotations. The priorities and behaviours appropriate to work were, as far as possible, abstracted from life – from birth, nurturing, compromise, feeling, and idiosyncracy. Work, the economy, came to be run, so far as possible, not for its human creators but in order to achieve some set of abstract goals, some internally rational ends which were themselves human creations. In this view, life and the people who live it must adapt to work. People, being reduced to "workers" or "labour," must move their homes, educate themselves, regulate their hours and their emotions, and socialize their children to conform to the requirements of these economic goals and ends.

Women, in the period after World War II, were not wholly successful in doing this, largely because they were defined in terms of the latter set of associations in the dichotomies – in terms of "life", the private reproductive activities. They worked as well as lived in the spaces designated for nurturing, emotion, childcare. They carried out the activities necessary to sustaining life. In the decades after the war, they began to

move in increasing numbers into the public set of spaces, the ones defined as productive, logical, work spaces. But when women adapted their
time and priorities to take on productive work in the 1950s, 1960s, and
1970s, they became not workers but "women workers," or "working
mothers," a recognition that they remained, to some extent, exceptions
to the "norm," that they also had another, primary job to do.

Being women in the post-war period meant that they encountered
constant spatial and temporal dislocation and contradiction. Due to their
separation from the market norm in the nineteenth and early twentieth
century, women had become not just different but "abnormal" and "exceptional."[13] In the mid-twentieth century, they either worked and lived
wholly in the idiosyncratic and secondary spaces of life, or moved back
and forth between work and life. The social definition of women as the
"other" permeated all of their actions and experiences. The language
of history and social analysis, ostensibly an human language, was based
largely on male experience.

The language used to describe women's experience and "nature" was
one which had become permeated with ideas of passivity, mystery, idiosyncracy, and unpredictability. Attempts to move out of this circle of
language and the experience it connoted were seen as a denial of "wom-
anliness."[14] In talking about their experience, women not only had to
reconcile the difficulties of two contradictory messages – one for people
and one for them – but simultaneously had to redefine the experience
and language of "woman" to include action, pattern, creativity, and
historical effectiveness and attempt to incorporate this new femininity
into the experience and language of "human."

It was this set of physical and ideological dichotomies which women
in Brighton were unravelling during the four decades from the 1940s
to the 1980s. As they altered their activities in the areas of biological
reproduction, domestic-community work, and wage labour, they gave
the gender category woman a new set of associations, a new, or amended,
content, and a new language. They created new resources and new
environments. They did so from the material base provided by the
separate home and community, and a separated city – an environment
which reflected and exacerbated the social and ideological contradictions
in their lives.

The city in which they did so, Brighton, occupies a special place in
the geographical and historical imagination of many Britons. Lying directly south of London, Brighton is a central point in what a *New Society*
writer in 1980 called the "wealthy and mysterious Deep South of England."[15] (See map 1.) The wealth, if not the mystery, is relative. Since
World War II, the long-standing cultural and economic differences between the North and the South of England have sharpened. Measured

Map 1   Southern England

by conventional economic standards, the southeast in 1980 was the most affluent area of England,[16] and Sussex, hugging the south coast and rolling into the downs toward London, appeared to epitomize prosperity and a timeless, bucolic graciousness. Brighton, together with the adjacent city of Hove, is the largest centre in East Sussex (see map 2). At its core, girdled by Regency terraces, sits George IV's flamboyant holiday home, the Royal Pavilion. Its central areas, though irrevocably stamped as once-royal, are now slightly tawdry. Still Brighton is a popular seaside resort.

Among the many resort towns which line the south coast, Brighton has been peculiarly favoured. By the early seventeenth century it was the largest town in Sussex. By 1750 its importance as a fishing and trade centre was overtaken by its popularity as a spa town. The visits of the Prince Regent, later George IV, in the late eighteenth century, increased its popularity.[17]. The opening of the direct London-Brighton railway

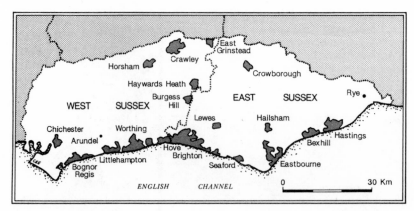

Map 2   East and West Sussex

line in 1841 made the town accessible to visitors of more modest means and to affluent commuters working in the London area. Throughout the nineteenth century and into the twentieth, the town continued to grow as a resort, commuter, and retirement centre.

Its "wealth and mystery" was, however, predicated upon the relative poverty of the majority of Brightonians. From its earliest development, Brighton was built and serviced by a large pool of poorly paid workers whose problems were made worse by a high cost of living.[18]

The invisibility of the base of Brighton's apparent prosperity was exacerbated by the fact that local authorities "have generally been loath to acknowledge, at least publically, the existence of such poverty and disadvantage."[19] The official political climate, dominated by the affluent, was a conservative one, and "compared with the situation in many other parts of Britain, the extent to which the public sector has ameliorated poverty is minimal."[20] The New Society envisaged in the post-war welfare state was either resisted or accepted only reluctantly by local governments. Brighton continued to be a low-wage, often high-unemployment area.[21] There was minimal public housing and even that concentrated largely on diffusing and isolating lower-income people into suburban estates. Social services were often gained only after concerted campaigns and considerable self-provisioning.[22] The conservative hue of local politics meant that, in the 1970s and 1980s, local authorities cut social service expenditure "with vigour and enthusiasm."[23]

These features of local place, history, and politics coloured the way in which women, and men, in Brighton contributed to the complex set of interlocking local histories and geographies which made up contemporary Britain. The interdependence of affluence and poverty, of conservatism and resistance, mediated Brighton's place in creating and changing British society and environment. In some instances the activities of Brighton women were typical of the activities of women throughout and beyond Britain in that they responded to and helped create national and global processes. In other instances the activities of the Brighton women were idiosyncratic, a reflection of the unique character of the people and place. Most actions were both typical and individual. Brighton, like anywhere else, is thus neither representative nor exceptional. It is an unimitative and inimitable part of the development of post-war Britain.[24]

The following chapters will trace this process. Chapters 2 and 3 set the stage, chapter 2 by looking at women's organization in Britain in the interwar and wartime periods and chapter 3 by describing the city of Brighton and the research carried out there. Subsequent chapters document the social history of women in post-war Brighton, focusing on changes in the urban fabric as a whole, and in women's domestic working conditions. Having outlined what women had to work with, chapters 5, 6, and 7 describe what they did with it, specifically how they acted and organized around issues of fertility, childbirth, childcare and wage work, and the concluding chapter pulls some strands together in a discussion of the Brightonian – and British – feminist tradition.

The tension inherent in this history is explicit in its telling. The book is written largely in a "feminine voice,"[25] and it is primarily about women. This is not, however, a history or geography of women. It simply writes about human experience from the relatively unfamiliar and, for some, uncomfortable perspective of the female part of humanity. Most pre-feminist history and geography writes about people as men, with occasional and specific references to women. This book does largely the opposite. It does so not from choice but because the experience of men and women is still sufficiently different, even contradictory, and the languages used to describe these experiences sufficiently diverse, that a truly "human" history or geography is not yet fully possible.

This book is, however, a human historical geography in that it recognizes that history and geography are never inevitable, because they are created by people whose activities and decisions can never be fully determined.[26] There were, in post-war Brighton, an infinite number of ways of doing things. The ways people chose and the choices that were forced upon them created, recreated, and changed a series of mercurial and powerful women and environments.

2 / Creating the Preconditions: Women in Britain in the Interwar and Wartime Periods

Throughout history women have been active and effective. They have changed things. They have done so neither easily nor freely. But neither have they been the eternal victims of forces beyond their control. Women can and do act. Their choice is not whether or not to change their lives. The problem, the choice, is whether or not they have the resources to take control of that change, to take responsibility for the implications of their actions, and to use these actions and their implications to achieve their goals.

Whatever those goals may be, taking control involves understanding both the constraints under which we act and also the power we have to change, not only the parameters of social constraints, but, much more significantly, the way we live on a day-to-day basis. It is these petty, routine details that make up the parameters of constraint, that reproduce or alter constraints. These details are, at once, most accessible to change and difficult to change. In many respects it is easier to alter gender differences in property laws than it is to change the way we speak to our children and friends over the dinner table. It is easy enough to put equal-opportunity legislation in place, although the campaigns to achieve this end may be long and arduous. What is difficult is finding new ways of talking to and thinking about fellow workers, new ways of allocating work tasks and organizing work places.

Action and understanding of this kind can never be complete. It is always muddy, often contradictory, frequently painful. Above all it is action and understanding that is never still. We are constantly having to re-evaluate the situation, to go back and begin again, to try another way, either because the present – the immediate context within which we think and act and remember – has changed, or because we have encountered a new set of memories and rescued another part of history. The implications of what we do are often evident only in retrospect. Even then, history, and our memories of it, changes as we live out its implications.

But retrospect, which is history women and those around them have made, can be useful. In fact, it is essential to the ordering of their lives. The world that women in post-war Brighton inherited was not a newly washed one. It was one which they, as well as their mothers and grandmothers, had helped create. Women's organization in the interwar period in Britain contributed to and prefigured the post-war welfare state and the new labour processes in the home and community and in the wage sphere. Post-war women were living out the results of their own actions and those of previous generations.

WOMEN'S ORGANIZATION IN THE INTERWAR PERIOD

Women's position in the interwar period was, at once, one of apparent powerlessness and one of central – although socially and economically unrecognized – importance. On the one hand women, confining their persons and concerns to the home, had become increasingly dependent on a single male wage while becoming progressively less able to affect the development of the wage-labour sphere. On the other hand, the demands women made and the networks they established to cope with these problems challenged the concept of a "family wage" and prefigured a new relation between family and economy. The actions of women were thus crucial both in the extent and direction of the social and economic upheavals of the 1920s and 1930s and in the course of regulatory change.

Women's Working Conditions

The home and community were the primary workplaces for interwar women. Women's entry into the labour force during World War I had been circumscribed with restrictions and with the insistence that the situation was temporary. The participation of women in the wage-labour force, especially that of married women, declined in most areas after the war.[1]

During the 1920s and 1930s women's domestic work was characterized by an identity of home and workshop. A woman "eats, sleeps, 'rests' on the scene of her labour, and her labour is entirely solitary."[2] While the association of home and rest rendered her work invisible to other family members, for these domestic workers, work was swallowing up every moment.

This was especially true of working-class women whose work in the home and community was materially difficult. Vera Brittain described it as going on in "semi-barbarous conditions – intensified beyond calculation by the War and its consequences."[3] These conditions yielded "a picture in which monotony, loneliness, discouragement and sordid hard work are the main features – a picture of almost unredeemed drabness."[4]

Health and life itself were often precarious. Numerous surveys testified that many families were living below the poverty line, meaning that, in the words of the Women's Group on Public Welfare, "they have not enough money for the mother, even if she were a perfect housewife, to pay for the bare essentials of rent, food, clothing, fire, lights and cleaning materials necessary to keep her family in health." This group goes on to say "in 1936, one-tenth of the nation's population, including nearly one-fourth of its children ... had a dietary lacking in all the constituents most essential to health."[5] Margery Spring Rice points out that "no unemployed married man with a family under the Assistance Board, nor any married man in ... poorly paid trades ... receives enough money to buy adequate food for himself, wife and children."[6]

It was the mother's work and her ability to cope which often made the difference between health and malnourishment, or even between life and death. The infant mortality rate in 1930–2 was 69.6 per 1000 and in 1939 50.6 per 1000, and this was concentrated among the "poorer classes."[7] Malnourished children, especially very young children who were the most susceptible to killing diseases, were frequently those whose mothers "suffered from anxiety, overwork, poor feeding and ill-health during pregnancy."[8] And it was, in turn, those mothers with large families and low incomes who tended to suffer most from anxiety and ill health. These women frequently had neither the time nor the resources to care for their own health, and compensated for inadequate household resources by eating less and using health services less frequently than their husbands and children.[9]

Yet both working-class and bourgeois women, whose lives were not so crushed by this "almost intolerable weight of unpaid domestic labour," were being freshly burdened with "home science" and rising "standards of family care." Compulsory training in domestic science was advocated for all women, and increasing numbers of consumer goods were advertised as "essential." Useful as such education and assistance may have been, it also increased the amount of work women felt required to do and decreased their time for external interests. Externally produced standards and goods also decreased the amount of control women had over the management of their own households. At the same time, a pragmatically conceived and commercially manipulated psychology was placing new demands on women's standards of "marital performance."[10] Wherever they turned women were exhorted to ever greater efforts in an ever dwindling space. Yet despite the dominance of the dependent-housewife role in all aspects of their lives, and despite the often crushing burden of work involved, women were neither passive nor silent in their homes and communities.

Compensating for the "Family Wage"

Throughout the interwar period housewives organized, from the basis provided by their work environment, to overcome the isolation and powerlessness of their position and to compensate for the fact that their working and living space was dependent on and separated from the wage-labour sphere. In these conditions of domestic labour, women's actions – both those of the poorer classes who suffered them, and those of the "new" professional women who researched them – were aimed toward gaining more control over and improving their conditions of work and life.

Many of these attempts were mediated through the male wage packet and the internal distribution of family resources, as the wage system provided no guarantee that the breadwinner would give the housewife sufficient housekeeping money even should his wages allow it.[11] Other attempts to change conditions were organized through informal networks of family and neighbours and through more formal women's organizations: Women's Institutes, Townswomen's Guilds, women's service clubs, and Women's Co-op Guilds, all of which acted to materially restructure working conditions in the home. Many Brighton women I spoke to talked about networks of friends and extended family which helped with childminding and small loans of food and equipment. The Brighton Townswomen's Guild and the Women's Co-operative Guild provided loans of sick room supplies. Such groups also provided information and education, as well as a source of companionship and social contact for women. In addition, the formal groups pressured for the extension of state services.

A growing number of formal groups became national organizations with branches spread throughout Britain. The National Association of Women's Clubs was formed in the 1930s to co-ordinate the activities of the increasing number of women's clubs providing social services and self-help networks.[12] Since one of the major aspects of women's work was the purchase of commodities, many groups had been established to provide consumer assistance. The Electrical Association of Women had been founded in 1924 to disseminate information on the use of electricity and "to provide a platform for the expression of users' views of domestic electrical matters."[13] The Women's Co-operative Guild, founded in 1883, became one of the largest of these consumer groups; by 1930 it had some 67,000 members.[14] Women in the guild were part of a wide-ranging movement where "the intelligent Guildswoman" shopped and saved in co-op institutions and, through the guild, "works loyally for all the objects of the movement, using her spending power to build up this great workers' organization. She knows that it contains within it the elements of a peaceful revolution that may some day transform our social system."[15] In its fiftieth anniversary year, a guild writer claimed that "what the Guild has done ... for the working class woman is to show her, and through her, the family, that she is a co-operator and citizen as well as a married woman, and that, all the more because she is a married woman, she and her services are wanted outside the home as well as inside."[16]

All of these associations, through acting to restructure women's working conditions, also helped women overcome their material and psychological isolation. They, in conjunction with welfare clinics and the church, were often the only regular outside contact that women had.

The dominance of the "family wage" meant that there was no market mechanism to match individual male wages with the size and special needs of a particular family. There were therefore constant pressures to "make up the difference" for large families, or for those without a regularly employed male wage earner, to build on the nascent recognition of the limitation of the family wage through directly supplementing family resources. Part of this pressure and much of the direct intervention was carried out by "rationalized" extensions of nineteenth-century charities. These were staffed by latter day "Lady Bountifuls," as well as by a new breed of professional social worker. The National Association for Maternal and Child Welfare and the Charity Organizing Society expanded and professionalized their roles to provide integrated service to the disadvantaged family.[17] Perhaps more significant was the formation of a range of professional women's groups and of co-ordinated pressure groups by these and community-based women's organizations. For example, the Women's Group on Public Welfare Hygiene Committee, an umbrella organization, had representatives from the Women's Public Health Officers' Association, Women Officers of the National Council of Social Services, The Society of Women Housing Managers, and the National Federation of Womens' Institutes. The Women's Health Enquiry Committee which initiated and carried out the study reported by Spring Rice included representatives of the Women's Co-op Guild, the National Union of Townswomens' Guilds, the Women's National Liberal Organization, the Standing Joint Committee of Industrial Women's Organizations, the Midwives Institute, the National Council for Equal Citizenship, the Women Public Health Officers' Association, the Council for Scientific Mangement in the Home, and the National Council of Women.[18]

The struggles for various forms of social insurance, for improved public health, and for legal protection were led by women, both in Parliament and in the community. These groups researched and campaigned for "the needs of the community as a whole," attempting to "build a coordinated structure of services which leaves no gap."[19] The recognition of domestic work *as* work, and of the limitations of the family wage, was most clearly expressed in the campaign for family allowances. This campaign initiated a fierce debate on the extent of state responsibility for the family and, under the auspices of Eleanor Rathbone's

Children's Minimum Campaign Committee, opened up the private sphere to fierce scrutiny.[20]

Education of young children was another area where private family life was opened up. The British Association for Early Childhood Education, founded in 1923, worked for the improved education and welfare of young children in all situations and especially for the extension of nursery schools. The Parent Teacher Federation was also formed in the 1930s to co-ordinate the growing number of Home and School councils and Parent Teacher assocations.

At the same time, bourgeois women were fighting to "reorganize society in such a fashion that its best women could be both mothers and professional workers."[21] The struggle for a larger role in public life was carried out by suffragist organizations and the professional groups mentioned above, and assisted by a profusion of new voluntary political groups. Pressure from these as well as the more traditional groups succeeded in "getting no less than 101 Acts concerning women's special interests onto the Statute Book between 1918 and 1950."[22]

Birth Control and the Urban Fabric

The campaign for birth control and family limitation was also a significant part of women's attempts to control both their physical health and conditions of work. Many bourgeois women had been controlling their fertility since the 1870s.[23] In 1920, the first birth control clinic in Britain was opened by Marie Stopes. By 1930, there were five birth control societies, which together formed the National Birth Control Campaign, the precursor of the Family Planning Association (FPA); by 1938, the FPA had sixty-one clinics.[24]

The birth control movement was always a movement by women for women. Its form of organization was "a type of women's self-help enterprise" with relatively autonomous clinics funded by voluntary efforts, along the lines of the Women's Institutes and other women's organizations.[25] The movement's campaign to force government responsibility for providing access to birth control was supported by a large range of women's groups, including the Women's Co-op Guild and the women's sections of the Labour and Liberal parties.[26] Women's control over their fertility thus became an increasingly important social issue, which was linked, both by campaigners and opponents, to wider movements. "The promotion of birth control became an extension of women's claims for the right to education, to property, to work and to vote."[27]

Through the clinics, through the often controversial publicity they generated, and through the educational campaigns mounted by the FPA and other groups, the use of birth control spread to more and more women (and men), including working-class people.[28] In 1934, in response to pressure, national legislation was passed obliging local authorities to provide guidance and give contaceptive advice to married women if pregnancy would be detrimental to their health. Subsequent provision of this service was, however, limited and patchy.[29]

Women having greater control over their fertility, especially through the use of the "female methods" advocated by the FPA, was seen increasingly as a threat to "masculine domination at home and at work" and to "the very foundations of family life."[30] In the late 1930s and early 1940s, these practices became seen as a "social crisis," as a result of growing panic over declining birth rates. This panic focused simultaneously on the so-called decline of the British race – the decline in average intelligence and fitness as a result of better educated and more intelligent women limiting their fertility – on the decline and destabilization of the family, and on a prophesized economic and cultural stagnation attendant on a static and perhaps dwindling population.[31] Women's ability to control their own fertility had, not for the first or last time, become a vital issue for "mankind."

Pressure was exerted to inspire women to produce more and "better" children. Some of this pressure was coercive. There were discussions regarding limiting the paid employment of women, restricting birth control, and restricting the occupations of and imposing extra taxes on "childless men."[32] The women's press, reflecting the exhortations of "professionals," castigated "wives who did not wish for a brood of 'wee darlings' for their selfishness."[33] On the related question of delaying marriage or permanent independence, the same writers evoked the tyrant of psychology. "Any girl who declares she prefers to stay single is only fooling herself. No matter how full of life she may be, it isn't complete without marriage. Nothing else can fulfill this fundamental need. If you are clinging to single blessedness, the chances are that there is something wrong with your emotional makeup or your attributes, or that you are the victim of false ideas. Knowledge and guidance may help you."[34] The choice was motherhood or misfit. Such threats were combined with more positive pressure, including a renewed campaign for the extension of social services to improve the conditions of family life and compensate for the costs of parenthood.[35]

Housing policies, developed partly in response to demands for better housing by women's groups and unions, and accelerated by the concern to provide adequate and healthy housing for the socially desirable large family, also created new problems. Slum clearance and relocation policies increased the isolation of domestic workers largely through "ending the extended family and community networks that previously helped informally to collectivize household work in urban areas."[36] This had the unintended effect of creating new problems out of previous "solutions." "The isolation of the housewife implies a diminution of social resources available to her to cope with crises associated with childbearing and rearing, thus rendering childbearing less attractive. Hence falling family size, increasing alienation amoung housewives/mothers, and increasing demands on the social services by 'normal' families are all different sides of the same coin."[37]

All of these interventions were accompanied by, and simultaneously reinforced the necessity for, renewed pressures for what some popular women's journals called "dear housewifeliness." But this barrage was already contending with fundamental changes in the nature of housewifeliness. The outbreak of World War II provided a decisive interruption in the housewife's progress towards nirvana within four walls.

WOMEN'S ORGANIZATION DURING WORLD WAR II

The mass mobilization of women during the war and the radical changes wrought in private households broadened both the basis and the scope of women's activities. The war experience also broadened women's expectations: as direct contributors to the war effort, at home and in the labour force, they became part of the "nation" again.

Elizabeth Wilson says, "the housewife was *the* heroic figure of the Second World War." She symbolized the national spirit. "She kept the Home Front going and the Home Front was what the boys were fighting for, for that and the Welfare State that was promised when the war was over. This wartime housewife was lapped round with state solicitude and with honeyed praise from the press; a striking contrast with her neglect in prewar years."[38] In the home, women were bombarded with appeals to "make do and mend" in the national interest. Their previous difficulties of domestic labour were compounded by wartime shortages, family separations, and relocations. These difficulties gave rise to a number of groups that pressed for more resources to "make do and mend" with, while simultaneously inventing and disseminating ways of "making do" without much.[39] And as more and more women entered the labour force, these domestic problems were compounded by the strain of a wage job.

Although women's entry into the wage labour force, as during the First World War, was bounded by "the assumption of their fundamental implausibility and unacceptability as real workers," women's groups were establishing a range of organizations to consolidate and expand this foothold.[40] The London Women's Parliament – an association of "housewives' clubs," Co-op Guilds, unions, professional organizations, and

other women's groups – demanded a unified plan for the mobilization
and protection of women wage workers, claiming that: "no consideration
of previous craft privileges or customs must be allowed to stand in the
way of this substitution [of women for men in wage jobs]. Neither must
the deplorable low pre-war rates of wages generally paid to women be
taken into consideration when laying down current rates. The discrepancies between male and female rates of wages hitherto accepted ... can
no longer be tolerated."[41] These and other groups also demanded the
extension of social services to facilitate women's entry into the work
force. The Women's Parliament, in conjunction with a variety of other
groups, pressured for nurseries and then backed up their pressures with
demonstrations of mothers pushing placarded prams. These groups also
pressed for the extension of hostels, home helps, convalescent homes,
nursing support, food subsidies, and provisions for infant welfare – all
in order to facilitate women's dual role.[42]

Evacuation also produced a crop of women's committees, both to
protest against and to assist the movement *en masse* of working-class
women and children around the country. Evacuation provided many
bourgeois Britons with their first personal knowledge of poverty. The
Women's Group on Public Welfare says "the effect of evacuation was to
flood the dark places with light" and to make the "ordinary citizen"
aware of conditions under which the urban working class lived. Evacuation also pointed up the state's ability to fundamentally alter the lives
and location of masses of people and led to growing demands for more
responsibility in the way this alteration was carried out.[43]

All of these increased women's concern for an integrated social service,
both to meet their own needs and the needs of the "nation." It increased
women's determination to have a role in creating the post-war reconstruction. The Women's Committee for Peace and Democracy put it this
way.

We want democracy in this country. And "democracy" translated into terms of
real life for the average woman means for her the right to voice her opinion
and to make her demands effective in the things which touch her own health
and happiness and the welfare of her children ... Democratic Air Raid Precau-
tions mean full knowledge, full participation, and the greatest amount of local
control. Insofar as evacuation is concerned it means the right of women and
women's organizations, on the basis of their knowledge and experience, to ask
from the government and the local authorities those things they know are necessary for the benefit of the children and get them.[44]

The great machine which moved people from place to place, which built
nurseries and hostels (after much pressure), which fed, clothed, and

deloused a mobile population, also laid the basis for an optimism about the possibility of mass planning and about the inception of a new relationship between family and state. Ferguson and Fitzgerald note, "war time shortages made the Government an arbiter on questions of social policy from which it had formerly stood aside and they also brought the Ministry of Health to the fore as an advocate for the daily and intimate requirements of mothers and children."[45] All these services, and especially the nurseries were "partly an expression of the *right* of the mothers willing to contribute to the war effort, to this sort of service ... The nursery was more than a mere device to get a maximum number of women on to the assembly line or into the weaving shed; it was a contribution toward the feeling of mutual responsibility between Government and family."[46]

The readjustment to peace was difficult, not only for the nation, but for its women who, again rather abruptly, were no longer a direct part of this nation. The resistance to women's re-domestication was vocal, both in the home and workplace. One contemporary wrote, "One of the respects in which the war has created a social revolution is in taking women out of their homes, and compelling them to lead a communal life."[47]

In the immediate post-war period many women, especially older women, wished to continue wage work. Many married women did, however, "return home," a process which Vera Douie describes as a "counter revolution" which "will present almost as many psychological problems as did the war itself."[48] Wartime services, which had been qualified by insistence on their emergency and temporary nature, were rapidly dismantled to make way for reconstruction and the new welfare state.

The war itself had not fundamentally altered the ideological view regarding "women's natural sphere," nor the material conditions which demanded that most women devote most of their lives to domestic duties. But it had extended concerns of the interwar groups for fundamental change in the relation of the family and state and accelerated the impact of these organizations on the development of the post-war welfare state.

WOMEN'S ORGANIZATION AND THE WELFARE STATE

Women's organizations in the interwar and wartime periods displayed an inherent tension, the result of simultaneous objectives: pushing for change and "making do." This tension informed the priorities and organizational structure of all these groups. On the one hand, women in the interwar period and during the war were pressing to change the situations in which they lived and worked: they were demanding more and better services and materials to work with, organizing to achieve better access to and more control over resources, and attempting to find new ways of working. On the other hand, women were faced with the need to find ways of coping in the immediate circumstances and to maintain, through their daily activities, the health or even life of other, often dependent, people.

It was this tension which gave rise to the "new feminism" of the 1930s, itself a concern which rejected "the focus on equal rights with men, and concentrated on improving women's condition in the family."[49] For these new feminists, organizing from "where women were" – the private domestic workplace – was both a limitation and a source of strength. For the poorest working-class women, there was "*no time* to spare for such immediately irrelevant considerations as the establishment of a different system ... they are not themselves going to be given the second chance, whatever reforms may be introduced, and meantime they have their twelve or thirteen or fourteen hours work to do every day and their own day to day life to lead. It cannot stop, it cannot be interrupted; no one else can do any of their jobs ... there is no margin whatsoever." (emphasis in original)[50] For all women a large part of their work was based in the mundane, peremptory and inescapable details which made up the daily conditions of human life: the illness or death of a child, failing health, and, for many, housing

with basement kitchens, with one w.c. either on the ground floor or outside in the yard; with one or perhaps two cold water taps in the back basement or outside wash house and perhaps on the staircase; no hot water supply, no means of heating except a kettle or saucepan, and no bath. Such a house may be inhabited by anything from two to ten families ... For people living in such conditions, there is hardly any privacy, there is no place for more than two or three people to have a meal together, no facilities for adults to have a bath or even a good wash, no adequate facilities for drying clothes. There is often no place to store food. A woman already sufficiently handicapped by these intolerable conditions frequently has to contend as well with damp, with smoking chimneys, with old uneven floors which are difficult to clean, and with bugs, beetles and other vermin.[51]

The unity of women's life and work ensured that there was no escape to abstraction and only rarely an escape to vision or concerted action. Vision was further limited and clouded by the acceptance of the private nature of reproductive activity and its concomitant naturalization. Women internalized expectations that marriage and motherhood were their "natural" roles, and that difficulties in these roles were themselves, in part, natural.

But the concern with immediate, concrete details also gave these women, and the groups through which they organized, a singular strength – a practical grasp on the necessary human *content* of reforms and, potentially, on the content of a new society. Precisely because they dealt with a private sphere that was separate from the imperatives and logic of the market, the women's interwar groups looked at resources in what Raymond Williams calls "a socially useful rather than a capitalist way."[52] Denied the basis for direct intervention in the economy, as well as for theoretical abstraction, they were thus prevented from developing grand models of social change which "either simplify or merely rationalize a social order."[53] These groups were forced to face the complex content of human needs not in terms of an abstract social order, nor only in terms of producing goods and services. Rather they saw needs primarily in terms of human interrelations, in terms of the relations through which goods and services would be produced, allocated, and used.[54]

These groups, in defining women's issues as domestic issues and in demanding immediate resources to assist women's work – consumer information, family allowances, contraceptive clinics, nursery schools, pest control, and laundry facilities – defended the private realm of the home. Simultaneously they opened it up by demanding public resources for, and recognition of, the social and economic value of women's work there. In their defence and specification of the private, they protected one of the main sources of the new and innovative ways of working and living developed by women in the post-war period. In opening up the domestic sphere to the community and the state, they extended the spaces for creativity and self-organization which, at least potentially, existed in the gender-bound unity of home and work.

At the same time this form of organizing did nothing to break down, and in fact reinforced, the idea of women as home-makers concerned primarily with family life. These groups provided no real or ideal alternative to the gender division of labour. They thus contributed to perpetuating the uneasy and problematic relation between an interdependent society and a gender-typed "private sphere."

Gender and the Welfare State

This concern for socializing aspects of the private family and supporting women's work, on one hand, and the limited vision of gender roles and ways of reproducing people, on the other, were incorporated into and extended by the post-war welfare state. In many areas the welfare state took over and either built upon or destroyed the pre-conditions for the networks of services which women had created in the preceding decades.

The architects of the welfare state were often identical to, or informed by, the professional groups which had researched women's conditions in the 1920s and 1930s. The formal groups – Women's Institutes, Co-op Guilds and the wartime organizations – also contributed to policy. In practical terms, for example, state responsibility for contraception eventually superceded the work of the FPA; social services and home helps took over the equipment loaning and care networks of the Co-op Guilds and Women's Voluntary Services, as well as many other functions of the "charitable" organizations. The form in which these services were produced – by "outside" agencies to "free" individuals – and the mass movement engendered by post-war housing policy broke down many informal and formal community-based networks.

The process of building upon certain elements of women's interwar organization, and inadvertently destroying the preconditions of others, meant that the welfare state incorporated and extended some of the tensions inherent in women's organizations. Welfare services, like those previously provided by women's organizations, were designed to support a "separate" family and to support women in their roles as mothers and housewives. The Beveridge Plan was predicated on full *male* employment and an adequate family wage.

Beveridge had written in 1909 that "society's ideal unit is the house-hold of man, wife and children maintained by the earnings of the first alone ... Reasonable security for the breadwinner is the basis of all private duties and all sound social action."[55] Thirty years later, as one of the most influential architects of the welfare state, he translated this ideal into policy: "In any measure of social policy in which regard is had to facts, the great majority of married women must be regarded as occupied on work which is vital though unpaid, without which their husbands could not do their paid work and without which the nation could not continue. In accord with facts, the Plan for Social Security treats married women as a special insurance class of occupied persons."[56] Married women's special status, including their exemption from insurance, meant that they had reduced claim or no claim to sickness or unemployment benefit.

The services and interventions of the welfare state were therefore based upon a specific definition of women's role, in which the "natural" role of women was seen as housewife and mother and in which women's wage work was both economically and socially worth less than that of men. Yet, by the end of the war, this definition of femininity and of women's activities was materially outmoded. Women's war-time work had forced experiences that precluded forever a quiet adjustment to a "proper sphere" which, in any case, had never existed in the ideal form envisaged by Beveridge and his colleagues. In addition the private and proper sphere was no longer in any real sense private; the interwar organizations had opened it up. The welfare state further opened up the family, making its activities more and more a public and political concern. The very inception of welfare services politicized the content of women's domestic role. Yet, blissfully, or perhaps deliberately unaware of the extension of the women's sphere and of their own role in this extension, post-war governments set out to provide a bare minimum of services based on the assumption of a female population blindly devoted to, or at least quietly confined within, Beveridge's 1909 "ideal family."

In thus contradicting the changing reality of women's lives, the welfare state services provided a new context for organization. Women's domestic struggles to "make ends meet" were extended into the arena of parliamentary debate and council deliberation. The establishment of inadequate welfare services based on an outmoded definition of women's activities opened up a new arena of struggle for them. The welfare state led to changes in the nature of work and life which rapidly and irrevocably altered women's role. The simultaneous expansion of welfare services and of the consumer-goods sector in post-war Britain led to a rising demand for wage labour. This expansion, coupled with the low "natural" increase in population in the 1930s due to family limitation, also resulted in labour shortages. These shortages, combined with a continued need for a family centred around the work of a housewife-mother, led to a new adjustment in the female labour process – the expansion and institutionalization of dual roles for women.[57]

Women thus entered the brave, new, post-war world supported by services that contradicted the changing reality of their lives, the aspirations they were forming, and the new demands these were prompting. The welfare state and dual roles at once multiplied women's activities and constituted a new force which had to be continually "taken on" in attempts to provide an adequate context for their lives, aspirations, and demands. This was the social and environmental material with which post-war women created new lives, new definitions of "woman," and new environments.

People in Brighton did not set out to alter themselves, their city, nor the fundamental basis of their lives. Rather they made a series of adjustments in the way they planned and formed their families, cared for their children and other adults, and organized domestic and wage-earning work. They made these individual small-scale adjustments through reorganizing the environments available to them and through altering their time schedules.

These incremental and common sense adjustments in time and space, which came in response to big events such as the creation of the welfare state, were carried out not only by Brighton women but by millions of women in millions of homes and thousands of neighbourhoods throughout the nation. It was these adjustments which made up the large, long-term changes in gender relations and social environments. Seeing the changes, it is all too easy to forget the lives in which they were created. Fully understanding these changes calls for entering into people's lives and into the specific places where these lives are lived.

3 / Brighton: Official Views and the Methodology of Unofficial Questions

Brighton is a city of a quarter of a million people, situated on the south coast of England, about sixty miles south of London. Like most seaside resorts, it is a city people "know about." Almost anyone who has lived in or visited Britain has an image of Brighton, and most of these images have an iridescent quality, compounded of lights on the piers, a regal past, stretches of pastel terrace houses, and acres of Mods and Rockers gambolling or squabbling beside the sea. Brighton seems a world away from the towers of finance in London and the dark, crowded centres in the North, where the real work of the nation appears to go on.

These images have some truth, most of it frozen in the landscape or carried away in the postcards and memories of the holiday crowds. Brighton is often radiant, sometimes gaudy, occasionally beautiful. It is also a working, breathing, quarrelling city of people. Its work-a-day side is no more real than its incandescence; Brighton is a city of contrasts. In 1919 its mayor described the city as a "ragged garment with a golden fringe."[1] Sixty-two years later, in 1981, the Brighton Community Health Services administrator told me that, "Behind all the glitter, the facade and the glamour, this is a pretty crumby place." This continuity of contrasts is a consistent feature of Brighton life.

In 1919 this contrast was reflected geographically, in the disparity between the "fringe" – the affluent major streets and the seafront – and the "garment," the "appalling" slums of the overcrowded back streets.[2] While the geographic contrasts were less marked in the early 1980s, the contrast between the city's official image and the life of many of its inhabitants remained. Brighton is an apparently affluent town, its economy based on holiday visitors, conferences, commuters, and commerce – with the commuters and vacationers moving faster and more frequently than did the Prince Regent. It is also a city where a large number of people experience low wages, crowded living conditions, and, frequently, high unemployment. This continuity of contrasts is woven into people's lives, the places they live, and the jobs they do. It forms a theme that links and engages Brightonians, more often than not, in antagonistic ways.

THE CITY: IMAGES AND
OFFICIAL VIEWS

The people who "planned" and publicized Brighton always seemed, understandably perhaps, to have concentrated on the fringe and on preserving and extending it as far as possible inland. The official image of Brighton as a resort permeated planning policies throughout the interwar and post-war periods. The first "comprehensive" planning document on the area – the 1932 Report of the Brighton Hove and District Town Planning Advisory Committee – says, "One of the chief conclusions arrived at in the Preliminary Report of the Committee was that the general prosperity of the Region as a whole depends to a large extent on its attractiveness, healthy residential communities and natural beauty and that the preservation of these three items will define the main purpose of town planning in the Region."[3] Nineteen years later, the first post-war plan stated that its first objective was to "strengthen the attractions of Brighton as a coastal resort without sacrificing its character."[4] The subsequent development of an extensive conference centre and marina reinforced these priorities, as did the consistent concern of the town council to preserve "amenities," free transportation and accommodation for visitors, and, where attention was focused on non-tourist related employment, to develop office blocks as opposed to industrial sites.[5]

Another official view of Brighton is found in a 1979 report by the County Council of East Sussex, the county within which Brighton is situated. "Summarizing evidence on census indicators of urban deprivation, the Council found that Brighton had several neighbourhoods ... that may be described as 'areas of special social need' ... areas usually in the older parts of towns and cities which contain abnormally high concentrations of those who are relatively deprived by national standards."[6] The report also notes that Brighton has "high levels of need indicators ... associated with 'social disorganization,' a high illegitimate birth rate," a high number of children in care, and a high infant mortality rate. Into the 1980s Brighton had some of the lowest average wage rates in the country. It also suffered from an unemployment rate which, since 1968, had often been above the national average, and a lower rate of employment expansion than the national average.[7]

Brighton has also historically been a retirement area. Since the turn of the century, it has had a higher proportion of people over sixty-five and a lower proportion of people under fifteen than Great Britain as a whole.[8] Housing and welfare resources have therefore been consistently directed toward meeting the very real needs of the elderly, needs which were all the greater since the majority of elderly were older women who,

in many cases, tended to have very low incomes.[9] This population structure, combined with the high cost of cleaning, servicing, maintaining,
and policing a town whose prosperity is assumed to rest on its beauty,
was reflected in Brighton's municipal budget. Compared to other local
authorities, the rates were consistently lower for education but higher
for social services, public health, police, and "amenities."[10]

All of these factors, to some extent, distinguished the lives of people
in Brighton in the early 1980s from the lives of those in other places.
The opposition between the fringe and the garment and Brighton's
demographic and social structure influenced the allocation of resources,
the structure of employment, and the location of housing. Competition
over, and alterations in, urban space and urban resources formed both
the backdrop and the stuff of the activities and organization of Brightonians.

ASKING THE UNOFFICIAL QUESTIONS

I moved to Brighton in September of 1980, thirty-five years after the
end of the Second World War, at a time when the "recession" and the
cutbacks in social services were not only beginning to dominate political
priorities and personal lives locally and nationally, but when these same
processes seemed to be heralding the end of the expanding wage economy and the "social wage" which had dominated the post-war period.
For two years I watched, read, talked, and sometimes acted, attempting
to construct a "map" of the liquid process of social and economic change
as it unfolded in my life and in the lives of those around me. Not only
was I, as a "foreigner," learning new things daily, but the context and
content of my life and those of my neighbours was altering daily. It was
altering because we were acting differently; in small ways we changed
the places we went and the things we did. And yet, as we readjusted
our shopping patterns, had children, changed jobs, and joined or left
organizations, we were creating patterns which analysts discussed and
which we – in the quiet times we reflected on them – could identify and
identify with.

The most challenging part of all this was trying to find a way of
describing the process, trying to build a bridge between the content –
"what we did on Monday" or "where we lived in the winter of 1950" –
and the broad questions that made up the context: how did women's
space-time patterns alter in post-war Brighton, and how did women
create new networks and resources to respond to these alterations? It
is one thing to say, as I have, that daily activity constitutes gender and
social environment in an interactive and constantly changing process.
It is quite another to collect the disparate and bewildering range of

actions, ideas, and opinions to describe this process in a comprehensive, comprehensible, and sensitive manner.

On the one hand answering these questions involves entering into the daily rhythms, the space and time of women's lives – their kitchens and sitting rooms, their conversations and meetings, their bus routes and strolls. This direct entry is essential because the activities that make up domestic-community life and the activities whereby women link this to the economic sphere as consumers, clients, citizens, and wage workers are fluid, idiosyncratic, and subject daily to small and unforeseeable decisions and choices. It is not possible to construct universal models about the form or sequence of the decisions and choices through which women arrange their lives.

In their domestic-community work, women do what is required. And what is required is, in most cases, concrete and obvious. The kitchen must be cleared of breakfast dishes before lunch preparations can begin, crying children must be comforted, new shoes must be purchased with yesterday's earnings. Unlike much wage work, which often has no immediate meaning or value to the person who actually performs it, the reasons for doing household jobs are inherent within the actions themselves. The ways in which women must link these concrete and essential activities to the more ephemeral activities that make up wage work necessitate a new set of arrangements, that is, dual roles. Women make multitudes of "small" daily decisions and choices in an attempt to adjust the time and space for giving birth and nursing, for care of children, for domestic-community duties, for sexuality, and for leisure. All these arrangements must take account of the fluid constraints imposed by the specific balance of resources and family needs. Women's allocation of space and time must attempt to balance the amount of money, the number of goods and services, the amount of time that is required to achieve a desired family lifestyle.

On the other hand, all of these processes leave patterns, the bare outlines of which can be traced by bringing together a host of official statistics and commentaries on things such as birth rates, ownership of household equipment, persons per room, women in the labour force, and journeys to work. It is thus possible to use statistical and secondary sources to glean some idea of aggregate changes and trends in regard to specific characteristics: changes in the physical structure and equipment of the home, in its location, and in the computable characteristics of families living there. And it is possible to get some overall picture of women's participation in the labour force and even of some of the adjustments this has caused in society.

Neither kind of information is sufficient. Aggregate data alone – whether assembled from secondary sources or through the separation out and statistical relation of survey results – are inadequate, largely because they obscure the way in which characteristics are combined in people's lives. It is the sum total of people's lives that change and that constitute social change. Lives, and society, alter through the alteration of each area relative to all the other, generally indistinguishable, areas. The interdependence of biological reproduction, domestic-community work, and wage work is the outstanding characteristic of women's lives. Interdependence forms the basis of the problems they encounter and their responses to them. This interdependence is also the characteristic which has been most consistently obscured in analysis. And obscuring the connections in people's lives, reducing lives to trends and prognostications, not only removes the richness of social change from social science but makes it more difficult for people to know how they can act and what effect their acts, their complex and integrated lives, will have on achieving their goals and aspirations.

Conversely, purely idiographic or autobiographical studies which make no attempt to contextualize or analyse individuals' lives are also severely limited. They make it difficult to generalize. And it is generalization which allows us to put ourselves "in context," to build upon shared experience and insights. As Sheila Rowbotham notes, "experience which is not theorized has a way of dissolving and slipping out of view ... We can retain attitudes and responses toward forms of organizing which we prefer but it is hard to pass them on or give them a more general validity."[11] This means, in Elizabeth Wilson's words, that "each succeeding generation of women has to make anew the effort to retrieve a past that continues to remain hidden."[12] So moving too far in either direction puts us at risk of producing work that obscures experience and obstructs the kind of understanding leading to effective social change.

The objective, then, is to find a way of summing up the daily, small decisions and choices made over a lifetime, and among groups of women, in order to discern a pattern and to see, analytically and perhaps strategically, the large changes: alterations in the nature of what is "required" and in how it is required to be done. I have tried to do this by examining how this summing-up creates alterations in space and time devoted to the various dimensions of life and alterations in the resources which are available or attainable within this space and time. What follows is therefore a discussion of how one group of women balanced and adjusted their space and time in response to specific constraints and opportunities, and of the possibilities for social organization that emerged from this balancing and adjusting.

Initially, in an attempt to develop background material on service provision, labour-force characteristics, and the development of Brighton's urban fabric, I used available library resources, consulted official documents, newspapers, and the records of various local groups, and questioned people in the statutory service sectors.[13] But understanding the process which creates these broad patterns, and understanding the problems and the response to these called for information which could only come from women themselves. My major "sources" were therefore women interviewed in Brighton between May and September of 1981.

There were two distinct interview groups. The first comprised the activists in groups and statutory workers in services concerned with birth control, abortion and childbirth, childcare, consumer services, and women's wage employment. This group included both women and men; it is referred to below as "activists" and "statutory workers." The second was a random sample of fifty-five women living in three areas of the city. I also visited playgroups, mother and toddler groups, nursery schools and classes, community centres, and local schools. I was invited to attend the meetings of many of the groups I spoke to (and sometimes to become an active participant in activities). With the co-operation of the PreSchool Playgroups Association, I was able to distribute questionnaires to twenty-four playgroups, twenty of which responsed.

The interviews with activists were intended to gather information on service availability and use and on organizational structure and aims within the field. The interviews with the community sample covered a range of topics, which were intended as a whole to build up a picture of women's lives. I asked each of the fifty-five women questions about family size, structure, and income and about her own history, including her wage-work history. I asked all these women about their homes and communities as a working environment and about their personal and social networks. Women with children were asked about their childbirth and childcare experiences, and each in the group was asked her opinion on a number of general social issues. The questionnaires for each set of interviews, though primarily used as guides to conversation, are reproduced in the Appendix.

The interviews were not only a means of gathering "data": they were, above all, social encounters with other women. As noted above, the kinds of questions one asks and answers in building up a picture of the rhythms of women's lives assumes entering into these lives. Personal involvement, as Ann Oakley points out, "is the condition under which people come to know each other and admit others into their lives."[14] This involves shedding the idea that social scientists, when they are actually engaged in the act of performing social science, must, and can, be apart from their object of study. Over the years, social scientists have developed a kind of protective colouration of "objectivity," based on an interview relation where an aloof observer questions a faceless and passive observee. This textbook relation, in which idiosyncracy, emotion, specificity, and the "interruptions" of ongoing life, have no part was, in this research, stood on its head. Entering into women's lives makes it necessary to recognize and to utilize the fact that a woman interviewing other women about being a woman becomes inescapably part of what she observes. And it is precisely the local, specific, and immediate that are important.[15]

Talking to people about their lives assumed that I entered into and shared women's domestic, living and working environments. The nature of the interview reflected the character and adequacy of this environment as a working and living place. Those interviews which took place in small, council-flat kitchens – the neighbour's radio competing with the children's television program from the sitting room and myself holding a mug of coffee in one hand, the toddler in the other, and tape recorder and notebook in the third – had a distinctly different, although no less satisfactory, quality than those carried out in cool spacious sitting rooms, with a table for my teacup and another for my notes. The relations between myself and the women I spoke to and the environment in which we spoke were a significant and informative part of the interview.

More important, entering into people's lives assumes one comes as an invited guest and becomes a confidant. The common courtesy required of a guest demands that one participate in a relation which, however brief, is based on mutual trust and respect. It also demands that one act, if appropriate and possible, in the way a guest and confidant would: help peel the vegetables for dinner, or amuse the baby while the mother is talking on the telephone, and – in textbook terms, even more unconventionally – share knowledge of and access to resources that your hostess requires.[16] This was the primary means whereby I could repay my hostesses' hospitality: by providing immediate information such as the names of contacts and also by using my less constrained time and space to "look up " things they wanted to know. Less direct means of reciprocating included involvement in the groups I was studying and, in some cases, taking women along to various groups that interested them. A less tangible reciprocity was what Oakley calls the "theraputic effect" of the interview itself.[17] A number of women commented to me that it was "good to talk about all this," and several said, when I returned, that subsequent to the inteviews they had had "good discussions" with husbands, mothers, daughters, and friends about issues raised in the interview. But the debt of hospitality remains mine.

Just as the immediate environments in which we spoke varied greatly, so did the communities in which these homes were located. The women I spoke to lived in three areas of Brighton: I chose the areas in order to discover the influence of different domestic-community workplaces (See map 3). These areas, an old central-city neighbourhood, an interwar estate in the inner suburbs, and an outer, post-war estate, represent different phases in the development of Brighton's built environment. They also incorporate class-differentiated sub-communities within one geographically defined area.

The oldest was the central Hanover-Queen's Park area, which combined two communities in one densely populated acre. Hanover, a privately rented/owner-occupied area of nineteenth-century terrace housing, is part of Brighton's traditional working-class residential area (and the setting for much of Graham Greene's *Brighton Rock*). Some of its pastel plaster houses were undergoing gentrification by young professionals in the early 1980s, but this steeply hilly, intensely busy, and densely utilized community remained primarily occupied by working-class people. Queen's Park, located more or less "across the street," was a largely middle-class area. Primarily owner-occupied, the houses were bigger, brick-fronted, and separated by lawns and gardens; they surrounded the spacious park. The Queen's Park community was quieter than Hanover (except in the immediate vicinity of a local nursery school and playground), cooler in summer, and flatter in all seasons. I interviewed twenty-five women in this area: thirteen in Hanover and twelve in Queen's Park.

The second community was Whitehawk, an area some two miles from the town centre. Whitehawk combined in a one-minute walk, although again not in one social community, two distinct areas. Central Whitehawk, occupying the bottom of a valley in the Sussex downs, was a large interwar council estate, with streets of occasionally attractive but largely monotonous grey and beige row-houses. In the 1950s and 1960s Whitehawk gained a reputation as a "dump estate," full of "problem families" and rising damp. In the early 1980s, it was undergoing a controversial redevelopment in which large areas of older housing were being demolished to make way for a combination of council-built and housing-association flats and houses. Despite close extended-family ties and active community associations, many of the women in Whitehawk felt isolated and cut off, especially with the low-lying winter fogs and the geographic barrier of the ridge which divided Whitehawk from the rest of the city. (This ridge was dominated by the oddly brooding presence of the Brighton Race Track buildings.) East Whitehawk, in contrast, was an area of self-built owner-occupied housing stretching along the gentler eastern ridge above the estate and down toward the seafront to the south. The houses were not only larger, with varied facades and floor plans, they gave the impression of being connected to the elegant seafront terraces

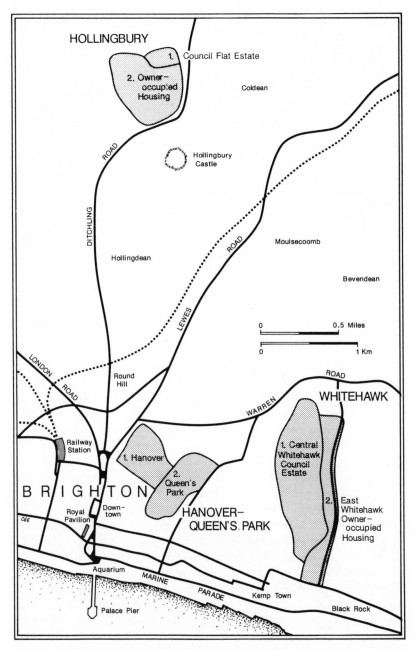

Map 3   Brighton: Areas Where Community Interviews Took Place

Table 1
Summary of Personal Characteristics of Community Interviewees

Characteristic	Number of Women	Characteristic	Number of Women
MARITAL STATUS		AGE CATEGORY	
Married	46[1]	20–29	11
Single	1	30–39	15
Separated	4	40–49	12
Divorced	3	50–59	10
Widowed	1	60–69	4
		70–79	3
HOUSEHOLD INCOME (PER WEEK)		TIME IN BRIGHTON	
Under £40	7[2]	Less than a year	0
£ 40 – 80	20	1 to 5 years	4
£ 81 – 120	16	6 to 10 years	4
£121 – 160	6	10 to 20 years	6
£161 – 200	2	20 or more years	15
£201 – 250	2	All her life	26
£251 and over	0		
Unable to estimate	2		

Source: Brighton Community Interviews, 1981
[1] 4 married more than once
[2] 6 female headed

to their south. I interviewed twenty women in Whitehawk: eleven in Central Whitehawk, all of whom were council renters, and nine in Eastern Whitehawk, all of whom lived in owner-occupied homes.

The third and newest area was Hollingbury, an extensive post-war suburban estate, some five miles from the town centre, juxtaposed against Brighton's largest industrial estate. Hollingbury as a whole contained both council and private housing, the latter often of very high standard. The Carden School catchment area, where my interviews took place, encompassed two distinct areas: one of owner-occupied houses, either purchased from the council (Hollingbury was developed largely as a "sale" estate) or privately built; and a one-parent family "ghetto" – three streets of barrack-like flats occupied almost entirely by independent mothers and their children. The latter were built on a steep hillside overlooking the owner-occupied housing; they rang with noise from children and televisions and were surrounded by small patches of scrubby grass. It was a crowded community "away from everything." I interviewed ten women in Hollingbury: five in the owner-occupied houses and five in the flats.[18] Some general information on the women interviewed in these three communities is included in tables 1 and 2.

Table 2
Summary of Characteristics of Community Interviewees by Neighbourhood

	Average Income	*Average House-hold Size*	*Average No. of depen-dent children*	*Average no. of Ameni-ties[1]*	*Average No. of Aids[1]*	*% with car*
HOLLINGBURY						
Council flats	£35	3.4	2.4	2.4	4.0	0
Owner-occupiers	£80	3.0	1.0	6.1	6.4	100
WHITEHAWK						
Council estate	£65	3.5	1.8	4.6	5.4	64
Owner-occupiers	£95	3.1	0.8	6.7	5.8	67
HANOVER-QUEEN'S PARK						
Hanover	£70	2.6	0.9	5.2	5.1	30
Queen's Park	£85	3.7	1.3	6.2	6.0	60
Average for Total Sample	£70	3.2	1.4	5.2	5.5	54

Source: Brighton Community Interviews, 1981

[1] These are average scores for amenities and aids for domestic-community working conditions. Amenities included gardens, number of bedrooms, telephones, central heating and hot water; aids included refrigerator, separate freezer, washing machine, vacuum cleaner, radio, television. Scores were obtained by allocating one point for presence of each amenity or aid, and averages by adding scores and dividing by the number of women in each specified area.

The creation and change of these three communities and the homes within them had been effected both by official policies and by the actions of individuals. These environments formed not only a concrete context for women's lives and organizations, they formed the material of contest.

4 / Changing Domestic-Community Working Conditions

> After the war, a lot of us thought everything could change. This town
> has changed a lot since the war. People moved ... into bigger houses ...
> and had baths and televisions and ate better too ... We worked hard for
> some of those changes, the men in the unions and the women right here
> ... at home. Some of them were good, what we wanted. Some things ... I
> miss some of the old ways. (Sixty-year old native Brightonian, life-long
> resident of Hanover.)

The city of Brighton in 1945 was a vast, complex, and spatially differentiated resource system in which bomb sites and small amounts of
temporary war-time construction had only marginally altered generations of building, paving, walling, and engineering. As local officials and
residents were well aware, it was a resource system fraught with problems
– inadequacies, health hazards, transportation bottlenecks – and one
where the allocation of resources was inequitable and often inefficient.
But in the apparently universal official euphoria following the war, it
was seen as a system of resources which could be "planned" into a new
city. Achieving this required pouring more resources into the urban
fabric to change it from an *ad hoc* collection of individual structures into
a system which would reflect and reinforce post-war human ideals. It
involved restructuring the physical basis for individual and family life
and, especially, altering the material setting of the housewife's role.

The relationship between restructuring the city and restructuring
family life was not one which went unnoticed by period planners and
social theorists. Post-war reconstruction, in both its physical and social
aspects, involved an attempt to build a new "classless" consensus based
on the family as the "central unit of society."[1] This consensus drew on
and embellished the historically specific definition of femininity embod-
ied in the welfare state. Women's "natural" and primary role was housewife and mother, and greater material support – in the form of new
products and services – combined with a growing ideological celebration
of this role, was seen to render all housewives equal. "The woman wield-
ing the hoover ... [became] the symbol of the social revolution that had
obliterated inequality; for women were above all classless."[2]

This was a more elaborate and collective, even democratic, consensus
than the rather bare one which had followed the First World War. It

promised women and, through them, everyone else more. One of the foundational promises was new homes in new or improved communities.

Homes and communities were fundamental to the way women created their lives in post-war Britain; they were also an outcome of this creativity. Throughout the post-war period, the work of maintaining the home and community continued to be primarily the responsibility of women, and often women's primary job. The home and community remained the primary resource base from which women acted and organized. Thus women's organization was often motivated by domestic-community issues. The ways women changed their activities were influenced by the form of their homes and neighbourhoods. The new or altered homes and communities of the post-war era, as built and supervised by the expanded state, were animated by women who were creating, even as they moved and cleaned and built and restructured their domestic-community resource bases, an increasingly mercurial and unpredicatable femininity and feminism. As they were doing so, the city, its neighbourhoods, and its homes changed further, in physical structure, contents, and in the activities which went on in and through them.

MOVING THE HOME: SLUM CLEARANCE AND SUBURBANIZATION

Prewar Urban Fabric

Brighton's prewar planning legislation was largely permissive, limited in intention and effect. Its primary concern, as part of national housing policy, was to co-ordinate the ongoing process of suburbanization.[3]

Until the 1920s most of Brighton's population was centrally located. Throughout the interwar period, however, satellite towns and ex-urban settlement grew at a faster rate than did the city itself.[4] In 1923, and again in 1928, the city boundaries were expanded to include these new areas, and the council began to plan central redevelopment and suburbanization for those Brightonians who could not or would not move themselves.[5]

Slum clearance and suburbanization were two sides of the same coin.[6] Brighton's 1928 area plan said that housing was generally overcrowded "and it would appear therefore that a policy of decentralization, slum clearance and the erection of smaller types of working-class dwellings at a lower rent is required to afford the necessary relief in this direction."[7]

Such conclusions not only reflected a prevailing British view of solutions to the housing problem, but recommended what was, in a small way, already in progress. Some redevelopment had been initiated in the

1920s, and, by 1934, the Housing Department announced that "slum clearance was now going ahead." Before 1940, 877 Brighton houses had been demolished as unfit for human habitation.[8]

Concomitant with this, as in other areas of Britain, was a growth of suburban council estates. Construction of one large council estate, Moulsecoomb, to the northeast of the city centre, began in 1919. In 1928 "the nucleus of Whitehawk estate appeared in the form of 60 houses." Whitehawk continued to grow: a total of 85 houses were built in 1929, 66 in 1931 and 248 in 1933.[9] By 1936 an engineering report could state, "This estate can be considered as a satellite town, since it has its own shops, senior boys and girls and junior mixed schools, a site for a church, a church hall, playing fields and police cottages."[10] By the late 1930s the council owned much of the land to the north and east of Central Brighton.[11]

Throughout this period, in Brighton as well as throughout Britain, there was considerable resistance to "slum clearance" and "relocation," those all-inclusive phrases for the complex process of restructuring previous generations' built environments in a manner intended to reflect a richer and more rational society. There were growing indications of emerging problems, which were attributed in part to the working-class "homogeneity" of the populations moving to the new estates.[12]

These problems were exacerbated by the location of wage jobs. The 1928 and a 1937 plan stated that industries were small and locally oriented, as well as centrally located. More important, so were most of the service industries, in which 85 per cent of Brightonians who were employed in 1931 worked.[13] Some recognition of the problem of a labour force living miles from its wage workplace is evident in the statement of the 1937 plan that "the lowest paid must be downtown" and that their relocation into flats is "inevitable" although "the necessity of reducing the cost of erection to the absolute minimum precluded the provision of all those features which make flats so attractive to the well-to-do."[14] The difficulty of living and working in the newly erected flats created an extreme reluctance on the part of some tenants to move into the new central blocks when they were completed in 1935 and 1938.

The war brought this program of restructuring working-class residential environments to a virtual halt. The loss of housing due to "enemy action" and the lack of repairs during the war were to provide the brave new post-war world in Brighton with its first major planning obstacle.

Post-War Urban Fabric

When I go back to where we lived just after the war ... it's so different. The house is gone now, there's flats there and all the people are different. They look different. I used to go visit a friend but she's gone

Table 3
Houses Demolished and Families Rehoused:
Brighton, 1940–44 to 1975–79

	Houses Demolished	Families Rehoused
1940–44	168	39
1945–49	26	0
1950–54	9	28
1955–59	112	707
1960–64	474	612
1965–69	318	682
1970–74	148	213
1975–79	21	244
Total	1276	2525

Sources: Brighton Corporation, Medical Officer of Health,
Annual Reports; Brighton Corporation, Housing Department,
Annual Reports; Brighton Corporation, Housing Advice
Centre, Unpublished Records

now ... there's nothing left at all. (Fifty-five year old native Brightonian, relocated from the Hanover area to a suburban council estate in the 1960s.)

In the post-war period, the processes of slum clearance and suburbanization accelerated as a result of the wider powers and obligations granted by the 1947 Town and County Planning Act. Although the action was plagued by delays, some housing was demolished and new housing, largely flats, was built in the clearance areas.[15] (See table 3).

The double problems of access to wage jobs and controlling costs continued to dominate the policies under which women's new working environments, and everyone's living environments, were being created. The Housing Manager in 1949 had warned, "An effort must be made to conserve the use of land by the erection of terraced type housing and flats in small blocks ... The question of transport costs will increase the difficulty of housing problems as and when it becomes necessary to build outside the three mile perimeter."[16] The 1951 Outline Development Plan said, "In order ... to reduce ... the amount of land which must be found on the outskirts of the town for rehousing, it will be necessary to consider the erection of large blocks of flats in the inner area."[17]

As the Housing Manager predicted that "there will be more aged couples and single persons to rehouse from clearance areas than in pre-war days," most of the flats built were small, intended to accommodate

small families and individuals for whom the "provision of new accommodation is costly" or the elderly "who do not settle easily in new surroundings."[18] Council construction in the 1950s consisted largely of "low
rise" flats in central areas.

The erection of flats, while ensuring access to central jobs and cutting
council land costs, created problems for those who actually lived in these
new developments. In 1955 the Housing Manager stated:

Flats do not provide the ideal solution for the re-housing of families from un-
healthy dwellings in congested areas. One of the objects of re-housing such
families is to place them in surroundings where they may have the opportunity
to "start anew," to raise themselves from their former level, away from their old
associates, and not herded together. When such families are rehoused in large
blocks of flats the bad influence one on the other continues; they complain of
noise and improper use of communal facilities; children are constantly in trouble
on flatted estates, they cannot play naturally lest they interfere with the comfort
of other tenants. They must have an outlet for their energies and this must take
the form of play under decent conditions. Barrack like buildings with paved
surroundings are not sufficient.[19]

The solution to this previous and problematic solution had been suburban estates. Private development continued to expand. Between 1945
and 1965 there was much "self-built" housing erected by co-operatives
of construction workers and "laymen" who acted as labourers. This
included the building to the east and south of the Whitehawk council
estate.

Several residents of these houses – the pioneers – said this was a
"wonderful time." "We were living in two rooms downtown. With the
two children it was really crowded, but we had the house to look forward
to and when we moved in here it was wonderful. So much space." "I
hardly ever saw my husband for years, he came right out here after
work. But we made friends with all the other families and there was a
good feeling when we moved." "We had to save every penny for this
house, and when we moved out, there was nothing here, just mud.
Anyway the kids loved it, and after a while it was all right. At least
everyone was pulling together."

Suburban council building also expanded as elsewhere in Britain. In
Brighton the building was concentrated in the new suburban estates,
including Hollingbury. The "nucleus" of the Hollingbury estate – 18
houses – had been built by 1938, but the bulk of Hollingbury's expansion
was primarily a post-war development. In 1947, 155 new properties
were built, and by the following year the number had reached 563,
including eight shops. The expansion continued throughout the early
1950s.

Hollingbury, like the other new estates, was intended primarily for young families. Its expansion was based on a set of assumptions about the importance of environment in influencing behaviour; if the working class lived in "middle-class" kinds of surroundings, they were more likely to act accordingly. Expansion was also based on the assumption that families with children had only one wage earner. The Housing Manager reported in 1953, "Young families with several children must as far as possible be given opportunities of living in houses in the suburbs, and the middle aged with several working members of the family can be expected to meet the higher rents of flats in central areas where the transport costs will not be as heavy as those in the outlying areas."[20] These estates were also, at least to the official eyes of the Department of Housing, new "paradises." According to the Housing Manager the new estates "reward us for the efforts we have made. The happiness of the tenants, the keen delight of children in country surroundings and sights and their general uplift in health makes us realize how much the entire deprivation of such influence in their lives must mean to their development."[21] The women who moved to Hollingbury and to the self-built areas of Whitehawk in the 1950s and 60s confirmed that, in many ways, their working conditions had improved, especially because of the additional space. "The children could play outside and I didn't worry." "They weren't constantly annoying the neighbours clattering up and down the stairs." "The garden was such a joy to us."

Part of paradise was presumably being able to walk to work. Hollingbury included an industrial estate. The juxtaposition of industry and residences in central areas was seen as a problem and a "conscious effort" was made to "rationalize industrial locations and more recently, by planning controls, to steer new industrial development to a few sites at more peripheral locations in the Borough."[22]

The 1951 plan for Brighton had recommended the limitation of existing industry to seven small central areas and a ten-acre site in an estate in the extreme east of the city. It had also stated "it is not expected that there will be any large scale movement of general industry to Brighton" and that therefore "provision for industry in the outer areas was limited to Hollingbury and Lower Bevendean."[23] These estates, combining "ideal" residences for the working class with appropriate and accessible jobs, were a keystone in the equitable and efficient planning of all aspects of social life. They "were established to encourage manufacturing employment which would redress the seasonal unemployment problems" and provide "a more orderly work environment and facilitate a more efficient means of production than many of the cramped inner area sites."[24]

The first factories on the Hollingbury estate opened in 1955. Throughout the late 1950s and 1960s expansion continued. By 1966 the Hollingbury industrial estate had ten firms employing 5,000 people. Industry in Brighton was both consolidating and suburbanizing, and doing so in a manner which appeared rational and efficient, as exemplified in the 1966 planning application in which machine tool manufacturers

who at present occupy two factories on the industrial estate and employ some 900–1000 persons therein, have requested the Council to make available to the firm an area of land in [Hollingbury estate] which immediately adjoins their no. 2 factory and upon which they can erect an additional industrial building. The company, who have 6 factories dispersed between Brighton, Hove and Little- hampton, have informed the Council that ... the full potential of the Company cannot be exploited unless virtually all their activities can be concentrated in one place ... The dispersal of their factories makes it difficult to control production to the desired efficiency ... It is their intention ... to close all the other factories except [one].[25]

Paradise, however, imposed its costs. Some of these were financial. The Housing Manager had warned in 1949 that "the growth of 'suburbia' is a very costly form of growth for all concerned; heavy demand is made on the Water, Gas, Electricity, Transportation, Cleansing, Street Lighting and Postal Services."[26]

Paradise also had costs for those apparently excluded from the officials' "all concerned" – the residents. In 1959 the Housing Manager pointed out that the 1951 plan had neglected to mention health centres and nursery provision for the estates. The people who lived and worked there had noted this, as well as the lack of shops, pubs, schools, and transport, some time before.

Women living in Hollingbury and in the self-built area of Whitehawk said: "It was like a wilderness, there was just no place to go"; "I felt cut off from everyone, and in the winter, alone with the kids, it was worrying ... lonely"; "I had so much to do in the house I never got out, and it was so far to town." For many of the women working and living in the homes on these estates, re-housing indeed meant more space and better domestic equipment, but it also meant more to look after and higher standards to maintain. Above all, it meant isolation. Husbands and children left home earlier for work or school and arrived home later than when they lived in their former, central homes. They rarely came home for lunch. Friends and extended family were often scattered onto different estates. Shopping was a tiring expedition involving buses and "no time to socialize." Women said, "I never saw a soul from morning until teatime"; "I spent all my time scrubbing, what else was there to do?"

The problems of mobility, although not those of isolation, were more severe for some women with dual roles. Those who worked on the

Hollingbury industrial estate, while they could walk to and from work, had long journeys to shop and to meet friends in a pub. "After a day in that place [the local factory] you wanted to have a chat somewhere other than your own kitchen ... we had to walk better than a mile to the closest pub. It was ridiculous." "That was the first time I ever gave the children canned stuff, when we moved up here. It was so far to go to the shops after work, that I just went once a week and took my son and we bought everything for the week and carried it all back on the bus."

Problems of isolation and mobility were especially acute for elderly people, the majority of whom were women. Many of them had lived in housing that was often verminous, cold, and unsafe. The relocation of older people into new "efficiency flats" helped ease some problems but created others. In 1964 the Medical Officer of Health said:

During the year, owing to development schemes, elderly people, many of them old Brightonians, have had to move from the centre of town to outer areas. This has meant breaking links long established and separation from familiar surroundings, acquaintances and friends. The threat to the security of the individual has resulted in a number of people who have previously been fairly active and self supporting requiring help from the domiciliary services ... The adjustment to new budgets because of changes in the rent, bus fares, shopping in general ... and applications for National Assistance has on occasion caused them to spend too little on food with its accompanying ill effects on ... health and well being.[27]

Partly in response to these problems, home nursing was expanded, as was the domestic help service,[28] although staff levels never reached numbers high enough to meet what the corporation social services committee called a "constant and unsatisfied demand." There was also constant pressure for the establishment and extension of the "meals on wheels" and laundry-service programs.

Experiencing particular problems were the one-parent families in the Hollingbury flats. Times of "financial stringency" had forced the council to build inexpensive flatted estates on cheap suburban land. Although without exception, these women felt that the area was better for their children than the central council or private accommodation in which they had previously lived, the problems of isolation and mobility were acute. Women mentioned the "bleakness" of the area, the distance from family, friends, and entertainment. Yet while these women felt that the flats were isolated from the town and even from the rest of Hollingbury, they complained that the flats never allowed privacy, mentioning overcrowded conditions within the flats and the constant intrusion of "other people's noise" within the buildings. "Here I am, in the middle of nowhere and I can't hear the baby when she wakes up ... it's so noisy." These problems were exacerbated by the stigma attached to the "ghetto."

Despite the protestation of the Housing Manager in 1956, the women in the flats felt "herded together," that their situation combined the worst features of council-flat estates with suburban isolation. One woman said, "We begged for a house but we got sent here. It's awful. It's so far from town and it *is* a ghetto, like they say." One twenty-five-year-old woman with three children who had been recently separated said: "If you live up here everyone thinks you're the lowest of the low. Everyone up here has had a hard time. That's why you end up here. And after you get here it's even harder in many ways. It's hard being alone with the kids, with no money. Some brought their troubles on themselves but some of us try really hard. But they lump us all together."

The separation of the two communities in Hollingbury was also reflected in the comments of women in owner-occupied houses. One woman in an owner-occupied house immediately below the flats said, "We don't have a lot to do with them up there. It's not prejudice, we just don't mix. You see them pushing prams up the hill there and maybe nod to some but that's all." Another, older woman said, "Their lives are different than ours were when we were young ... They have different standards, for themselves and their children."

For families living in bedsits and basements, while waiting to move up the council waiting list, or for families bringing up young children on the tenth floor of a council high-rise, however, such isolation must have seemed attractive. One woman, who had recently moved to Hollingbury, said of her former two-room flat in the centre of the city: "I could never keep the place clean. The kids were everywhere. Sometimes I wanted to scream. I did once, at the council office."

As this comment suggests the job of exerting individual and collective pressure for council houses was generally assumed to be a "woman's responsibility," although as a rule such pressure was applied in less spectacular fashion. One Hollingbury woman said: "Well, I have to work in the place don't I? So I went down there [to the Housing Office] every week until we got the place, and now I go down when something goes wrong. It's my responsibility." Another woman recently relocated to the area of Whitehawk slated for demolition said: "We were desperate. We had the two boys in a one bedroom flat down town and when I had her [a daughter] I asked 'Is it a girl?' I was so relieved. It was strange. I'd just had my daughter and all I could think of was 'now we can get a three bedroom place.'" Others took more collective forms of action. A twenty-seven-year-old mother had organized other mothers to get a council closing order on a damp, structurally unsound building of bedsitters in central Brighton and had "pestered the Council day and night, got doctor's letters, sat in the office with our kids" until offered council houses.

Housing policy, especially the issue of how scarce, council-housing resources were allocated, became a major focus of the debate about how Brighton should be planned in the post-war period, as it was in many communities throughout Britain. As in other places, squatting and other forms of direct action complemented more individual and "legal" forms of pressure. Groups of "vigilantes" took over empty properties in the immediate post-war period and, by the 1960s, squatting had become a major political focus. Throughout the late 1940s and 1950s, wage-work-place based organizations such as the Brighton and District Trades Council had discussed inadequate housing. By the late 1960s there was a growing number of housing pressure groups.[29]

As more families and industries were suburbanized, the town centre was left largely to elderly people living in newly erected council high-rises and small private bedsitters, to wealthy owner-occupiers, to a few council tenant families and to pockets of working-class row-house dwellers, the last concentrated in Hanover, the fringes of Queen's Park, and the less affluent sections of the eastern seafront. Many of this latter group sold their houses or subdivided them into flats or bedsits or, if renters, had this done to them. Others, failing to qualify for "Improvement Grants," lived with the constant problems of repapering damp, crumbling walls, recovering sinking floors, and reroofing improvised bathroom extensions. One young woman who lived and worked in a home she had inherited from her mother said, gesturing around her kitchen, "Every week I have to spend a couple of hours fixing something. We don't pay rent ... but the repairs are a big expense, and a bother."

These changes in the nature of central domestic-community environments were all evident in the adjacent and contrasting areas of Hanover and Queen's Park. Although the dividing line between the two communities – Queen's Park and Hanover – was not as sharp as that in Hollingbury, there was a social distinction demarcated by a geographical division. It was exemplified in the remarks of the head teachers in the two schools. The first – Queen's Park School – serviced the former slum-clearance area and much of Hanover. The second – St Luke's – serviced the Queen's Park area. The headmistress of Queen's Park First School called her catchment area "the ghetto of city planning in Brighton," saying council housing in the area was of very poor quality and private rental housing often worse. She added that conditions were often worse than those in Educational Priority areas such as Whitehawk, a remark echoed by Whitehawk teachers. In contrast the headmistress of St Luke's Terrace First School said of her catchment area "this is not a problem area. It's a stable area. Often a child's parents and grandparents went to St Luke's." However, even in the stable Queen's Park area, people were encountering problems making ends meet. By the 1970s some of those in large houses around or above the park had taken in boarders, or subdivided part of their home into flats or rooms; such strategies either increased women's domestic work load or reduced the space for carrying it out. Many older Hanover residents commented on the "community breaking up," both as a result of slum clearance to the south of the area, the concentration of "problem families" in the older council flats, and an influx of "new people," mainly young families, many of which had higher incomes than long-time residents and had "gentrified" their homes.

The increasing separation of most wage jobs – from housing, from many services, from shopping, from other people's homes – led simultaneously to more movement and greater congestion.[30] It also led to more protests about increasing amounts of "machine space" and inadequate public transport and to the formation of groups to protest transportation-related issues. The groups included those campaigning to resist fare increases and cutbacks in train and bus services; residents' associations formed to resist demolition of housing for a proposed road extension; and environmental groups protesting traffic pollution. In the 1970s several residents' groups were formed to resist "road improvements" and piecemeal traffic plans which divided communities; they also pressed to have crosswalks and roundabouts redesigned for greater safety. One activist, quoted in the alternative newspaper the *Brighton Voice* said: "The road threats have not weakened but strengthened local communities. New friendships and acquaintances have been made. People formerly reluctant to participate in joint action now agree ... it can be effective and worthwhile." The use of urban space became an increasingly political issue, and opposition to transportation "improvements" became more and more associated with the "defence" of communities.[31] In one widely publicized transportation struggle, a group of mothers from the Moulsecoomb council estate resisted the elimination of school-crossing patrols – the "lollipop ladies." To them the issue of community control of road space within the neighbourhood was seen as a matter of life-and-death.[32]

Meanwhile, the old prewar council suburbs, especially the largest – Whitehawk and Moulsecoomb – were "in decline."[33] Problems in Whitehawk had arisen before the war. In 1938 the Medical Officer of Health expressed criticism "of the large number of houses built at Whitehawk, away from the centres of industry" and, in the same year, the Brighton Town Mission said that the rents were too high. "Too often the story was one of dire proverty where the woman tried to stretch her money beyond all possible limits."[34]

During the 1950s and 1960s Whitehawk, which had become an "inner suburb," had developed a reputation as a "dump estate." In the early

1960s the first flats were built at the north end of the estate; this added relocated council tenants to the influx of "new people" moving into the new self-built housing. The two social communities, in the words of one resident, "kept themselves to themselves." Several women in the self-built houses said the estate children were "rough and noisy" and that they didn't want their children to go to Whitehawk schools or the community centre. Others did have friends on the estate, which they had met either through mother and toddler clubs at the community centre or through local playgroups. One mother of a lively toddler said, of the mother and toddler group: "That's neutral territory. It's more important that we are all mothers with our children than where we live or where we went to school."

By 1970 one local social worker described Whitehawk estate as "one of Brighton's first slum clearance estates built before the war, spread out in a valley between a race course and a downs at the far end of the town. A dead-end estate, cut off, isolated, socially and geographically drawn in on itself."[35] Five years later a community worker reported that the area had a high rate of one-parent families, petty crime, patients suffering from depression and nervous disorders, "in care" families, vandalism along small selected roads, and an increasing deterioration of family life. But, she added, it was a highly inter-related family area. "Families remain in the area, or if they leave, return after a few years, and there is a good spirit of loyalty, neighbourliness, pride and forthrightness."[36]

This contrast of images was clearly reflected by the women I talked to. While most spoke of overcrowded housing, families with problems, lack of facilities for teenagers, and the unsettling effect of the demolition and redevelopment, they also spoke of what the headmaster of the local high school called "a genuine heart and soul in the estate." One woman who had grown up in Whitehawk said: "When I was a child we lived in each other's neighbours' houses. The back door was open. You'd just go in and your mother used to find you in one of half a dozen houses. She didn't know where you were but she knew you were safe. There was a feeling that everyone was your friend on the estate, and you could talk to anybody. You always knew your neighbours."

This spirit was both a cause and an effect of the fact that Whitehawk, although always a relatively "underprivileged" area, had always been an active community, both in terms of the "community of women at home" and the more obvious political organization around the issues of urban fabric and urban process. Throughout the post-war period Whitehawk residents organized around the issue of their housing conditions, and even went on a nine-month rent strike. From the early 1960s residents had pushed for redevelopment and gained support from a variety of groups, including the Trades Council.[37] Some of these processes were successful in helping residents gain more control over their domestic-community environments. In 1971 the residents of the tower blocks formed a tenants' association, which campaigned and petitioned about dampness and condensation in the flats and against rent increases and inadequate heating. The association pressured for, and three years later won, a playgroup facility in the flats; in the same year it got the council to agree not to place any more families with children under twelve in the tower blocks. The East Brighton Residents Association (EBRA) – formed to represent the entire East Brighton area – and other, more localized groups, organized and petitioned for better play areas and school facilities, better street lighting, and "speed bumps."[38]

In 1973 Brighton Council, in an attempt to "uplift" the area around the new marina south of the estate, approved plans for the demolition of the centre of the Whitehawk estate, the downed buildings to be replaced by a 1,000 new council houses and 7,600 "private flats." The East Brighton Residents Association and other groups initiated a struggle to control and guide development in the interest of Whitehawk, a struggle which was partly successful and which considerably strengthened community ties. The East Brighton Residents Association also co-ordinated "street wardens," who listened to and helped advise residents on their concerns, and ran a fortnightly advice centre. One street warden told me that it was most frequently women who brought grievances to her: "It's their job to straighten out the electric meter if it doesn't work or to apply for a larger house or even to deal with vandalism. Men don't even notice most of these things unless you tell them, and then they say 'oh, you go off and see Sarah about it.' But of course it's still the men who speak up in meetings, about the big issues, or even these little things. You can see their wives pushing them up to speak." All the residents I spoke to on the Whitehawk estate had had some contact with the EBRA, and many had used the centre to deal with problems ranging from electricity bills to suspected child battering.

These three communities, like those of the city as a whole, were therefore created by a combination of planning, protest, negotiation, and individual adaption. Structuring the urban fabric and restructuring the inheritance of previous generations was a matter of social and political contestation, contestation in which women – often individually, occasionally collectively, sometimes dramatically – attempted to improve the material context within which they carried out their domestic work. Some elements of these communities certainly were concrete, fixed, and inanimate. But they were never neutral, never simply a background. The communities were both the base and the motivation for women's organization.

STANDARDS IN THE HOME: WORKING CONDITIONS AND COMMODITIES

> It was really hard work trying to get the playgroup going in the flats, and trying to do all those other things to improve things up there. We had meetings after work and we worked on the place all the week-ends ... But you'd come home from a meeting, feeling good because there were all those people and we'd agreed and worked together and there it was, as you walked in the door, the damp running down the wall and the kids stuff all over, and our bed was in the living room because there was nowhere else. I'd get so angry, all my good feeling would disappear. But this place, it never lets you forget what you were fighting for. (Whitehawk mother, active in the protests about the flats.)

Integrally connected to the nature of the community is the home, the place in which women actually do most of their domestic-community work. The home is actively linked to its community through the daily movement patterns which household workers carry out. Like the community, the home is also changeful.

Wherever women went in the course of a day and whatever they did, their homes, as responsibilities, work, and occasionally as pleasure, awaited them on their return. Throughout the post-war period the nature and the quality of what was there altered, both in terms of the physical environments into which women stepped when they entered their front doors and in terms of the kinds of relations they were creating when they went out those front doors again.

All the women I spoke to agreed that there had been tremendous changes in the conditions and processes of domestic-community work over their lifetimes. Most stated that these changes – notably improved physical working environments and more state services and commodities – had made things better or easier. Many also suggested that the arena of women's activities and the number of things they did in the course of being domestic-community workers had expanded. A fifty-eight-year-old Hanover woman with three married daughters and a mother living close by said, with some amused animation: "My daughters are always rushing about, they're never at home, always saying they 'have to' do this and that. My mum now, she worked at home. In those days when they said a woman stayed at home, she *stayed* at home. She had too much work to do there to be off organizing things and earning money like the girls do now. Me, I'm somewhere in between. I go out more than mum did, but I'm not always rushing about."

In contrast, however, many women felt that the home itself and the family had become more "closed." Older women, speaking of their early married life, and young women, remembering their childhood, saw a decline in informal communal childcare arrangements where "we all lived in each others houses" and in sharing and borrowing networks. These networks had all assumed that most women were at home, or at least in the immediate community, and that they were available to one another for most of the day. This as an assumption precluded, as people noted, women taking on wage jobs. A number of women stated that they and their neighbours, while engaged in performing household duties, were more likely to be alone than their mothers' generation and that they were less likely to engage in informal collective work where neighbours helped with preserving, cooking a celebration meal, or caring for a sick child.

Changes in the time and space of domestic-community work took place in a number of ways, the basis of which was the house in which they took place and, as noted above, the community in which that house was located. The standard of housing, together with concerns over where to locate the housing, was a theme that wove through Brighton's post-war social planning and much of its political organization. It was also the context within which alterations in boundaries of women's "living" and "working," "public" and "private" space and time took place.

Throughout the post-war period statutory agencies emphasized improving domestic-working standards. And there was great room for improvement. The Medical Officer of Health reported that, in 1951, 43 per cent of Brighton households had no bath or had to share a bath with other households.[39] Two years later the Housing Manager saw overcrowding and unsatisfactory housing as the greatest problem in the city: "A great many families are living in old dilapidated houses and in dark damp basements. Domestic friction among two or three families sharing kitchens and other communal facilities continues." He mentioned "urgent cases" of "serious overcrowding" where "up to three children share parent's bedrooms."[40] Not surprisingly, there were reports that couples were delaying marriage or marriages were "breaking down" due to bad housing.[41]

Many of the older women I spoke to had experienced such conditions. They had lived with their mothers or mothers-in-law when first married, then rented a one- or two-room flat when the first child came, and finally moved into a council or private house just before or after the second child arrived. Often living with parents or in one room had been a wartime "make-shift," extended beyond the war out of necessity. Overcrowding was often mentioned as exacerbating the strains of readjusting to the return of husband and father. One woman said: "It was hard to get used to having another to look after. I was happy he was home safe of course, but my goodness ... he was so big! The children and I had fitted in but poor [her husband] never knew where to put himself ... It wasn't all roses after the war you know, whatever they say in the books."

The 1949 Housing Act provided financial assistance "to be available to local authorities and private owners for the improvement of dwelling accommodation by way of Improvement Grants." In 1954 this program was expanded and "for the first time a standard of fitness for human habitation has been included in the legislation."[42] This standard, which had been suggested by the 1956 Central Housing Advisory Committee, was incorporated into the 1957 Housing Act and required "regard to be paid to the condition of the house in respect of repair, stability, freedom from damp, natural lighting, ventilation, water supply, drainage, the sanitary conveniences and facilities for storage, preparation and cooking of food and the disposal of waste water."[43]

Throughout the 1950s the Housing Department reported "innovative" improvements in council and private housing: sub-floor electric heating, which cuts down the cleaning associated with coal heat, keeps "the decor fresh longer" and is a "protection to health"; provision of "shower rooms instead of baths," intended to save water and to assist the tenant's wife who "appreciates its secondary use as a washroom."[44]

This uneasy alliance of concern for housewives' working conditions and concern for the efficient allocation of social resources had its effect on the equipment and routine of the household. By 1958 the Chief Public Health Inspector reported that environmental hygiene had progressed. The food hygiene regulations had "focussed the attention of the public on the standards adopted in shops and this is again reflected in the storage and keeping of food in the home. The fitting of refrigerators in Corporation houses no doubt had a great deal to do with this improvement. It brought what was a few years ago considered to be a luxury article, into the class of necessity for reasonable living. Household routine has been improved and is reflected in better household management by the housewife."[45] In the same report, he stressed that "the improvements in housing standards and the ability of many to purchase the numerous aids which are marketed to ease work in the home are much in evidence in the daily round of the Inspector."

The contents of the home were, more and more, influenced by the decisions taken not only by environmental inspectors and housing agencies but by consumer goods manufacturers, the retail sector, and the advertising industry. The celebration of "mechanical slaves" which would simultaneously take the drudgery out of housework and render women "equal" – to one another and within the family – was an important part of post-war consensus. The advertising industry, whose expenditures rose throughout the post-war period, utilized the women's press to help create demand.[46] Although the distribution of household "labour-saving devices" did vary over class, there was a general rise in their ownership in the 1950s and 1960s, as well as a rise in the availability and use of ready-made clothing and "convenience foods."[47]

These improved standards were invariably mentioned by the women to whom I spoke. Several older women said they had homes their mothers "never dreamed of," and commented on the amount of household equipment they owned. Younger women, contrasting their lighter domestic workload with their mothers', mentioned their mothers' larger families and the fact that their fathers never "helped out" as their husbands did. One woman of fifty-two said: "My mother used to say every day 'If I make it through today, I'll live forever.' Me, I only say that once a week."

Older women vividly remembered the purchase of specific household aids: a wringer-washer, to replace boiling and hand scrubbing clothes; the first refrigerator; the vacuum cleaner which meant one did not have to beat the rugs in the back yard. "That was the worst job: backbreaking it was getting them out and in, and then there you were, choking in the dust, arms hurt, and covered in dirt." "It seems silly now," one woman said of her first electric cooker, "they're so commonplace. But I cried when I first turned it on. I was so happy. It was the first day for thirteen years, all my married life, when I hadn't had to light a fire." Women remembered buying an item of children's clothing for the first time instead of buying the material and sewing it up in the evenings, or the first use of an electric sewing-machine. They remembered electric irons and also the first time they burnt one of the new nylon blouses. "It just melted right away." Women commented on paper handkerchiefs and on disposable nappies, frozen lamb, and teabags.

But, as the disappearing nylon blouse hints, women also began to experience new problems in working with these new products. Things broke down, went wrong, tasted funny, and cost a lot more than expected. More and more items were made of new materials; clothing had to be "scientifically" washed, or dry cleaned; food was "less likely to be what it said it was" or was "full of chemicals and covered in poison." Shopping was not only more central to household work, it was becoming increasingly complex.

Throughout Britain the regulation of consumer standards and comsumer education was becoming, increasingly, a public function. "Experts" intensified the interwar plea for "domestic science" training, at least for working-class girls. Domestic science became more "scientific" and included chemistry and household accounting, so that students could attain an "A" level paper acceptable to universities. Women commented that their daughters and granddaughters "were learning in school what I learned from my mother" or, in contrast, "I couldn't teach her all that, it's all science and things I never heard of, let alone did."

Shopping patterns also altered as large, central self-service stores replaced both corner shops and the small Sainsburys "where you had to queue for every item." In the Brighton area, although the overall shopping floorspace increased in the 1960s, there was a gradual decrease outside the central areas.[48] By the early 1970s the city had clearly defined central shopping areas, while the smaller commercial parades in residential areas were almost wholly devoted to "convenience goods." Shopping became a more spatially extensive process.

Of the fifty-five women I spoke to, only six shopped entirely in their local area. Four of these were elderly women and two were mothers with young children; none had cars and all had limited personal mobility. Thirty-three shopped only "downtown" at supermarkets (thirty-one of these had access to a car), and sixteen shopped both locally and downtown. Forty shopped weekly and fifteen daily. Again, this latter group tended to be elderly or had young children and no access to a car, and were all lower-income people. They not only had less to spend on "big" shopping trips, but tended to have inadequate facilities for storing large quantities of food.

This pattern of retail provision and shopping presents some very real difficulties. Although thirty of the fifty-five women I spoke to preferred supermarkets, as cheaper and more convenient, almost all experienced some difficulty with this aspect of their domestic-community work. Problems were especially acute for women in Hollingbury. Prices in local shops were high. They "never had specials." Women with young children described their attempts to go shopping downtown by bus as "a nightmare," as "awful," as "the worst part of my week." They were often obliged to use taxis to come home. Three of the women from one-parent families said they "clubbed" together with other women to take care of children while others shopped, or they went on shopping trips together and shared the cost of a taxi.

Women in Whitehawk and Hanover who were elderly or had young children and no car also had difficulties. They all spoke of infrequent and expensive bus service, and those with children spoke of the difficulties of getting prams, bundles, and toddlers on and off buses. Prams and pushchairs (strollers) were "impossible" in supermarkets. "You can't push a pushchair and a cart and if you put the baby and the pushchair into the cart, where do you put the groceries?" Prams and pushchairs did not go easily through checkouts and turnstiles, nor did they easily go up and down stairs and escalators. "Children's shoe departments are always upstairs or downstairs. It's ridiculous." Prams do not weave easily through heavy pedestrian or vehicular traffic near large shopping centres. And shopping centres rarely have facilities for feeding or changing babies. "I've changed her on a bench in the middle of [a shopping centre]. It was awful. I felt so embarrassed. But what could I do? I couldn't let her go on crying." Although their prices were generally higher, small shops were easier for mothers with young children. Prams and pushchairs could be left outside the door or parked in one spot inside, although double pushchairs would not fit through the doors. Shopkeepers were frequently friendly; they talked to the children and gave them small treats. One woman in Whitehawk said her husband would take the children shopping in the local shops "but not to big shops. He says people stare."

Elderly women frequently resented the impersonal nature of super markets. Shopping in local shops had been "a social event" and they felt that products and service had been more reliable, or at least that redress was easier if goods were unsatisfactory. "I don't know why" one Hanover woman of sixty-seven told me: "When I go to the supermarket, I come home completely tired, and very depressed. I have these bags full of groceries that no one I know cares about, and I've given my money to people I don't know and I've seen lots of people and I haven't really talked to anyone. All I have at the end of a day are bags of groceries I can't trust and a sore back."

The greater centrality and complexity of this aspect of women's do-mestic-community work led to more consumer groups throughout Brit-ain as a whole pressuring for consumer protection legislation.[49] These consumer groups included a large number of women's groups. A 1949 commission on the organization of a domestic-consumer advisory com-mittee for the British Standards Institute recommended that the small advisory group of National Council of Women representatives, which had been set up in 1946, should be expanded to comprise "the extended use of women's organizations, several of which are of nation-wide stand-ing, and have in recent time done useful work in advising on various questions connected with Utility Schemes, fuel supplies and other mat-ters arising out of Government controls ... Some consumer represen-tatives might not be possessed of technical qualifications ... but might well know the practical needs of the domestic user and the practical defects of any existing equipment."[50]

In 1951 the committee was expanded into the Women's Advisory Committee, with eighteen "national women's groups represented." Until 1973, when the Consumer Standards Advisory Committee was formed with "mixed membership and government bodies," this constituted the major, domestic-consumer advisory committee to the British Standards Institute.[51] In 1961 the National Federation of Consumer Groups was set up and, in 1973, the National Consumer Council, a quasi-government body, was established with a special mandate to assist the "underprivi-leged consumer." In the same year the Ministry of Consumer Affairs and the Office Of Fair Trading were also set up.

The Brighton branch of the National Federation of Consumer Groups was, like other local groups, autonomous and locally directed. Its secretary stated, "People write or call and say 'I'm upset about this, are you doing something about it?' and we ask them to come along and we do something." The group had worked on issues ranging from community health services to planning enquiries to the prices of children's shoes. In all the local groups women, as the primary household consumers, had played the most active part: they often entered community politics through their work in the groups.

Throughout Britain, as consumer interests became more central to domestic-community work, the more traditional women's consumer groups expanded their campaigns and branched out, becoming, increasingly, bases for women's greater participation in "public life." The Electrical Association for Women designed new and more comprehensive courses for "homemakers, students and professionals." In 1958 it established an educational trust fund for women in scientific fields and set up a travelling lecture series, the high point of which was the 1970 series advocating "Women in Management."[52] The Women's Co-operative Guild redoubled its campaigns not only for women as consumers but "to prepare women to take part in local, national and international affairs."[53]

In 1964 the Medical Officer of Health stated that, in Brighton: "a better informed public is demanding changes in all aspects of life. There is a more lively appreciation of design, colour, order and the material aspects of home and family life. Viewing from the standards of living obtaining ... forty years ago, this difference amounts to a revolution. There is a quickening pace and the next twenty years should be dramatic."[54] In the same report he noted that "in the housing field, the public expects more vigorous action in regard to slum clearance, unfit houses and the improvement of older properties so that they can live more comfortably."

COMMUNITY NETWORKS AND PATTERNS

Life isn't what it was around here. It's all changed. People's doors are always closed ... all the young women go off in cars with their children ... they seem so busy and lively. (Older woman who had lived all her life in Hanover.)

The pattern of women's domestic work, as well as their space-time paths through the city, was influenced by the homes and neighbourhoods in which women lived. They, in turn, influenced these homes and neighbourhoods. The environments in which they lived and carried out their domestic work were not static: they represented an active, mutable set of resources providing opportunities and constraints. After the war, the nature and the use of home and community resources altered, in meaning, in location, and in equipment.

However homes and neighbourhoods varied, over time and over the space of the city, two things were consistent in this period. First, the home was a working environment; it provided variable sets of resources for use in work and influenced women's access to the wider resources of society. With the new locations of neighbourhoods came new transportation routes, affecting mutual access, changing the way women worked and shopped, and changing their social networks and family relations. Second, the home could not be separated from the community in which it was situated. The relation of the home to the community changed, largely through changes in women's activities, but the link remained active. It took two forms: the immediate personal networks of friends and extended family, which women established and sustained in their daily life, and the more formal groups, statutory and voluntary, which attempted to provide necessary communal resources for family life.

The amount of access to the city women had through networks and travel patterns varied over the three communities. All the women in Hollingbury expressed feelings of isolation and of being "trapped," especially in the winter. The women in the flats tended to have friends all over the city and to travel downtown to shop, visit, or "go out." All the women in Hollingbury relied mainly on weekly supermarket shopping trips and used more canned and frozen or dried foods than women in other areas. Among the women in the owner-occupied houses, there was little evidence of strong informal networks, although these were important to the "survival" of the women in the flats. Any formal networks were associated with playgroups or the school.

In contrast, the women in the Hanover-Queen's Park area had the most complex set of formal and informal networks and the smallest geographic range of the three areas. Long-time residents had strong and complex family and community ties. Of the thirteen women I spoke to in Hanover, seven had lived there "all their lives" and had family in the immediate area. All of these relied heavily on family and neighbours for support and exchange of services. Women helped one another with shopping and childcare and offered advice on pregnancies and jobs. The long-time residents were always "in and out of each others houses"; their conversations included references to "what your mother did" in a similar situation and to changes in networks stemming from alterations in the community fabric. The more recent arrivals to the community tended to get involved in formal community networks such as the community associations or the childbirth and childcare networks discussed below. This was especially true of the higher income, often professional "gentrifiers." Hanover-Queen's Park had the lowest incidence of weekly supermarket shopping and the highest number of women who "bought fresh daily." Almost everyone who frequented pubs used the local ones, of which there were many in easy walking distance, and several women said they met other mothers there for a drink outside at midday with the children.

The women on the Whitehawk estate also had strong and complex family ties, often extending over four generations. One woman I spoke to lived in between her mother-in-law and her older daughter, and said, as her seventeen year-old daughter introduced me to her fiancé, "She's next, we're going to take over the whole road soon." Such extended family situations were common. Teachers remarked that different extended family members brought and picked up young children, and a conference with family over a child's progress could involve up to five adult relatives. These extended family networks, along with informal groups of neighbours, provided the major source of support and information for the Whitehawk estate women. Women in the owner-occupied housing were less likely to have family living locally, but the long-time residents, especially the pioneers who had been part of the first self-build movement, all had close friends in the area who provided support. As two pioneers commented, "We all arrived here with young children, and we've all raised our families together and now we are watching them begin families together. We've shared a lot." "All our friends are up here." Younger women in the area, even if they were second generation, were more likely to find their support networks through the formal groups such as the local playgroups and mother and toddler groups, and were thus more likely to have friends, or at least acquaintances, on the estate than were those in the older group.

It was within this city-wide context, and within neighbourhoods like this, that women's post-war domestic working environments were located. The rationalization of the urban fabric (and concomitant problems and resistance) were part of a growing socialization and politicization of domestic-community working conditions. The history of post-war domestic-community work may be characterized as a growing penetration of "society as a whole" into the home and a parallel extension of domestic processes and activities into the community. This mutual interpenetration was not a straightforward, linear process of "opening up the home." Rather it was a process of constant, and subtle, alterations in where and when life and work went on, of overlapping of public and private space and time, and of mutations in the boundaries and definitions of home and community.

While the organization of women in the interwar period had opened the home, placing it within a web of social concerns and social services aiming to match the needs of the family with the resources which could be purchased with the male wage, this opening was greatly extended in post-war Brighton. Women's domestic work continued to be carried out, to a large extent, in isolation, in parallel in thousands of homes. But it was an isolation increasingly mediated, both vicariously and directly, by a growing range of public agencies and informal organizations which impinged on the way women organized and utilized their domestic-community space and the time they devoted to these responsibilities. The public sphere extended into the home through direct state intervention in domestic performance, through the growth of standards of performance and the growing use of consumer goods, and through intervention in the milieux through which these were provided: the physical home and community itself.

In the interwar period, many forms of pressure in the domestic-community sphere had continued to be mediated by the family wage packet. Attempts to improve conditions had increasingly meant taking on the state (generally, as noted previously, the local state) or the retail sector, as well as creating individual and collective alternatives to gaps in state and commercial services; in short, women had extended the domestic role into the community.

Some of this extension of the work of the home into the community had been foreseen and encouraged by the architects of the reconstruction. Recognizing the gaps in state services, including the lack of rehabilitation and recreation for housewives and of facilities for the communalization of household work, Beveridge had seen women's voluntary work as a means to meet these needs. The Fabian Society's brief to the 1949 Commission on Population went further, to insist on the social necessity for women's voluntary work outside the home and warn that, for "society's" sake, "the mothers who choose to spend their whole time looking after the children when they are small ... must realise that they should give part-time service to the community when the children are older ... A democratic society cannot tolerate parasites, and married women who are not pulling their weight should be recognized as parasites."[55]

But the form in which the home, in the shape of volunteering and campaigning women, was to spill into the community was unratified and unexpected. As the persons primarily responsible for domestic work, women were especially provoked to campaign in their communities for better and more equitably located services, for better home and estate management and maintenance, for more and better designed housing. However, their concerns and campaigns went beyond the form and content of the home to include pressures for social resources to change the nature of family life. In a move which startled post-war planners, women acted to alter those most private and natural areas of life, the nature of fertility and childbirth.

5 / *Extending Control over Fertility, Childbirth, and Family Patterns.*

> For me, being a woman wasn't all that difficult until I had the kids. Then I realized how superficial all those things like Equal Pay acts are. (Thirty-seven year old mother of two preschool children, former teacher and member of National Union of Teachers.)

Being a woman and being a person with the biological capacity to bear children is not the same thing. But the social definition of what a woman is and of what she should be doing has always focused on this capacity, a capacity which men do not share. Women's capacity for motherhood and motherhood itself has been a consistent organizing principle in the constitution of "woman," one around which other social constituents are created, grouped, and altered.

All the women I spoke to who had children saw motherhood as the most fundamental change in their lives. For most the change was simultaneously rewarding and restricting. But it was change – fundamental, irrevocable, and cumulative change. Becoming mothers altered women's daily activities, their mobility, their associations, and, for most, their income. It changed all aspects of the "where," the "when," and the "with whom" of their lives. And these continued to change as the children grew older.

The discussions I had with women in Brighton indicated not only that motherhood was fundamental to their lives, but that childbirth, maternity, and the households in which they went in were, in part, like their environmental contexts, human creations. People decided when and how to have children in the context of social and individual resources available to them. The amount of control which a woman exerted over her fertility and the process of childbirth was thus one of the primary conditions upon which – within the constraints of the resources available to someone in her class position – her conditions of life and work depended.

In the post-war period this control was increasingly recognized and articulated by women. For the women to whom I spoke, fertility and birth were no longer seen as wholly "natural" processes but as a part of their lives which, like other aspects, could be planned and which had to be "fitted in." In fact, control over fertility and childbirth was, in fundamental ways, the foundation of women's attempts to control their lives and extend their access to resources.

This was reflected in the National Abortion Campaign's 1980 *Statement of Principles*: "Women will only be able to take an equal part in society when we can decide for ourselves whether and when to have children."[1] Adrienne Rich, in her discussion of motherhood, said that "as long as birth – metaphorically or literally – remains an experience of passively handing over our minds and our bodies to male authority and technology, other kinds of social change can only minimally change our relationship to ourselves, to power, and to the world outside our bodies."[2]

This recognition by women, along with their subsequent demands and organization, was a response to the growing social control over conditions of fertility and childbirth. At the same time, it extended and altered the quality of such control.

REDEFINING BRITISH POPULATION POLICY

The concern for a "balanced" population of "adequate" people and the debate around the means of achieving this had lurked in British social planning since Malthus. Although successive governments had resisted forming an explicit population policy, post-war reconstruction governments fashioned an unsystematic series of legislative regulations on the "means" of demographic regulation – contraception and abortion – and increasingly intervened into the health and fitness of the "units" of this change – women and their infants. Policy and service provision were fragmentary and often contradictory, but they increased, nonetheless, the socialization and regulation of the conditions of women's biological reproduction.

Throughout the 1940s and 1950s, the fears of population decline that had haunted interwar social analysts continued. There was a general mood of pro-natalism, largely fostered through the "pro-family" social services. But, by the late 1960s, the pendulum had swung and overpopulation became the concern. The "population bomb" had hit the British media. All the arguments put forth during the late 1930s were reversed. Suddenly those who gave birth, as opposed to those who did not, were being castigated as selfish, shortsighted, and in need of control. Fear of the consequences of the "bomb" gave rise to a proliferation of groups advocating a "balance" of population and resources.[3] It also gave rise to a new wave of birth controllers.

In much of this excitement women were seen, if seen at all (except in back rooms making tea for the meetings), as units to which pressure was to be applied in order that they produce the correct number and type of children. For women, however, "population figures" and "demographic trends" were the outcome of decisions, or accidents, which, as noted above, structured the conditions of their health, their mobility, their daily activities, and the resources available to them. During the decades after the war they made this evident with increasing force. For more and more women, control over their own fertility had become a social and political issue. Only occasionally did the issue correspond to the prescriptions of the state, the media, and the population groups. In 1970 the first national women's conference made "free contraception and abortion on demand" one of its four demands: "We want to be free to choose when and how many kids to have, if any. We have to fight for control over our own bodies, for even the magic pill or (in the case of mistakes) abortion on demand only gives us the freeedom to get into a real mess without any visible consequences. We still can't talk of sex as anything but a joke or a battleground."[4] The question of balanced population and demographic change had taken a new and unexpected twist. The three elements of the demand – contraception, abortion, and self-determination of sexuality – constituted a new field of campaign.

EXTENDING CONTROL OVER CONTRACEPTION, ABORTION, AND SEXUALITY

Contraception

Until the development of oral contraception, the British medical profession as a whole saw birth control as outside its province. Birth control was not "real medicine." The Family Planning Association (FPA) therefore continued to function as the main provider of professional advice on birth control, a service it had developed in the interwar period. At the same time, in the tradition of women's organizations, it pressed for better facilities and more state support for women's control over their fertility.

This general pattern for the provision of contraceptive services was reflected in Brighton. At the close of the war, Brighton had one family-planning clinic run by the local authority. In 1951 Dr Rose Morrison, the assistant medical officer of health for maternal and child welfare, announced the opening of a "second session" at the clinic, in response to the fact that "the post-war rise in the birth rate brought its sequence of an increasing number of women requiring contraceptive advice on medical grounds."[5]

Until 1967, however, the local authority clinic in Brighton, as elsewhere, took only "medical cases." Even after the inclusion of "social criteria" subsequent to the 1967 Family Planning Act, it met only a small fraction of the need. In Brighton, as elsewhere, the major service was provided by the Family Planning Association.

Nationally, FPA clinic expansion continued throughout the 1950s and 1960s. The FPA also pioneered research on new and safer contraceptive methods and on domiciliary birth control. In the post-war period, the FPA was still an organization by women for women. In 1960, nationally, 89.7 per cent of its branch members were female and all but 1.6 per cent of its clinic doctors were women. The majority of these doctors (85 per cent) were mothers, most of whom worked part-time. Only 0.7 per cent of clients were male.[6] The Brighton FPA was also staffed and used almost entirely by women.

Birth-control use continued to increase, both nationally and in Brighton, especially among those women whose husbands were classified as non-manual and skilled workers. Among women whose husbands were manual workers, male methods – sheath or withdrawal – were still favoured. The "female" methods advised and provided by the FPA were used most widely by women whose husbands were non-manual workers.[7] Oral contraception and, to a lesser extent, the IUD, introduced in the early 1960s, rapidly changed these user patterns. First young people and then the majority of users attending clinics adopted the pill.[8] Birth control had always been a "woman's problem." Now it became almost wholly a women's responsibility as well.

Oral contraception also radically altered the attitude of British doctors to birth control. "Hormonal contraception required medical supervision and therefore provided a legitimate professional interest: the prescription of drugs as distinct from the fitting of caps which smacked of 'improper medicine.' Birth control became truly 'medicalised.'"[9] A debate carried on in the *Lancet* between 1960 and 1962 called the pill "a subject second in importance only to the nuclear bomb." Women's demands for the pill were increasingly met by GPs. Unfortunately, most doctor's major professional concern was "focussed on securing adequate payment for this extra service." The Family Planning Association, in conjunction with its offspring – the Council for Investigation of Fertility Control, established in 1958 – was the first agency in Britain to carry out preliminary tests on oral contraceptives. It also tested the IUD and began distributing it in 1964.[10]

Relatively reliable contraception whose use, although not production, was controlled by women themselves was probably the most significant factor in changing women's lives in the post-war period. As well as giving women some control over their conditions of health and work, reliable female contraception opened up the potential for women to explore their sexuality. The subsequent "sexual revolution" had ambivalent results.[11] It changed forever the lingering Victorian myth of female asexuality and opened up a new and, as always, problematic arena for women. But "freedom from fear" of unwanted pregnancies raised new dangers and led to new campaigns.

The first reports on thrombo-phlebitis, migraines, and jaundice in connection with use of the pill appeared as early as 1961. Medical and governmental inaction forced both individual women and women's health groups, including the Pill Victims' Action Group and the Campaign Against Depo Provera, to press for better controls on and safer means of contraception.[12] By the 1970s more and more women in Brighton expressed a reluctance to go on the pill or continue its use.

While fighting the effects of "medical miracles" and "contraceptive revolutions" with one hand, with the other women were pressing for the extension of fertility-control facilities. In 1967, as a result of extra-parliamentary pressure and the "population bomb" scare, the NHS (Family Planning) Act was passed. It liberalized family-planning law by extending local-authority contraceptive services and allowing the perscription of birth control for women who wished to limit their families for "social" as well as medical reasons.[13]

In Brighton the local authority took advantage of the 1967 act to expand provision in some directions. Expressing concern about the rising rate of VD and increasing number of children born to independent women, the Medical Officer of Health in 1970 urged better contraceptive services in Brighton and free universal provision of these services for the country as a whole. In 1971 he recommended that part of an urban aid grant be allocated to the setting up of a domiciliary family-planning service.[14]

Throughout the 1970s women's groups across the country, led by the "feminist" FPA offshoot, the Birth Control Campaign, pressed for fertility control to be available on the NHS.[15] Finally, in 1973, the NHS Reorganization Bill made family planning part of the NHS and, in 1974, a newly-elected Labour government implemented a "free family planning service." It was a victory, but a limited one. The FPA and other "voluntary" groups and charities continued to provide most of the innovation and protection and some of the services.

In Brighton administration of the FPA's Family Planning Clinic was transferred to the Area Health Authority. Since few GPs provided a full contraceptive service, this clinic was the main source of birth control advice. The change-over was, however, a difficult one. Charles Forster, regional administrator for the FPA recalled that: "A lot of people didn't like it because however big we [the FPA] grew, we were a big family. Everybody who worked for us was dedicated toward women's health and well-being through contraception. They believed in family planning, they saw it ... as a women's right. So we did have a very special kind of staff. Unfortunately now the selection of the staff [is based] on administrative background rather than attitude."

More severe problems arose when the Family Planning Clinic was threatened with a cutback, as an economy measure, on the grounds that it was a duplication of the GPS' services. FPA clinics throughout the country had to face such threats. The Brighton clinic survived two such attempts. The first came in early 1978, when the Area Health Authority proposed a cut of one-sixth of the budget allocated to the Family Planning Clinic and to cervical cytology. The second came in 1979–80 when proposed cuts of £650,000 would have virtually eliminated the service. (In 1980 the exchange rate £1$ Canadian averaged about $2.00.) On both occasions campaigns of lobbying, demonstrations, and petitions to MPs and the Area Health Authority, led by the FPA and supported by the National Abortion Campaign and the Brighton Trades Council, resulted in reprieves. Forster recalled: "We made a hell of a noise and saved the clinics. But it's not finished. When they look for economies, the Family Planning Clinics will be considered each time. Each time we will fight."

No longer responsible for clinics, the FPA continued, in the words of its national chairman, to fulfill its "responsibility for progressive thought. After all, the government likes others to do bold things."[16] The remaining activities of the eleven regional branches varied. The relationship was one of local branches developing services to meet local needs, services which were sometimes assisted and often taken up by the national office. In the Brighton area, the FPA ran courses, campaigns, and a weekly women's health centre. It concentrated resources on the sexual needs of the handicapped and on women who experienced menopausal problems and premenstrual tension. These programs had all developed in the same way. According to Charles Forster:

Someone comes in with a request, a problem – and we work on it together and we look around and find someone who knows about it and call a public meeting and they come and speak. Every meeting we've filled the theatre, and had to turn people away. People have come from all over, women realising that they're not the only one concerned about the problems. And lots of them speak up, in a meeting of hundreds of people, they're that relieved to have someone to listen to them. And then we set up smaller day meetings and then courses for professionals and in 1979, we sponsored a women's health week and out of that, set up the women's health centre.

The FPA also ran sex education courses for health care and teaching professionals and designed syllabi for schools. In conjunction with the Health Education Council, it published "mounds of literature" and worked on ways of getting it to the "right people." Distribution efforts included sending out a van stocked with contraceptive information to tour local shopping centres and, with union co-operation, factories. Above all the FPA, in a variety of ways, some of them ingenious, pushed for better services and for services which more closely met women's needs.

Abortion

The national struggle for contraception pales beside the controversy surrounding abortion. Despite long-standing pressure by groups such as the Abortion Law Reform Association (ALRA), formed in 1936, and despite the 1939 Birkett Commission recommendations for liberalization of abortion laws, it was 1967 before the Abortion Act was proposed (at the request of the ALRA,) and, after massive extra-parliamentary controversy, passed.

Even after 1967 abortion services continued to be inadequate. Availability varied regionally. In the 1960s the National Health Service performed less than 67 per cent of all abortions in England and this rate dropped steadily throughout the 1970s.[17] In Brighton the percentage of NHS abortions had always been especially low and the NHS service often unsatisfactory. Women said that they were given insufficient information, no choice about the type of operation they received, and that these operations were often more complicated than necessary.

The greatest barrier women encountered was what British Pregnancy Advisory Service chairman François Lafitte and others called the "NHS Abortion Hurdle Race": the constant confusion, delays, and obstacles that drive many women into a late and expensive "private" abortion or into continuing an unwanted pregnancy. The initial difficulty involved finding a sympathetic general practioner. Many GPs refused to recommend abortion, and sympathetic ones were reluctant to take on patients solely for this reason. Women were frequently forced to argue and plead in the face of "moral" disapproval. "It's almost as if they wait for you to grovel before they will do you a big favour and agree to 'help,'" one woman told me. In 1975, Lafitte said: "Some delay is attributable to patients themselves ... but the chief obstacles are erected by doctors. They result from the medical profession's legal monopoly of the authorising of abortion combined with doctors' freedom to abstain from helping women obtain it, so obliging them to seek private treatment facilities."[18] A 1981 National Children's Bureau survey of abortion services in Wessex reported that doctors were also affronted by the fact that women asking for abortions had done their own diagnosis and proposed a "cure."[19] A further difficulty arose in delays in pregnancy test results. In 1975–76, for example, although "87 per cent of the women consulted their doctor before eight weeks of pregnancy ... less than 65 per cent of NHS abortions were done before twelve weeks. Delays were found to occur in establishing proof of pregnancy."[20] Further delays occurred in finding hospital accommodation.

In response to the inadequacies of the NHS services, the Brighton National Abortion Campaign, in co-operation with the Brighton Women's Centre, offered "instant" pregnancy tests, as well as advice and assistance, which included researching and providing information on local facilities to women requiring abortions. In the tradition of women's organizations, they also pressed for improved NHS services. For instance, in 1978, they sponsored a campaign for improved day care and abortion which involved some GPs and hospital staff, the Trades Council, the Co-op Party, the Sussex University Student Union, and some individual unions. This campaign won the support of the Community Health Council.[21]

The inadequacies of national NHS services had necessitated the formation of a range of groups to press for fuller implementation of the act while attempting to fill gaps in the service. One such group was the British Pregnancy Advisory Service (BPAS), formed in 1968 "by a small group of volunteers in Birmingham." By 1981 the BPAS was a national organization with twenty-four branches and four nursing homes. It offered pregnancy testing and counselling, contraception, abortion (in the nursing homes), sterilization, artificial insemination, sperm freezing and storage, sex education, and psychosexual counselling and training. A national worker said, "It is likened by our ... visitors ... to a cottage industry but ... it has continued to be, as it was originally, a group of friends working together to a common end, because we all still believe that what we are doing is right."[22]

Nationally, the Pregnancy Advisory Service (PAS), also set up in 1968, had similar aims and a similar history. It and the BPAS pioneered in the research and provision of vasectomy and female sterilization. Similarly, the Birth Control Trust was set up in 1972 to carry out research and provide public information on contraception, sterilization and lawful termination of pregnancy. All of these groups exemplified combining pressure for change with making do.

The first BPAS nursing home, Wistons, was opened in Brighton in 1971. By 1981 it had thirty-eight beds and accommodated about 650 patients a month, most of whom sought to terminate a pregnancy. The majority of abortions in Brighton, up to 91 per cent, were performed by the BPAS/Wistons nursing home.[23] Renee Smith, the administrator, said demand for termination fluctuated, but the home was generally "full to capacity" and sometimes "we are doing operations seven days a week" in an effort to meet demand. Several BPAS/Wistons staffmembers said that they wished fewer women were forced to use their services. According to Renee Smith: "the fee for termination is a burden to many patients. We try to help with that, but our resources are limited. The NHS could do a good deal more."

Since passage of the 1967 act, there have been repeated challenges, on a national level, to even this inadequate level of service. Six separate bills advocated restrictions to the act. The national campaigns to defeat these bills, which were supported by BPAS, PAS, and by some branches of the FPA, gave rise to a number of groups who expanded the issue from that of a defence of abortion services to "a women's right to choose." By the early 1970s, as indicated above, women's right to control their fertility had become a central issue in the growing feminist movement. In 1972 the Women's Abortion and Contraception Campaign was formed. Three years later the National Abortion Campaign (NAC) was formed; it led the campaign against bills attempting to restrict access. Joining in the resistance campaign were trade union branches, women's charter groups, constituency Labour parties, and a revitalized ALRA. In 1976 the Labour Abortion Rights Campaign was set up to pressure within the unions and Labour Party against the 1976 Beynon Bill. In the same year, the Co-ordinating Committee in Defence of the 1967 Abortion Act (Co-ord) was set up to "represent a wide variety of national and specialist organizations which are concerned with women's needs and want to unite in defence of the 67 Act." Co-ord had sixteen founding members; by 1981, it had fifty-five member affiliates.[24]

Building on the networks and experience of the Brighton Women's Centre, the Brighton National Abortion Campaign (NAC) group was formed in 1974, the year of NAC's founding. The Brighton campaigns against the bills mentioned above were spearheaded by NAC, which organized popular fronts, including strong trade-union support.

Shifting the Boundaries

The struggle for women's right to control their fertility had become increasingly central to the feminist tradition. It was seen as a fundamental precondition of other struggles to change women's living and working conditions and to redefine the nature of "femininity" and sexuality. And it was an issue about which nearly all the women to whom I spoke had opinions – often forceful opinions.

This struggle, which continues to this day, has been one of the most bitter of all women's campaigns, largely because it directly challenges one of the most sacrosanct elements of the division between work and life: the "private" and "natural" area of sexuality and biological reproduction. The challenge, in itself contradictory, has thrown into stark relief the conflicts and the wide-ranging implications inherent in all women's struggles.

In the process of historically separating work and life, biological reproduction and sexuality came to be defined as private. The implications for women were ambivalent. On the one hand, this separation "naturalized" sexual experience, giving women little basis upon which to raise questions about their sexuality, or the form of lovemaking they shared with their partners. This view of sexuality also made it difficult to question the natural course of repeated and often health-destroying and painful pregnancies. This naturalization was also a basis for extending women's childbearing capacities into a natural responsiblility for other aspects of reproduction. On the other hand, the privatization of sexuality and biological reproduction provided an ideological and material basis for the campaigns for a woman's control over her fertility and, by extension, her sexuality: for "a women's right to choose."

The campaigns for safe, effective, female-controlled contraception and for abortion on demand were seen as campaigns which asserted and defended the right of individual women to make the ultimate decision about whether, when, and how to have children. They were also an assertion and defence of the "free space" allowed as a result of the separation and privatization of biological reproduction and sexuality. Yet, as a number of the women I spoke to pointed out, this defence was in itself contradictory in that it extended the collective elements of sexuality and biological reproduction.

This happened in two ways. First, women's right to have free individual choice assumed the provision of resources to back up her choice, resources which, given the state of medical and social technology in the early 1980s, were only provided collectively. Several activists in the area noted that the possibility of realizing a woman's individual decision about having, delaying, or regulating the spacing of children necessitated collectively produced, distributed, and defended contraceptive technology and abortion facilities. Second, the struggle to gain, maintain, extend, and defend these "public" facilities was itself collective, and compelled women to express their rights to free choice as collective and public demands.

A fundamental strategic problem also arose from the contradictory basis of the separation of public and private. By virtue of the historical necessity to defend this sphere of individual freedom and a women's right to choose, feminist campaigns necessarily accepted and perhaps reinforced the separation of this part of life and its designation as private. This, as Himmelweit points out, may have blocked the development of thinking and strategy about a collective response to sexuality and biological reproduction.[25]

The comments of both the activists and the community women I spoke to indicate that the collective struggle over a woman's right to choose may be providing ideas about how to break down this barrier and to develop ways of talking about and acting on biological reproduction and sexuality in a supportive, social way. For many of these women, however, the question still remains one of how to extend this or, more fundamentally, of how far it is possible or desirable to make biological reproduction and sexuality social. Many women said sexuality would "always be a private thing," although a number said they discussed sexuality, as well as the related issues of contraception and abortion, with women friends and relatives. "It's easier to talk to another woman" one woman, a mother of four, told me. "My husband would be embarrassed. And it's not his concern anyway." Some women, especially younger ones, had different attitudes. "Sex is a partnership" one said "and it affects everything else."

It can be argued that the possibility of thinking about and acting on these issues in a collective manner assumes the existence of the right to, and resources for, individual choice. To the extent that these are now more available than ever before in history – however artificially limited and tenuous that availability is – the question of their defence also begins to involve the question of how they should be developed in the future in order to break down the oppressive elements of the separation and privatization of sexuality.[26]

Meanwhile, the boundaries of the public and private were being "softened" and shifted once again by the demographic implications of this struggle for greater fertility control.

DEMOGRAPHIC IMPLICATIONS: NEW FAMILY PATTERNS

During the post-war period, people in Brighton and throughout Britain utilized the new resources available in order to change the kinds of families in which they lived. Demographic trends – due in part to women's increased control over their fertility – contributed to new household patterns and to a new life cycle for women. At the same time, women's actions furthered the development of new *forms* of family.

Although British birthrates rose somewhat in the immediate post-war period, they remained low relative to early twentieth century standards and then declined in the 1970s. The number of children per family also remained small relative to the early twentieth century and then showed a decline in the 1960s. These trends, it seems likely, were at least partly

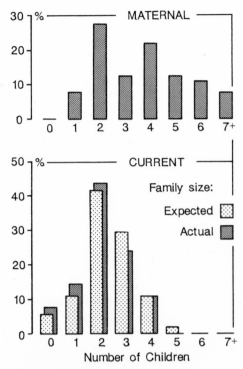

Figure 1   Maternal Family Size and Current
Family Size

due to the greater availability and reliablity of contraception. More striking evidence of this was the continued compression of fertility in the
decades after the war, a trend which implies deliberate and successful
fertility planning. On the whole then, in the 1970s and 1980s women
in Britain were having fewer children and having them in a shorter
span of time than did their mothers and grandmothers.[27] These trends
had implications for household patterns. The compression of fertility
and decline in family size meant that children were likely to have left
home by the time couples were in middle age. In conjunction with the
decline of the three-generation family, this led to more, and smaller,
households.[28]

As elsewhere in Britain, the birthrate in Brighton remained low relative to nineteenth-century standards.[29] Almost all the women I interviewed had fewer children than did their mothers. Households were
therefore relatively small. Slightly over half of the women lived in
households which were nuclear families with dependent children and
only four were three-generation households. (See figure 1 and tables 4
and 5.)

Table 4
Household Size

Persons per Household	Number of Households	Percentage
1	1	1.8
2	16	29.1
3	13	23.6
4	21	38.2
5	2	3.6
6	2	3.6
Total	55	100.0

Source: Brighton Community Interviews, 1981

The women to whom I spoke, especially the younger women, confirmed the British pattern of compressed fertility and were conscious that their childbearing period was short relative to that of their mothers. On the whole, women had positive feelings about their ability to plan their families and about the compression of fertility. A twenty-seven-year-old mother with children aged one and two said she had completed her family, adding, "We decided that's the way we wanted it. I didn't want to be pregnant all my life." Another, thirty-one-years old with three children under five, said, "It's better to have them all at once. Then they're friends and in a few years when they're all older and in school I can go back to work." Others contrasted their own family history with that of their mother, "who was always pregnant" or "always had a baby under her feet."

Families were not only smaller, they were taking new forms. Women appeared increasingly conscious of and concerned about evolving family patterns. Those women who had controlled their fertility made it clear that maternity need not be a life-time job. The growing number of women in female-headed single-parent households and other "non-traditional" families also made it clear that the male-headed nuclear family was not the only family form in which to live and bring up children. One of the most frequent comments women made about changing family form related to the rising numbers of one-parent families. The growth of one-parent families was seen as a result of the increasing number of divorces and of (the less well-documented) legal and informal separations, as well as the growing number of women who were having children independently and keeping them.

Brighton always had a relatively high number of one-parent households. Although the reliability of data is questionable, there are strong indications that the number of such households rose over the post-war

Table 5
Household Type

Household Type	Number	Percentage
Married couple only	14	25.5
Couple with 1 dependent child	10	18.2
Couple with 2 dependent children	16	29.1
Couple with 3 dependent children	3	5.5
Couple with independent children [1]	4	7.3
Woman only	1	1.8
Woman with 1 child	1	1.8
Woman with 2 children	4	7.3
Woman with 3 children	2	3.6
Total	55	100.0

[1] Independent children refers to children over 18 and includes married or separated children living with their parents, in all cases with their own children.
Source: Brighton Community Interviews, 1981

period. This was due to the increase in births to independent women (see table 6) and to the greater demand for and ease of separation and divorce. Mrs Shane, the headmistress of Queen's Park First School in the Hanover area, said that in 1979–80, 40 per cent of the nursery class intake came from single-parent families. Headteachers of Whitehawk schools also said that their areas had a large number of single-parent families.

All of the women in one-parent families to whom I spoke said their roles were difficult and often lonely. Coping was a struggle. Difficulties mentioned included unaided shopping and travelling with toddlers, managing on limited incomes, and coping with feelings of isolation and frequent exhaustion. All expressed concern about whether this was the "best way" for their children. But without exception, the separated and divorced women felt a one-parent situation was preferable to a bad marriage, and the independent women felt it was preferable to "giving up the children." One divorced woman with two children said: "It's so much easier now. Years ago I couldn't have got separated and kept the kids. I couldn't have supported us. I wouldn't have had any friends. I would have had to stay with him like my mum did."

While fully aware of the continued "stigma" of one-parent families and the difficulties of their situation, these women were also aware that family patterns were changing and that they were part of that change. Although not active in them, the women were also aware of the national and local organizations formed to deal with the specific disadvantages

Table 6
Births to Independent Women as Percentage of
Total Births: Brighton and England and Wales,
1946–50 to 1980

	Brighton[1]	England and Wales
1946–50	9	6
1951–60	8	5
1961–70	13	8
1971–75	13	9
1976–80	13	11

Sources: Brighton Corporation, Medical Officer of Health,
Annual Reports; East Sussex Area Health Authority, Information Services Division, *Child Health Statistics*

[1] 1946 to 1975 for Brighton County Borough, 1976 to 1980
for Brighton Health District. Brighton Health District includes Brighton and Hove on the west and stretches east to
Newhaven and north to Lewes. See map 2.

suffered by single parents. Groups such as Gingerbread and the National
Council for One-Parent Families had been established to press for better
services and, on a local level, to provide mutual support.

All the women I spoke to were conscious of general changes in the
position of the family in society and women's lives. One fifty-three-year-
old Queen's Park woman with four children summed this up saying:
"Families are smaller now. Women go out to work. The family isn't the
whole world to women any more." Many, especially older women, felt
that the family was "breaking down." They mentioned divorce, lax discipline, and children's "lack of respect." Most agreed that these changes
were attributable to "society" rather than to individuals within the family.
Women frequently mentioned the penetration of "society" into family
life in the form of women's wage work and the media – especially television advertising which emphasized high levels of consumption for
children – and a generally insecure future, compounded of nuclear
warheads and unemployment. One forty-six-year-old woman in Whitehawk with two teenagers said: "All these changes, they happened so
fast. It's hard to know what to do or think. It's frightening to think how
insecure it all is for children."

The younger women, in particular, felt that changes had also improved family life. Children were more often planned and "wanted."
And smaller families, in combination with greater participation by husbands, were resulting in a better quality of care. One young woman with
two children under five years of age said: "Families are a lot more open

Table 7
Maternal Mortality: Brighton Hospitals, 1940 to 1980

Years	Mortality Rate per 1,000 Live and Still Births
1940–44	2.9
1945–49	1.1
1950–54	0.2
1955–59	0.5
1960–64	0.5
1965–69	0.4
1970–74	Nil
1975–79	Nil
1980	Nil

Sources: Brighton Corporation, Medical Officer of Health, *Annual Reports*; East Sussex Area Health Authority, *Community Health Services Statistics*

now than they used to be. I can relate to my kids, talk to them and to my husband about anything, even sex. I had no relationship with my mother at all. She was too busy. I don't think she ever really talked to dad."

On the whole greater fertility control and the resultant smaller families, as well as more open family relations, were seen as the product of greater accessibility to social resources and as a factor in the new forms of internal family organization. These, in combination, led women to a new examination of the process of birth and motherhood itself.

EXTENDING CONTROL OVER MATERNITY AND CHILDBIRTH

If you're only going to have two kids all your life, you become a lot more careful about when, where and how you have them, and about their health." (Twenty-seven-year-old, from a maternal family of six, living in Hanover with two toddlers.)

This "greater care" was evident from both the state and women themselves. As facilities for maternity and childbirth became more of a social responsibility, and as the supervision of birth and parenthood extended, women responded with increasing pressure to exert control over maternity and childbirth processes.

Concern to improve services to mothers and infants was an important feature of Brighton's post-war medical services. Maternal and infant mortality steadily decreased throughout the post-war period, as did the rate of stillbirths. (See tables 7, 8 and 9.)

Table 8
Infant Mortality[1]: Brighton[2] and England and Wales,
1920–29 to 1980

Years	Brighton	England and Wales
1920–29	63	74
1930–39	52	60
1940–49	50	46
1950–59	25	26
1960–69	18	20
1970–74	18	18
1975–79	16	14
1980	8	12

Sources: Brighton Corporation, Medical Officer of Health,
Annual Reports; East Sussex Area Health Authority, Information Services Division, *Health Statistics*

[1] Deaths under 1 year per 1,000 live births.
[2] 1920–74 for Brighton County Borough; 1975–80 for
Brighton Health District. For description of Brighton Health
District, see note, table 6.

In 1951 Dr Rose Morrison had attributed this to the "discovery of
antibiotic drugs and improved preventative methods together with better conditions," as well as to the general expansion of maternal and
infant services due to "recent advances in medical research and treatment which have increased the Authority's obligations under the NHS
Act."[30] The rate of decline of infant mortality slowed after the 1950s.
This, combined with the fact that infant mortality in Brighton in the
1970s often exceeded the British average (see table 8), led to renewed
pressure for improvements within and outside the health service.

Part of the extension of services had been a "medicalization" of childbirth. Fewer and fewer women had babies at home in post-war Brighton
(see table 10), a pattern which was evident throughout Britain. The
number of community midwives dropped steadily, while the number of
hospital midwives rose.[31] During the 1950s and 1960s this trend was
generally welcomed, both by the medical service and by mothers. The
medical staff saw hospital births as safer and more efficient. Most of the
women to whom I spoke, although critical of the hospital service in some
respects, also felt hospital deliveries were safer and easier. Many said
that their stay in hospital combined a rest ("you could sleep right
through"; "it was like a holiday camp"; "to have your meals brought! I
felt like the Queen."), good company ("I never had so many people to

Table 9
Stillbirths: Brighton,[1] 1940–49 to 1980

Years	Rate per 1,000 Live and Still Births
1940–49	26
1950–59	20
1960–69	13
1970–74	10
1975–79	9
1980	7

Sources: Brighton Corporation, Medical Officer of Health, *Annual Reports*; Great Britain, Office of Population Censuses and Surveys, *Community Health Service Statistics for Brighton Health District*

[1] 1940 to 1974 figures for Brighton County Borough, 1975 to 1980 for Brighton Health District. For description of Brighton Health District, see note, table 6.

talk to. I often think back on that time"; "we had some real good times, laughed about everything"), and the assurance that everything was "being looked after" ("it's good to know it's all right there if something goes wrong"). The Brighton Women and Science Group pointed out, however, that after the "holiday," the return home could be difficult: as others had taken control of the mother and child in hospital, it was often difficult for them to reassert control later.[32] Most of the women I spoke to, especially multigravidae, said they "felt better for the rest." Most first-time mothers, however, found readjustment difficult, and nine of the eleven women who had had both home confinements and hospital deliveries said the integration of the new child into family life was easier and pleasanter after a home confinement.

By the mid 1970s a growing number of women in Brighton were asking for home confinements. Of the women I interviewed, thirteen had had home confinements, mostly older women who "hadn't any choice." Of these, seven said they preferred them, at least in some respects. Both of the two younger women who had had home confinements had chosen them; one said she had had to "fight" for hers. "It was my baby, I told the doctor, not his." Eight younger women said they would like to or intended to have home confinements in future. In 1977 and 1978 the local Community Health Council supported the "right of choice for a home confinement." After considerable pressure the Area Health Authority began supporting home confinements through the provision of community midwives' services and an emergency "flying squad." How-

Table 10
Percentage of Domiciliary Births: Brighton Hospitals,
1940–49 to 1980

Years	Percentage of Domiciliary Births
1940–49	27
1950–59	19
1960–69	11
1970–79	1
1980	1

Sources: Brighton Corporation, Medical Officer of Health,
Annual Reports; Great Britain, Office of Population Censuses
and Surveys, Community Health Statistics for Brighton Health District; Royal Sussex County Hospital Records

ever hospital staff still preferred women to come into hospital, even for
stays as short as six hours, and then return home accompanied by the
community midwife.

Moving confinements into hospital was only one aspect of the medicalization of childbirth. After the war there was an increase in the use
of drugs and instruments to accelerate the birth, "calm" the mother, and
otherwise render the process of childbirth more efficient. Some of these
methods were undoubtedly helpful – as the infant and maternal mortality statistics reflect – but more often they were undertaken in the
interest of a generally understaffed hospital delivery system. The Brighton Women and Science Group stated: "The hospital regime pivots
around the idea of illnesses and of compliance by the 'patient' to expert
advice. Birth is increasingly seen as something that cannot be left alone,
that must be interfered with, monitored, 'helped along.'"[33]

Many women I spoke to were critical of the delivery system. They
observed that "they [hospital staff] don't have time to tell you what's
happening"; "they don't tell you what they're giving you"; and that they
treat mothers "as if the baby was the hospital's." Of the forty-four mothers who had attended hospital ante-natal clinics, thirty-nine criticized
what they saw as the "conveyor belt atmosphere" and the subsequent
lack of continuity in care.[34] In short many women felt cheated by the
process of hospital delivery and resented the passive role the hospital
had assigned them.

A range of informal and increasingly formal groups formed to artic-
ulate these grievances and press for a more humane service. Ruth
Bryant, divisional nursing officer for community and midwifery in
Brighton said:

There are definitely a growing number of pressure groups which put demands on the [maternity and childbirth] service ... One of the things we are being asked to look at, and I think probably rightly, is the humanizing of the services ... There was a trend for many years for hospital delivery ... a great emphasis on the technical development of care. Maybe we swung a bit too much that way which meant a swing away from the natural and human aspects of care. We're swinging back again, which I think is right. You've got to get the right balance.

Nationally, the Association of Radical Midwives (ARM) was formed in 1976 to "encourage midwives in their support of a woman's active participation in childbirth." The Maternity Alliance, an umbrella organization formed in 1980 by the National Council for One-Parent Families, the Spastics Society, the Child Poverty Action Group, and others, began campaigning for improved medical, financial, legal, and social support for pregnant women, parents, and their babies. The Society to Support Home Confinements provided practical advice and assistance and pressured for increased state support for women who chose to have children at home.[35]

In Brighton all of these activities were co-ordinated by the Birth Centre. Established in the spring of 1979 by two midwives who felt the need for a supplement to the NHS facilities, especially in the area of ante-natal classes, the centre included representatives of ARM, The Society for Improvement in Maternity Services, and the LaLeche League. It gave advice and support on all aspects of birth and offered the services of alternative practitioners, including homeopaths, acupuncturists, and yoga teachers.

Even more active in this field was the National Childbirth Trust (NCT). Nationally, the NCT had been founded by a group of women in 1956 to "improve women's knowledge about childbirth and to promote the teaching of relaxation and breathing for labour."[36] The Brighton group, which began to meet informally in the early 1970s, largely through its ante-natal classes, was incorporated in 1978. It organized around the push for a "humanized" hospital delivery system. To this end the branch met on a regular basis with hospital and community midwives to exchange views; it also invited health-care workers to its seminars and courses. Members visited mothers in hospital and often acted as companions at the birth. The following list of suggestions submitted by the NCT at the invitation of the Royal Sussex Hospital reflected and summarized many of the comments women made to me.

1 Open visiting for fathers, to support mothers and increase bonding.
2 Open ante-natal clinic in evenings, to enable partners to attend and

ease the problem of looking after other children as well as easing overcrowding.

3 Ante-natal courses should be given by the same person throughout the course.

4 Fathers should be allowed to be present at all times during labour and birth.

5 Allow the baby to stay with the mother after the birth.

6 More flexible approach toward the length of stay in the hospital. Some first time mothers only want to stay a short time, some multigravidae would prefer to stay longer and need the rest from domestic responsibilities.

7 A general increase in flexibility in the process of birth.[37]

While pressuring for better services, the NCT also ran alternative networks, including ante-natal classes, breast feeding counselling, and an extensive network of post-natal support groups. The ante-natal classes were run by NCT-trained teachers and included contact with a breast-feeding counsellor. Christine Bedford, an "experienced breast feeding counsellor," said she met with each class to provide information and invite new mothers to coffee mornings in her home. But "most of my work is done on the telephone. People with problems, but others too, once they get confidence in you and understand that you have a sympathetic ear, will ring you up about all sorts of things. I get calls at four in the morning and on Christmas Day."

The branch also ran training meetings on parent craft and produced a monthly newsletter which included – in addition to information on new publications, second hand equipment, and its frequent activities – accounts of women's experiences of childbirth. The branch chairperson, Sarah Playforth, had also instituted a register for disabled children and mothers.

Eight of the women I interviewed had had contact with the NCT (and two were active members). Four of the eight said that in some respects it replaced their absent extended families and that, when their children were very young, it constituted their primary or sole network of social support. For others the NCT was a vital supplement to family and community ties. Almost all the mothers to whom I spoke said the most difficult time of their lives – and, for some, the most rewarding – came immediately after the birth of their first child. They felt isolated, confined, and often "overwhelmed by it all." Mothers and older friends were a help, but the women also mentioned inter-generational disagreements over appropriate childcare measures; most frequently these involved questions of discipline and the amount of medical care and purchased goods necessary. Many older women felt there was too little discipline and too much buying of goods; younger women said their childrens' grandmothers and older female relatives "spoiled" the children and interfered with the routines the mothers had set down. In the words of one woman with close family ties: "You need people who have a baby the same age, who have the same problems. The advice mum gave me was good but things have changed. We [the interviewee and her contemporaries] used to get together and figure out new ways of doing things. And then we stuck together. We still meet sometimes."

Almost everyone I interviewed – health care professionals, activists, and women in the community – saw, on the whole, a growing knowledge of the medical and social processes of pregnancy and childbirth, as well as a growing confidence among women about demanding more knowledge and more control. Groups such as the NCT both articulated and extended a more knowledgeable assertion of women's control over childbirth. Progress was often slow, and achieved only after many battles.

A few women I spoke to felt childbirth was a difficult and painful experience, one which was out of their control and to be got over quickly. One older woman remarked that "interference" by women in their children's birth was unnatural. "It should be left to the doctor." However, all activists and many women in the community would agree with the comment Sarah Playforth made in our interview: "It's all part of a movement to greater self-awareness among women, wanting to improve the quality of life. Improving the birth process is an important part of that."

EXTENDING CONTROL OVER WOMEN'S HEALTH

Women's chances of bearing healthy children and living to see them, and of doing something other than bearing children, had improved since the 1940s. Gaining the facilities to control fertility, to prevent unwanted childbearing, and to preserve and enhance women's health was difficult, as has been defending them against constant challenges. But as the dangers of repeated maternity and childbearing abated, other aspects of women's health came under increasing scrutiny. Many women felt that the medical profession as a whole still saw women primarily in terms of their roles as biological reproducers; they began exerting pressure for the development of health services which recognized other aspects of their lives and, concomitantly, mounting campaigns against new and ambivalent "medical miracles." They were critical of doctors' insensitivity to their general health needs and of the assumptions many GPs made that women were "unbalanced if they weren't married and didn't have kids" or "never have any responsibilities. They [doctors] can just give us tranquillizers."

In response to these problems, women also set up a variety of alternative services. Women's health groups such as the Brighton Women and Science Group, which did some of the initial British research on toxic shock syndrome, and the Brighton Women's Centre campaigned for and helped provide more sensitive health care. Their services included informal discussion groups and therapy sessions, as well as referral and advice. In 1981 St Gabriel's Family Centre, which was affiliated to the Church of England Children's Society, sponsored a weekly Women's Health Day. The event pooled the resources of a variety of groups in informal discussions of topics ranging from contraception, nutrition, and child development to the most effective use of health care professionals. These discussions emphasized the relation of women's health to other aspects of the "status of women." Joy Adamson, the project's initiator, observed, "A big part of it is the demystification, getting people to actually think about their health, because usually women don't get a chance to come together collectively and look at those things."

Inadequacies in medical services were especially evident in the failure to meet, or even recognize, the needs of women who were beyond childbearing age – menopausal and post-menopausal women – and those who suffered from non-pregnancy related problems such as premenstrual tension and depression. Not surprisingly, these problems were frequently dealt with in informal women's health groups and by voluntary services such as the FPA Women's Health Centre.

This centre, in fact, concentrated on menopausal and premenstrual tension problems. Do Freeman, the co-ordinator, said she got a wide cross-section of women, "many of whom literally don't know what's happening in their own bodies, and want information." The centre provided information and referrals to sympathetic doctors and gave women the "confidence to demand more attention and better treatment from the GP." Kate Page, of the Brighton NAC, summed up both the range of issues and the consistent need to "make do" while pressing for change when she said: "We need to discuss alternative ways of providing women's health care, what sorts of facilities we need and want. It's very slow. In the meantime we try to create them, work with what we have, learn from that, but it's a constant struggle."

SOCIALIZING THE FAMILY

For most of the women I spoke to, motherhood and family remained the most important influence on their space and time. But the quality of this importance, and the social context within which the family was perceived and experienced, appeared to have altered significantly in the post-war period. The processes previously outlined have removed some constraints on women's lives and imposed others.

On the one hand, the experience and attitudes of the women I spoke to who had come to maturity in the post-war period contrasted sharply with the recorded experience and attitudes of interwar women. Fertility, childbearing, and family relations and processes were no longer seen as "inevitable" or wholly "natural" occurrences. Families could be, and were, planned. The number and spacing of children was a matter amenable to women's control. The institution of the family itself was "in question." Rising divorce rates and the growing number of single-parent families indicated that marriage was not necessarily an irrevocable life-time decision, or even necessary at all. In the areas of fertility control and childbirth and health women expected more information and active participation. One young Whitehawk woman, with two planned children, a job she enjoyed, and active community ties, said: "For my mother, all that generation, the family was their whole life ... they just took whatever came. I don't think my mother ever thought about what she did. She just did it. The family just smothered her."

On the other hand, though the "smothering" inevitability of family life had lessened, greater control had imposed new burdens. Women's vulnerability to "nature" had been replaced by a vulnerability to "society". More decisions could and had to be made about family life. More and more these decisions, including decisions about the "most private" aspects of family life, had to be made with reference to a widening range of complex social factors outside the family's control. As the socialization and medicalization of fertility control, childbirth, and general health care extended, women were either constrained to accept another sort of inevitability or to actively reassert their right to knowledge and control. Women noted that they were making decisions about when to have children and how many to have in response to such "outside factors" as council house availability, prospects for their own or their husband's employment, and mortgage rates.

Women in both single- and dual-parent families also felt vulnerable to "the break-up of the family." Reflecting the ambivalent effects of these changes on their lives, women's attitudes toward the simultaneous removal of old constraints and imposition of new ones were also ambivalent. Mrs Shane, the headmistress of Queen's Park First School summed up these fears and hopes: "What kind of children are we producing? Girls know, most of them, that marriage isn't a meal ticket like it used to be. But boys in their twenties are very broody. They want a home of their own, don't realise women aren't like their mothers, full-time housekeepers. Will this generation be able to come together? We are not bringing them up in a family community setting such as we knew. Maybe they will create a new kind of community."

The problems and possibilities of a "new community" were even more evident in the lag between the medical technology available to assist women in bearing children and the social infrastructure and support available to help women care for them. The development of childcare services, the most vital of these, is the subject of the next chapter.

6 / Extending Control over Childcare

> I work nights, and I get off at seven and my husband picks me up with the kids in the car and we come home and have breakfast and then he takes the older children to school [two different schools, four miles apart] on his way to work and I take [the toddler] back to bed with me and try to get some sleep but he usually fusses and I've a lot to do around here, and then my husband picks up [the oldest child] after school and [the middle one] walks home and then we have dinner and then we all drive back to [where she works] and then he puts them to bed when he gets home. (Thirty-seven year-old Whitehawk woman.)

If the fact of becoming a mother is the most important change in women's lives, the women I spoke to indicated that the arrangements they were able, or forced, to make in order to care for their children constituted the most significant factor in constraining their space and time or in opening up new space and time. This was true both for women with dual roles and for full-time domestic workers.

Childcare arrangements – as with fertility control, childbirth, and family patterns – were part of the constitution of a particular kind of motherhood in post-war Brighton. Women carried out parenting activities on a day-to-day basis, making thousands of decisions which, summed up over many years and many mothers, made up "motherhood." They shared these decisions and activities with other people – fathers, relatives, friends – and in so doing created specific kinds of households and communities. The environment where childcare took place, the course of daily activity, the "rules" people followed, or broke, were influenced by a complex interweaving of statutory and public resources, individual circumstances, and organizations which women had created themselves.

In the immediate post-war period, the concern of statutory agencies for the physical structure, that is the equipping and siting of the home, was parallelled by a concern for the adequacy of its internal processes. The subsequent intervention into domestic performance was largely an intervention into parenting.

The statutory services in the 1950s and 1960s were based on a socially specific definition of adequate parenting: the assumption that mothers were the primary care givers and by implication, that only a female could give adequate care to children. Fathers were shadowy figures, largely excluded from day-to-day care. This vision was delivered to mothers both directly through the assistance of infant welfare workers and through "sociology, psychology, and psychoanalytical theories, massively popularized."[1] The most influential of these theories was a body of work promulgated as "maternal deprivation theory" or "Bowlbyism."[2] This work "proved" the child's inherent need for a mother's care, at least in infancy, and promoted the ideal of a maternal instinct which would meet this need. By thus "scientifically" reinforcing women's "natural" desire to stay at home full-time with her children, this theory provided an external standard of maternal performance against which a growing army of health visitors, social workers, and environmental health inspectors could measure maternal performance. It also led women to regulate their own standards of performance. Mothering became a complex and demanding process, fraught with formerly unknown dangers.

However, women were not passive recipients of this vision of motherhood. The difficulites of living out Beveridge's outworn definition of female domesticity and Bowlby's prescription for mothering led women to make a series of unratified and unexpected responses which altered both the activities and the understanding of motherhood. This following chapter looks at some of these, first at the growth of statutory services for mothers and children, and then at some of the ways in which women created alternative services.

SOCIAL SERVICES TO THE FAMILY

Given this prevailing definition of parenting and of the woman's role, it is hardly surprising that Brighton social services in the post-war period regarded women primarily as pregnant and nursing mothers. This resulted in an increase in the socialization of care for pregnant women, mothers, and young infants. In 1951 Dr Rose Morrison, the assistant medical officer of health for maternal and child welfare announced that rhesus testing, blood grouping, and analgesics were to be made available to all Brighton mothers. She also noted that the council was already providing ante-natal classes, as well as lectures and demonstrations on the process of childbirth, breast feeding, and infant care.[3]

Throughout the 1950s and 1960s there was an increase in the number of Infant Welfare Clinics and health visiting staff. The number of community midwives and ante-natal classes also grew. By 1958, nine weekly ante-natal classes were being offered; the following year, parent-craft classes commenced both in the centre of town and in Whitehawk. This activity was supplemented by the work of the Dyke Road Mothercraft Centre, a charity centre opened during the Second World War, which offered ante-natal and mothercraft classes as well as "Well Baby Clinics." In 1961 a mobile clinic was provided "in order to meet the demands for child welfare centres in areas where premises are not available." Throughout the early 1960s, it served the suburban estates, including Hollingbury, as an ante-natal clinic, welfare food distribution point, and child welfare clinic. In 1967, a new custom-made van was provided, and the inclusion of family planning services suggested.[4]

All of these improvements were accompanied by exhortations to the family to be more self-reliant and to the mother to achieve "better standards." In 1954 the Brighton Children's Department reported that as it was "firmly established that accommodation problems are now less acute" attention must be directed to "rehabilitating families" and "preventing the separation of children from parents." The report added, in a burst of Bowlbyism, "the removal of a very young child from his mother may have an adverse effect upon his whole life."[5] Five years later the department stated, "As social conditions improve and unemployment is reduced to a minimum, there are few excuses for parents to abandon their children to the care of the Local Authority".[6]

Along with this push toward "self-reliance," there was an increase in the supervision of domestic working-standards and conditions. The fruition of the wartime reformist vision of a new relation between family and government had produced greater external demands on the domestic worker, as well as an increase in the number of visits and letters she received to make sure she achieved these demands. Motherhood was still largely contained within the family, but it was no longer a wholly private or natural process. Society had a responsibility for children in parallel to its responsibility for the family.

During the 1950s, the "Decade of the Child," public institutions felt they had moral authority to increase their intervention in the family. One area that saw increased activity was family law. In response to public debates concerning the care of children of divorced parents and the surveillance of one-parent families on social security, as well as pressure from traditional women's groups and several other newly formed groups, the laws regarding family were reformed.[7] Increasingly, in relation to matters of family intervention, legal institutions came to parallel social welfare institutions.

Family legislation is now moving closer to welfare legislation, and is also adopting interventionist strategies that have been more common to the latter. For example, the courts have increasing powers to investigate incomes, to deduct monies at source, to vary property ownership and to investigate the family through the agency of welfare officers. Intervention into and surveillance over the family is becoming more extensive and the prevailing strategy of family law is not to construct a semi-autonomous institution within which one patriarch has absolute power, but to regulate family members ... and to contain economic dependency within the family unit.[8]

Part of this was achieved through the extension of infant welfare not only to the child but to the whole family in which the child lived. In 1951 the Medical Officer of Health described the reorganization of the infant welfare service, saying the service must "meet its new task with the change of emphasis from infant welfare alone to that of providing medical and social advice to all members of the family."[9]

The most striking instance of this was the creation, discovery, and re-creation of the "problem family." The problem family had been first officially discussed in Brighton in 1953 at a conference on problem families. This was followed by the formation of a council committee which approved special loans for the "purposes of purchasing suitable properties for occupation by substandard families."[10] The problem was subtly reversed the following year when the Medical Officer of Health convened a co-ordinating committee to help all agents, including voluntary groups, "in continued efforts to rehabilitate and prevent deterioration or break up of family life in these substandard homes," noting that these families need more supervision as "improvement is usually very slow and backsliding is frequent."[11]

At the same time, the school was also being extended into the home. One of the most obvious ways in which the school "aided" the family in providing adequate care was through the school meal programs. These had been initiated during the war; the first school canteens offering "hot midday meals" were opened in 1942 in seven locations. By 1944 there were twenty-seven canteens in operation and the following year all schools but one had canteens. School records and the reports of the School Medical Officer claimed that the program assured better standards of nutrition. The numbers of meals served increased rapidly throughout the 1940s, 1950s, and 1960s.[12]

School authorities were urged to extend their responsibilities to include the whole family. The School Medical Officer, in his 1952 report, affirmed "the basic principle of the desirability of a single health team dealing with the preventative and socio-medical problems of the mother and her growing family."[13] Two years later he reported, "When there is proper appreciation of the significance of home conditions ... and when there is proper liaison with the facilities of the Health Department to put things right, a child can make the most of his education without carrying a millstone around his neck by reason of coming from a bad home."[14]

By the end of the 1960s, in the spirit of the Plowden Report's emphasis on the "whole man," the schools were extending their role in a new way through the expansion of domestic science into mothercraft and guidance classes. In 1963 the School Medical Officer announced the commencement of a new course "designed to help the developing child to understand its emotional needs in relation to growing up and becoming a citizen and parent. The importance of accepting responsibility in one's relations with other people is stressed throughout the course ... Great stress is laid on the need for stable family life with the mature approach to the problems of a happy and healthy marriage."[15] The syllabus listed subjects such as "marriage as a vocation," "the stability of family life," and "statutory services for the family." Four years later the Medical Officer of Health outlined an ambitious "cradle to grave" program for health and guidance education.

While the interventions outlined above were taking place – while the organizations responsible for them were "opening up" the home – these same organizations were being opened up by groups of clients, parents, students, and patients. This reciprocal opening succeeded in many ways in directing or redirecting the course of health and education to meet the need of its "consumers."

The educational philosophy of involving the whole family increasingly led schools to draw parents into schools. Mrs Coates, Brighton area advisor for early childhood education remarked: "We aren't just educating children. We have to bring the mums and dads in as well. At one time there was a cut-off line, that was home and this is school. But we're all becoming intermingled. And we're using parents. If parents have a skill we say 'come and use it' ... People are more aware about education. That's why they come and then they become even more aware." All the first-school teachers to whom I spoke said they ran "open schools"; they involved parents in outings and in the classrooms and held "open days" and social evenings. All of the schools had Parent-Teacher associations. This involvement, concomitant with the increasing intervention of the schools into family and community life, made education more of a "political issue." This, in turn, provided parents with the motivation and confidence to intervene. The Queen's Park area Save Our Schools Campaign, set up in 1974 to oppose the merger of three small infant schools into one large one of more than 600 pupils, was, according to one former activist, begun and largely sustained by "mums" who had met through school-based voluntary work and through talking after dropping off or collecting their children from school.

Such direct intervention by parents, while it could increase the control some women – primarily those with the time and skills to organize and contribute – had over their domestic-community work places and their children's education, also imposed another area of responsibility on parents. Despite the extension of the concerns of the educational and health authorities, the post-war relation between family and state assumed vigorous and unpaid "voluntary" work by parents, not only in the home, but also in the community. The family was supposedly self-contained and yet its boundaries were permeable, both to standards from "outside" and to the extension of women's parenting work into the community. Nowhere was this more evident than in the area of care for children under five.

Statutory Services and Pressure for Change

Most of the women to whom I spoke regarded caring for children under five as the most rewarding and most demanding period of childcare. Care outside the home and contact with others – other mothers and professionals – was crucial. Yet despite a long history of interest in and action around early-childhood education and care, statutory provision in Brighton reached relatively few children. It was also fragmented, with responsibility for various services split between the social services and education sectors.[16]

Day nurseries. Day nurseries, which concentrated on "care" for younger children, were always seen as a limited part of the Health Service. In 1945 a Ministry of Health circular specified that "day nurseries are to meet the needs of children whose mothers were constrained by individual circumstances to go out to work, or whose home conditions are in themselves unsatisfactory from the health point of view or whose mothers are incapable of understanding the full care of their children."[17] This was still policy in the early 1980s. In 1976 the Social Service Department of East Sussex said its principal objective in the provision for children under five was "to leave the family with the main responsibility for bringing up children, but to assist those families which cannot fully cope and by exception, to provide services for children where the family cannot cope at all."[18]

In 1981 Brighton had one day nursery, with places for fifty children.[19] Admission to the nursery was difficult. It was granted largely on the recommendations of Health Visitors and social workers, which gave priority to children from "problem homes." All the mothers I spoke to either dismissed nursery care as "impossible, I couldn't get in" or as "not for me." Other comments I heard were "it's not for middle-class children," "you have to be a single parent to get in," "you have to pretend to bash your kid to get a place." Some saw its integration into the social services and its reputation as a place for "children under stress" as threatening. One woman said: "I don't want [her son] to go there. They'll put him in care if I went there. I've heard that they watch you if you go there."[20] In addition, the hours of service were restricted, the nursery was closed on public holidays and weekends, and it was unable to accommodate older siblings. Nevertheless the waiting list, although officially limited, was long, as was the wait in most cases.

Since the 1950s there had been various private nurseries in Brighton accommodating an average of seventy children. Their fees were beyond the means of many parents. Even so, many were forced to close in the early 1980s, due to high costs and an inability to realize a profit.[21]

Nursery schools and classes. Nursery schools and classes, concentrating on "education" for children aged three to five, were the responsibility of the Department of Education: "The 1944 Education Act allowed Authorities to provide Nursery Education if they wished to do so. This led to very uneven provision. Circular 8/60 prevented any expansion of Nursery Education from 1960 to 1973 when the rest of the educational services were undergoing a rapid expansion. Since 1973, successive economy cuts have curtailed expansion."[22] In 1981 Brighton had three nursery schools, each of which had been gained after a lengthy campaign by parents. Tarnerland opened in 1933. Whitehouse opened in 1947; threatened with closure in 1951, 1952, and 1977, it was kept open on each occasion by parent pressure. The Royal Spa, in Queen's Park, opened in 1976 after a three-year campaign to stop the site from being developed as a casino. Mrs Coates, the Brighton area advisor for early childhood education said: "Brighton has always had a lot of people wanting nursery schools. That's why we've got them. Thirty years ago people were working for them."

The demand was still there in the early 1980s. Nursery schools had long waiting lists – up to two years. Teachers reported that parental involvement was high. Mrs Rayment, headmistress of the Royal Spa Nursery School said: "We depend on parents. I visit their homes, parents visit us here. We have parties, picnics, a lot of small interactions. Mothers have a support group. Some of them have set up networks to help women with new babies, through meeting at Nursery School." Many of the women I spoke to confirmed this high level of involvement, at least among the full-time domestic workers. One woman, who had recently moved to Brighton, said most of her friends were "nursery school mums," and added, "I was really active in lots of things at home ... since we've moved to Brighton the [nursery] school has been my biggest activity. My husband laughs at me sometimes, but I feel it's important for the children to see me involved with their education." After a pause she went on, "It *is* important." Another said she structured her day around taking the children in to the school and picking them up, "and in between I go shopping, visit friends, talk to the other mothers, or I stay on for a while." But women with wage jobs found such involvement difficult. One woman said that her younger child had gone to nursery school but was now with a childminder (babysitter). "It's no good now I have a job. Even if the hours were right, I couldn't pull my weight."

There were nursery classes in nine of Brighton's twenty-one first schools. Each class provided places for forty children, all on a part-time basis.[23] Although there had been a slight rise in places over the period 1977–80, in 1980 there were still only enough places in state facilities for a minority of children.[24]

A number of groups were set up, nationally and locally, to press for the extension and improved quality of these services. The British Association for Early Childhood Education (BAECE), founded before the war as the Nursery Schools Association, had had a Brighton branch since the 1960s. It acted primarily as a research and educational forum for "early childhood education specialists" and interested parents and childcare workers.

In the mid-1960s the national BAECE assisted in the setting up of an activist campaign, the National Campaign for Nursery Education (NCNE). Affiliates to this campaign included the British Association of Social Workers, the Health Visitors Association, National Union of Teachers, National Union of Public Employees, the National Council of Women, the National Association of Women, and Save the Children. The group lobbied, petitioned, and staged local and national demonstrations for increased free, state nursery education. At the same time, it kept up a running battle to defend both the level of nursery education which existed and to make it more responsive to women's changing needs: "Although society accepts the idea of equal opportunities for women, at the same time the care of young children under five is usually regarded as being mainly the concern of the mother. This puts her in a dilemma. We think that women should be treated as responsible adults, free to make up their own minds as to what course they follow. This implies adequate provision being available."[25]

In 1981 the more militant and explicitly feminist National Childcare Campaign (NCC) was set up, claiming that "a comprehensive child care service is essential to women's equality." The NCC aimed to build a national campaign around "the demand for comprehensive, flexible, free childcare facilities provided by the state."[26] Local affiliates organized pressure campaigns – on a small scale in Brighton, mainly within the National Union for Public Employees – and in some communities even occupied threatened daycare centres.[27]

In the 1980s these groups and a number of local *ad hoc* campaigns found themselves involved in resisting the threatened cutback or closure of state childcare facilities. In 1977 the East Sussex County Council proposed the closure of all nursery schools and classes as part of a £2 million cost-cutting package. A Save Our Nursery Schools Campaign, which organized petitions and demonstrations at County Hall, succeeded in having the proposal shelved.[28] Then, in 1980, the East Sussex County Council Education Subcommittee on Expenditure "rumoured" that all nursery schools would be closed, justifying this on the grounds that the birthrate was falling and that costs could be cut by transferring children into nursery classes in first schools. Parents formed the Brighton Nursery Schools Joint Action Committee, with representatives from each of the three schools, and mounted a Save Brighton's Nursery Schools Campaign. The campaign printed and distributed literature and window stickers and promoted lobbying and letter writing. This group affiliated with the National Campaign for Nursery Education in 1981. Jane Goldsmith, the local organizer and the former national president of the NCNE said: "We have not become so militant that we would lie down and take over nursery schools. The national campaign is not anxious to get involved in that form of militancy. What the actual local group [Save Brighton's Nursery Schools] would do I don't know, if it actually came to the crunch of closing."

Participants in these groups said that their activities had not only raised their own level of awareness but had impressed upon the public the importance of nursery education. The activities had also involved a growing number of parents in the schools. Lyn Ashworth, a member of the parents' committee of the Nursery Schools Campaign said that when the announcement of possible closures came "headmistresses were inundated with calls from people who wanted to put their child's name down." Such involvement was even more evident in the groups which had been established to fill gaps in statutory provision.

Parent-run Networks and "Making Do"

The inadequacy or inaccessibility of statutory services led to a growing range of networks which co-ordinated parent-run "alternatives." Like the more open schools and the pressure groups described above, these alternatives extended the prewar welfare concern with the infant to include concern for the mother's conditions of life and work.

The largest of these in 1981 was the Pre-School Playgroups Association (PPA). Formed in 1961 after an "overwhelming" response to a letter in the *Guardian*, by 1981 it had, nationally, an estimated 13,500 affiliated playgroups serving an estimated 270,000 children.[29]

Table 11
Playgroups in Brighton, 1981

Date Started	By Whom?	Outside help?	Supervisor?	Hours Worked Per Week	Pay (£ hr.)	Supervisor's training	Parents Rota?	Parents Stay?	Parents Fund Raise?	Other Financial Help?	Other Sources of Funds?	Child Minders Use?	Mother and Toddler Group?
1 1980	Supervisor/ parents	PPA	Yes	9	1.30	NNEB	Yes	Sometimes	No	No	Fees 1.00	No	No
2 1967	Parents	Social Service Fire Dept.	Yes	12	—	PPA	Yes	Yes	Yes	Milk	Fees	Yes	No
3 1968	Parents	PPA	Yes	12	1.15	PPA	Yes	Yes	Yes Sales	Milk	Fees	No	Yes
4 1967	Parents	No	Yes	15	Varies	PPA	No	No	Yes Donations	Milk	Fees 1.00	Yes	No
5 1962	Parents	No	Yes (2)	6 + 9	1.15	PPA	Yes	Yes	Yes	Milk	Fees	Yes	Yes
6 1970	Church members	—	Yes	9	1.00	PPA	Yes	Yes	No	Milk	Fees .45	Yes	Yes
7 1965	Parents	No	Yes	20	1.45	NNEB, PPA	Yes	Yes	Yes	Milk	Fees	Yes	Yes
8 1971	Parents	PPA	Yes	10.5	.80	NNEB, PPA	Yes	Yes	Yes	Milk	Fees	No	Yes
9 1970	Parents	—	Yes (6)	6–12	1.15	PPA	Yes	Yes	Yes Sales, Dances	Milk	Fees .70	Yes	Yes

10	1965	Supervisor	No	Yes	18	1.45	PPA	No	Some-times	Yes Bazaar	Milk	Fees	Yes	No
11	1977	Parents	PPA	Yes	8	2.00	PPA	Yes	Yes	Some Sales	—	Fees	Yes	No
12	1967	Parents	—	Yes	9	1.00	PPA	Yes	Some-times	Yes Sales	Milk	Fees .50	Yes	No
13	1970	Parents	—	Yes	12	Varies	PPA	No	Yes	Some Sales	Milk	Fees	No	No
14	1973	Parents	PPA	Yes	9	1.15	PPA	Yes	Some-times	No	Milk	Fees .60	Yes	Yes
15	1968	Parents	PPA	Yes	15	1.10	PPA	No	Some-times	Yes Sales, Donations	No	Fees .75	Yes	No
16	1970	Parents	—	Yes	12	Varies	PPA	Yes	Yes	Yes Sales	Milk	Fees	No	No
17	1968	Parents	Soc. Serv./ PPA	Yes	15	1.00	PPA	Yes	Yes	Yes Sales	Milk	Fees	Yes	No
18	1974	Parents	PPA	Yes	9	1.15	PPA	No	Yes	Yes Sales	Milk	Fees	Yes	Yes
19	1971	Parents	—	Yes	12	—	NNEB	No	Some-times	No	Milk	Fees	No	No
20	1966	Parents	—	Yes	10	Varies	PPA	Yes	Yes	Yes Sales	No	Fees	Yes	No
Summary					Average 11 Range 6–20	Average 1.20 Range .80– 2.00	PPA 17 NNEB 4 None 1	Yes 14	Yes 19	Yes 16	Milk 16		Yes 14	Yes 8

Source: Brighton Playgroups' Questionnaire

In 1980 there were 95 playgoups in East Sussex, of which 30 were in Brighton. Most (75 per cent) were parent-run; the remainder were private, mostly nonprofit groups. On average these playgroups ran two to three hours a day, two to five days a week.

The playgroups were co-ordinated by a regional PPA branch, which ran local training courses for playgroup supervisors, helpers, and "mums," and gave advice and support on setting up and running groups. It also ran a supply depot, providing material, furniture, and a duplicating service to playgroups at cost. Of the 20 groups I contacted, 17 had supervisors and 14 had "mother helpers" who had taken PPA courses; and 17 indicated they used the depot. (See table 11). Although the playgroups had problems of the constant need for fundraising and of sustaining parental involvement, many were long-lived. One had run for nineteen years, while most were from ten to fourteen years old.

There had also been a tremendous increase in the number of mother and toddler groups – informal meetings of mothers with their "under threes" for a few hours a week. These too were often parent-initiated and run, sometimes with the help of the PPA, social workers, or Health Visitors. In 1981 there were "around" 30 such groups in Brighton; they met in venues ranging from clinics to church halls and community centres to people's homes. Several people I spoke to said that their waiting lists were "amazingly long." One organizer commented: "You wouldn't think we'd have a waiting list for a thing like this, just a chance to sit and chat and drink tea. And the tea is always terrible too. But we do, people are so desperate to have a place to go, we have to put them on a list and call them if someone leaves the group."

In addition, there was a range of self-help networks throughout the city co-ordinating childcare services. Groups such as the Parent-Teachers Association and the National Childbirth Trust post-natal support groups organized babysitting exchanges, crèches for group functions, and events where mothers and young children could get together.

The largest of these self-help groups in Brighton was the Working Association of Mothers (WAM). In 1981 WAM had a network of 600 members exchanging skills ranging from household repairs to baby sitting – on the basis of a token exchange – as well as running regular and varied social events and holiday playschemes. They organized largely through informal contacts, ran a (more-or-less) monthly newsletter, and had almost daily neighbourhood events: sales, coffee mornings, barbeques ("husbands invited too"), pot luck dinners, wine evenings and meetings at pubs, collective lunches for mothers with their children, or gatherings for children held by group members ("to give you two hours of peace and tranquillity"). One WAM member said: "I went from the NCT into WAM when [her son] was four months old and I guess in a few years I'll

Table 12
Mothers[1] Using Collective Childcare Facilities
(of the 51 who had children)

Facility	Number of Mothers Using	Percentage of Mothers
Day nursery	1	2.0
Private nursery	1	2.0
Nursery school	3	5.9
Nursery class	12	23.5
Playgroups	23	45.1
Mother and toddlers	9	17.6
WAM	2	3.9
None	17	33.3

Source: Brighton Community Interviews, 1981

[1] Total exceeds 51 and 100% because some mothers used more than one facility.

get into playgroups, and then maybe into the Nursery School Group and of course the PTA. It's great, I know no matter what happens, there will be a group of mums around to help me out." "Parents," her husband said. "Oh, yes ... all right, parents."

As this brief exchange indicates, some men were becoming more active in "public parenting." A number of women commented that "there seem to be more men around the groups." In 1980 WAM added the subtitle "self-help group for parents" to its name, largely to reflect the growing involvement of fathers in parenting and in the organization, especially as male unemployment increased. Other childbirth and childcare groups also encouraged participation by men, although they were still initiated and run primarily by women.

Most of the mothers to whom I spoke used some form of collective childcare facility at some time and often more than one. (See table 12.) However, both the teachers in part-time state facilities and workers in the voluntary groups said these facilities "were not set up for women with wage jobs" largely because the hours were too short. Most parents, especially those working for wages, relied on other forms of childminding.

In the early 1980s it was almost as difficult, for official purposes, to define what a childminder was (a person who cares for the children of others in his or her home) as it was to come up with an estimate of their number. For Britian as a whole, 200,000 has been suggested as a conservative figure.[30] Local authorities had no obligation to provide childminding services nor to provide services to childminders, although they were permitted to subsidize both playgroup and childminder fees for children in special need.[31] Local authorities *were* required to inspect and register childminders, but relatively few childminders registered. A 1979 study of Huddersfield, in Yorkshire, discovered in one area "at least ten times as many ... children ... were being looked after by illegal minders as by day nurseries and official childminders combined."[32] The Brighton Medical Officer of Health remarked frequently on a "large" but unspecified number of unregistered minders.[33] Brighton had 55 registered childminders in 1980, for whom the social services provided a friendly if minimal service.[34]

Of the 3 childminders I met, only one was registered: I spoke to 11 other women who regularly "helped out" a friend or neighbour, either for a small payment or on the basis of service exchange, but who did not see themselves as minders. In fact, the majority of women I spoke to did regular or occasional childminding for relatives or friends. This was described as "having the grandchildren twice a week while my daughter goes shopping", as "exchanging with my cousin some evenings so we can both go out with our husbands, just to a cinema"; or as "we're always running back and forth between the houses, leaving the kids when we need to go shopping or to the dentist." More regular arrangements were also made: "My neighbour two down works in a shop three afternoons and I look after [her three year old]. It's no real trouble ... he plays with [my son] but she gives me a bit now and then and also gets things at the shop for me and brings them up here."

In general, then, childcare services in Brighton were a complex combination of statutory and collective, parent-run facilities and informal individual arrangements. Most of the facilities had been initiated and run by mothers themselves, for themselves and one another.

For the women to whom I spoke, general mobility and satisfaction with mothering was strongly influenced by their access to these varied networks. The extent to which women had access to informal exchanges and parent-run networks in turn varied with their location in the city. In general Hanover-Queen's Park had the most complex set of networks, while Hollingbury appeared to have fewest, especially of the relative and neighbour "helping out" variety. Access to such networks also varied with length of time in the area and the presence of relatives, although there were no significant differences evident between the women who called themselves working class and those who called themselves middle class. Most women used a combination of all these services and relied mainly on fitting their hours around those of their children.

The most complex and difficult arrangements were those pulled together by women who had wage jobs. Of the thirty-five women I spoke

Table 13
Childcare Arrangements of 35 Woman Who Had
Wage Jobs and Children

Arrangement	Number Using[1]	Percentage of Women Using
School[2]	27	77.1
Husband	15	42.9
Friends or neighbours	14	40.0
Mother/sister/ grandmother	8	22.9
Minder	8	22.9
Took child to work	5	14.3

Source: Brighton Community Interviews, 1981

[1] Number who mentioned each type of arrangement as part or all of childcare arrangements, current and past. Total exceeds 35 because most women mentioned more than one arrangement.

[2] Includes nursery schools and classes.

to who had children and wage jobs, most used a combination of fitting into school hours, husband's hours, relatives' help, and occasional minding, generally described as "my friend helps out." (See table 13.) Only eight regularly used minders and only six relied even partly on nursery school or classes. Five took their children, or some of them, to work.

These arrangements were often astoundingly complicated. Almost all depended on the mutual exchange of services with relatives and friends, varing from "swapping" minding, to picking up children from school or playgroups. Almost all were characterized by incredible feats of juggling time, jobs, and transportation, as was noted in the experience of the woman quoted at the outset of this chapter. Her story was not atypical. Nor was another told to me by a twenty-four-year-old divorced single parent with an eighteen-month-old daughter and four-year-old son. She worked mornings as a private cleaner, taking the younger child to work with her while the older was at nursery class.

Taking the baby to work, it's a problem but it's the only thing I can do. It's the only job I could get where I could take her. [Her employer] said it was OK but I don't think she likes it. The baby makes trouble sometimes and I can't concentrate on my work. It's OK if the buses are on time because I have to get back before [her son] is out of nursery class. I get furious, so worried if the bus is late. It can reduce me to tears. Then the baby cries and we're all miserable. [Her son] is miserable if I'm late, he tries to go home by himself and that's dangerous with the traffic. Sometimes he goes to the neighbour's but if she's out he just sits on the step and looks so sad until I come. It's awful. I feel awful. I may have to quit my job in the holidays because [her employer] says I can't bring [her son]. A neighbour said she might help if I helped her out in the evenings. She's got two, both older than mine. That might work out, I guess. It's the only thing I can think of now.

CROSSING THE BOUNDARIES

From the perspective of its providers and its users, childcare has three major roles: it is an element in woman's domestic-community work; it is a fundamental precondition of women's wage work; and it is an important source of wage employment for women.

Childcare networks and facilities are a resource around which the space-time patterns of women's domestic work are structured. Many women to whom I spoke saw the state and informal groups as "substitutes" for the extended family and the "old" community networks. As greater geographic mobility, housing policies which emphasized suburbanization, and women's growing participation in the labour force broke up the extended family and community of full time housewives, more and more women with young children found themselves isolated. Many of the activists I spoke to emphasized the isolation of women with young children. Diane Bewley, the PPA co-ordinator for mother and toddler groups in Hove said that in her job "things are always happening, like someone phoned me up the other day and said 'I feel awful for phoning you, but I'm ever so lonely and I want to know someone. I feel very strange talking to you on the phone. I need somebody I can talk to.'" Both supervisors and users of playgroups attributed their increase not only to the lack of statutory nursery provision, concomitant with a growing awareness of the importance of early childhood socialization, but to the "need to break down mothers' isolation." Jo Withess, the East Sussex co-ordinator for the PPA said: "Society forced the playgroup. It's a substitute, on one hand for the nursery ... we said 'we'll do it ourselves' ... and on the other for the old community. And over the years the movement has become almost an extended family."

People attributed the increase in playgroups, above all, to the need "for mothers to make friends" and to "find time to pursue their own needs." One supervisor told me, "Sure they care about the kids, want them to have friends, but they come for themselves too, to have a chat with other mothers." For many of the mothers I spoke to, the playgroups were a "godsend," both a chance for a few hours "for themselves" – generally devoted to shopping or catching up on domestic work – or for meeting with other parents. Women said "It's the only time I talk to anyone all day"; "I look forward to it all week. We both do [she and her child]." At some of the groups I visited, mothers, and occasionally fathers, stayed at the group "just to chat." This "chatting" however, was largely an exchange of vital information on problems of childrearing, access to local resources, or arrangements for mutual service exchange. Almost all users said they had made new friends through the groups and established networks to exchange services.

Users and organizers of mother and toddler groups said similar things. According to Diane Bewley: "It's mainly for the mothers. Usually when you talk to people you find that's why they come along, because they're so lonely. I stand in the [infant welfare] clinic and talk to people and then go with them the first time." Sister Doust, who helped co-ordinate the Mothercraft Centre Mother and Baby service group said that "long-lasting friendships are made through the group. Often people pal up and go off and we don't see them again, but we've given them a service. Young mothers are often so lonely."

More open schools, pressure groups formed to extend state provision, and the growth of parent-run services directly altered the time and space of women's childcare role, extending it more and more from the home and immediate neighbourhood into a wider community. Increasingly, a regular and accepted part of women's daily work involved helping out at nursery school or playgroup, attending a mother and toddler coffee morning, or, for some, picketing the council office to defend their nursery school.

Childcare networks had also directly altered the community environment and created new kinds of environments. For many users the greatest value, especially of the parent-run groups, was that they provided a physical place for mothers, and a few fathers, to go with young children. Despite the fact that "common sense" ideology defined all women in terms of their capacities for biological reproduction, the public resistance to dealing with the results of the fruition of such capabilities was tremendous. Women with young children were not welcomed in many venues, and many other environments were actively hostile and dangerous to them. Cafes are difficult to enter with pushchairs and prams, and drinking a quiet cup of tea while her toddler investigates other customers' shoes and its pushchair blocks the service area is far from restful. Breast-feeding or changing a baby in public, even in parks, is likely to draw stares, hostile comments, or worse.[35] With the exception of a few "official" spaces such as infant-welfare clinics, the collective spaces for women and young children were almost all created by women themselves.

Being a mother of a young child is a full-time job, if not a lifetime job. It is therefore not surprising that many mothers of young children had lives which were almost entirely oriented toward childcare in the home and the collective creation and use of places to support women such as themselves. Their network was an interconnected, noisy and very lively one. Whether or not they had wage jobs, their lives were almost wholly bounded by the needs of – and restrictions imposed by – their children and by the political activities surrounding these needs and restrictions.

At the same time, childcare services were a fundamental element in structuring the space and time of parent's, especially mothers', wage work. The availability and quality of childcare, its location, hours, and cost determined, to a large extent, the kind of wage work women with children were able to do, the hours they could work, and the distance and direction they could travel to wage jobs.

Childcare services also provided employment for a growing number of women. The majority of workers in statutory sector services were women. Throughout Britain, in 1980, 99 per cent of day-nursery staff and 91 per cent of all nursery-school and class staff were women.[36] Estimating the rate of employment growth in the informal sector is difficult. However, it is reasonable to assume that the number of play-group supervisors expanded concomitant with the expansion of the services, and Jackson and Jackson estimated a growth in childminding.[37] Molly Evans, pre-school care officer for the Brighton Social Service Department, stated that numbers of registered minders grew between 1970 and 1980, and other activists noted a growth in unregistered minders.

There were also problems and divisions within the childcare networks. The most evident split, both nationally and in Brighton, was between those women – many with wage jobs – who wanted, needed, and demanded full-time, state financed provisions staffed by professionals, and those women – with irregular or no wage jobs – who wanted, needed, and had created parent-run facilities.[38]

This division and the resulting general fragmentation of services was reflected in divisions among the wage workers in childcare. Wages in the non-statutory sector were low and often erratic. Although some playgroup supervisors, especially in the more established groups, received a regular hourly wage, most playgroup workers worked for minimal and irregular wages. These were often based on "what is left over" out of daily fees after expenses were paid. Fourteen of the playgroups responding to my questionnaire gave information on supervisors' wages, which ranged from 80p to £2 an hour, with an average of £1.20. Four more said that the wages varied with the number of children attending each day. In 1978 a PPA report on parental involvement noted: "There is no proper 'salary' or 'wage' for the supervisor or any regular helpers, for the very simple reason that if there were, then the daily costs would be so high that families could no longer pay their share. The very small amount of money that each receives ... is only a token of appreciation contributed by the parents in recognition of the fact that a commitment is made to be at every play session, as distinct from the parent's occasional days with the children."[39]

This attitude not only opened the groups to potential exploitation as "cheap alternatives" to statutory care, but opened supervisors to involuntary exploitation by low-income parents with little to contribute to this "token of appreciation." Given that many supervisors were themselves working-class women who depended on their wages for household needs, there was often a conflict between their dedication to the playgroup and the children and their own financial needs. One former supervisor said that although she had "loved the job" and "was never happier" than when she worked at a playgroup, she had been forced to find another job as "I couldn't afford to go on working there."

Childminders worked long hours at a highly demanding job, and also received relatively low pay. A national survey by the Childminders Association in 1978 found that most childminders cared for at least three children and "over a third also looked after school-age children before and after school and nearly half were doing so in school holidays." The survey found that hours were long, generally exceeding ten hours a day, and the range of charges varied from £3 to £15 a week with an average of £8.32 a week.[40]

These long hours and low wages were confirmed in the discussions I had with Brighton minders and mothers who used minders. One full-time registered minder estimated she made "about 45p an hour" (about $1.00 Canadian) but that it often "worked out to less if I give them a treat for lunch or we go to playgroup or on the bus somewhere." Another said: "It's a long day often, up to twelve hours, and sometimes if the mother has to work overtime it's longer. Sometimes when they take the children I'm so relieved and tired, and then my son wants a lot of attention to make up for all the time I spend with the others." She added that being both a mother and a childminder: "feels sometimes like I'm working all the time. My husband sometimes complains if things aren't done when he gets home. I wonder how he'd feel if he found his line [assembly belt] in the living room when he got home from work."

The pay and conditions of non-statutory workers not only created difficulties for women working in this sector who were trying "to make ends meet," but also threatened statutory childcare professionals. Statutory workers were themselves divided by a discrepancy between the pay of day nursery and nursery education workers.[41]

Despite these divisions childcare networks, those either set up or adapted to help women cope with the new conditions and constraints of their lives, were themselves changing the nature of both the domestic and wage-working environments and forging new links between home and wage workplace. This was occurring primarily as a result of the increase in collective organization among all groups and the concomitant growing ties to, and interventions in, "traditional" employment-based organizations. For example, in 1977, the National Childminding Association (NCA) "was started by a group of childminders and parents and other interested people ... during the first showing of the BBC TV series 'Other People's Children.'"[42] By 1980 it had over 500 member groups and associates across the country. The NCA acted both as a professional association and a union. It pressed for recognition of the childminders' role in childcare and attempted to facilitate communication, education, and the standardization of pay and conditions among childminders.[43]

A 1976 East Sussex Social Service Department report stated: "There has recently been much publicity about making minders into 'professionals' who are 'employed' by their authority to care for children, and a small step toward this is for the Authority to bring the minders together for group discussions with child care advisors, educational psychologists and so on."[44]

This the Brighton Department, mainly under the auspices of Molly Evans, the Brighton social services pre-school care officer, initiated in 1980 with the co-operation of staff at St Gabriel's Community Centre. Chris Warren of St Gabriel's said that after a year of monthly meetings and a short course run by a member of the St Gabriel's staff, the minders were taking on the organization themselves; they declared themselves a branch of the NCA in 1981. Although the branch had only thirteen members by the summer of that year, Warren observed that "its networks are much wider." Activities of the group included workshops, training sessions, coffee mornings, consultations with "experts," and parties with the children. The growing recognition, training, and use of women's "natural" parenting skills was reflected in the PPA courses and in the growing range of federated groups attempting to co-ordinate childcare services, collectively articulate their problems, and press for more support. These included not only the PPA organizations at the city, county, regional, and national level, as well as similar federations in WAM, but also the Brighton Liaison Group for Under Fives and TUF (The Under Fives), which brought together statutory and parent-run sector workers.[45]

These networks often provided women with opportunities to gain confidence and develop in new directions. Jo Withess recounts of playgroup work: "One woman said, after the Christmas bazaar, 'You know I didn't have any talents before I came to the playgroup. Well they think I'm marvellous, I can do these Christmas decorations.' No one had ever told her how clever she was before. Women, after motherhood, have lost their confidence to bring out these skills and suddenly they have a new lease on life." Pauline Wright, the PPA Brighton co-ordinator, said the object of playgroups was to: "bring the whole community to work with the under fives and develop people, especially the mums, who go from feeling 'just a mum' as they say and often work their way up to be a supervisor and beyond. Everyone has developed. The tutors have become very skilled now, the whole structure ... has become so professional. It's bordering so near being a professional body in some ways. Everyone has all got so much confidence and they go on to greater things. They go on to teaching and into social services and hold quite key positions in different places." A PPA Vice-president said that play-group workers "are professionals in a new field" and urged opportunities for crossovers from parent-run sector work to statutory employment.[46] The National Childcare Campaign argued that community-controlled nursery care "would employ and provide opportunities for training for local mothers and fathers, thus offering those who want it an alternative community-based form of employment, at the same time freeing other parents for outside employment."[47]

The growth of these networks also had an effect on the trade-union movement. Most workers in statutory services were union members.[48] And a growing number of parent-run and pressure groups had national and local ties to trade unions. The National Childcare Campaign had a Trade Union Liaison Committee while the NCNE, the PPA, and the NCA encouraged contacts with the trade unions. This resulted in increasing pressure for, and some success, in making childcare a "union issue."[49]

All of these groups were explicitly attempting to alter the relations between the home and wage workplace so that they more closely conformed to women's changing lives. Groups were campaigning for recognition that wage workers were also parents and that parenting was work which must be socially and economically valued and accommodated. Suggestions for facilitating this included altering parents' wage-working hours to fit the school day, providing more secure and flexible part-time work, and extending community-controlled alternative employment in the field of childcare.[50]

Childcare services and networks thus provided a concrete link, for users and providers, between the home and wage workplace. And these ties were being increasingly articulated by childcare groups and by union women in the childcare field.

The following chapter examines such links from the "opposite perspective," that of women's involvement in wage work and "traditional" employment organizations, and outlines some of the other links developing between these sectors.

7 / *Extending Control over Wage Work*

> Well, I certainly never thought I'd be working at my age. I thought hav-
> ing a home and a family would be my work. I don't mind the job, but it
> just shows you doesn't it? (Forty-seven year-old Whitehawk woman with
> two school-age children and a part-time cleaning job.)

Domestic-community work in the post-war period was characterized by
complex changes in the rhythms of household processes and in the
resources available for, and utilized in, these processes. The altered life
cycles of women, changing household structures, and the new goods
and services potentially easing women's domestic work loads, demonstrated, in combination, that maternity and domestic-community responsibilities were not necessarily full-time lifetime jobs. In general, in
this more extensive urban fabric, a "patchwork" of specialized estates
and districts, women did more things – drove to supermarkets and
department stores, attended ante-natal clinics and child welfare centres,
met teachers, lobbied housing offices – and were urged, by statutory
visitors, the media, and by domestic science, to do them "better." They
also relied more and more on purchased services and commodities to
achieve and maintain these standards.

Changes in post-war domestic-community life – the larger homes, the
equipment and supplies to furnish and maintain them, the growing use
of cars and public transportation, declining informal networks – all cost
money. The escalating cost to the family of providing the commodities
and infrastructure deemed necessary to an adequate family life called
for a supplement to family resources. As children stayed in school longer
and as, due to better housing conditions, they often married and left
home earlier, traditional sources of supplementing the wage declined.
In 1968 Myrdal and Klein reported that "the pressures of mass production and competitive advertising have created a situation in which
the employment of married women is, for large sectors of the population, the key to a share in the much publicized 'affluence' of our society,
and the conditions of the labour market are such that jobs of one kind
or another are not difficult to find."[1]

Pressures to supplement family resources with a second wage were
especially acute in Brighton. Due largely due to its economic base as a

Table 14
Average Earnings in East Sussex as a Percentage of
Average Earnings in Great Britain for Male Workers,
1974 to 1977

	Manual Workers	All Workers
1974	89.4	92.2
1975	87.4	89.0
1976	87.4	90.1
1977	86.3	88.9

Source: East Sussex County Council, *Resource Allocation Statement and Departmental Information Gazette*

service centre and resort town, life in Brighton consistently featured relatively low wages and high living costs.[2] A 1978 East Sussex County Council report, *Evidence of Social Needs*, stated that "the average earned income in East Sussex is consistently below the national average," and it "is likely" that the cost of living "is higher than the national average and certainly is as far as housing costs are concerned."[3] (See tables 14, 15, and 16.)

Wage work by married and independent women in Brighton had long been a feature of the city's economy, at least for the working class. This was partly due to this history of relatively low wages and high living costs and partly due to a high proportion of service jobs. (See table 17.) Throughout the post-war period, as women attempted to meet family needs and balance resources, the majority began "supplementing" the family wage as part of their reproductive role.

EXTENDING INTO THE DUAL ROLE

The "Jobs Explosion" and Deindustrialization

Looking back now, it was really different then. My neighbour had a job down in the town and she told me they wanted more [shop assistants] and I went along with her one day and got hired on the spot ... I had that job for a while and then moved to [another shop] closer to home. (Fifty-year-old Whitehawk woman.)

After the war it was hard around here ... My husband's works closed and my [son] he left to go up North, said there was nothing for him here. (Sixty-two-year-old Hanover woman.)

For many women in Brighton, especially those with some professional skills, finding a job in the period from the late 1950s–70s was not dif-

Table 15
Average Hourly Earnings[1] (pence): Great Britain, Southeast England,
and East Sussex, 1980

	Male		Female	
	Manual[2]	Non-manual[3]	Manual[3]	Non-manual[3]
Great Britain	240.5	361.3	170.4	206.4
Southeast England	245.2	391.2	180.7	226.9
East Sussex	209.3	316.2	—	197.4

[1] Excluding effects of overtime.

[2] Age 21 and over.

[3] Age 18 and over.

Source: Calculated from the 1980 New Earnings Survey by Brighton Anti-Low Pay Unit, unpublished information.

ficult. In fact, judging by the records of the education and health departments, and the recollections of the women I spoke to, avoiding a wage job must have been difficult.

As Myrdal and Klein imply, throughout Britain, the push factor of the need for two incomes was reinforced by an interdependent pull factor, the increased availability of certain types of jobs. The welfare state did not simply provide services to the family, it also employed an increasing number of people who worked to provide these services. Similarly, the increase in commercial services and goods consumed by the household created demand for wageworkers in the service and light manufacturing sectors.[4]

Women in post-war Brighton found jobs opening up to them largely in social services and "semi-skilled" factory work. As elsewhere, the demand for female labour led to concessions over part-time work and homework. Some employers paid lively lip service to expanded childcare facilities. Throughout the 1960s, the School Medical Officer reported persistent difficulties in recruiting staff and the necessity of hiring "part-time married women." By 1966 the Medical Officer of Health claimed there was a "crisis of medical man power in the Government service." It was, in fact, a crisis of woman power. With regard to doctors he suggested a two-tier system involving "the establishment of a small, well-trained and well-paid core of senior medical administrative staff and the employment and imaginative use of part-time women doctors who should be offered career prospects to match their family commitments and the stimulus of any necessary post-graduate courses."[5] He went on to detail provision for expanding the day nursery to admit the children of mothers who have "vital occupations – nurses, midwives and teachers."

Table 16
Average Rates of Pay per Annum (£), American Express:
Brighton and London, 1981

Job Description	Brighton	London
Trainee computer operator	2,000	4,000
Copy typist	2,250–2,500	3,000
Junior clerk	1,872	2,340–2,500
Clerical worker	2,300	4,200

Source: Information supplied by Brighton Anti-Low Pay Unit, unpublished information

That same year work began on the long-awaited new day nursery; it went into operation in 1968, with places for fourteen more children. Close to that time the whole nursery policy underwent a review, basically revolving around the question of how to provide more places to care for the children of mothers required to care for the children of other mothers.

Throughout this period, for the Brighton home nursing staff, "the married part-time nurse continues to be of value ... the number fluctuates during the year due to domestic responsibilities."[6] By the 1970s almost all home helps, those who assisted ill, disabled, or elderly people, were "married women with families."[7] This created difficulties as "they are unable to start early or finish late at night which is often essential." Despite the disadvantages to the smooth running of services imposed by the domestic responsibilities of women with dependents, married women were seen as a "permanent" and "necessary" part of these services, especially in the case of the home help service where "the pay and career structure for home helps is not good enough to be suitable for single women."[8]

In parallel with the demand for women workers there was a constant though rather less successful demand for childcare facilities. In 1971 the Brighton Hospital Bulletin reported: "Radiographers, occupational therapists, physiotherapists, and social workers are in desperately short supply. Other departments too, rely on married women – kitchens, pharmacies, medical records offices and domestic services for example. The provision of facilities for the care of children of all types of staff would almost certainly ease staffing problems throughout the hospital ... School holiday periods when married women either resign or take annual or unpaid leave, have been causing [small hospitals] difficulties for a number of years."[9] The campaign for a hospital crèche continued throughout 1971. Under the headline "Crèche demands greater than realised" the *Bulletin* reported "hospitals could do a better job if facilities

Table 17
Employment by Sector as Percentage of Total
Labour Force: Greater Brighton Study Area[1] and
England and Wales, 1966

Sector	Study Area	England and Wales
Primary	0.7	5.2
Manufacturing	23.2	35.3
Service	76.1	59.5
Total	100.0	100.0

Source: Brighton Corporation, Planning Department

[1] Area stretches from Lancing on the west to Seaford on the
east, including all the coastal communities in between, as well
as Brighton and the area north to Patcham. See Brighton
Urban Structure Plan Team, *Summary Draft Written Statement.*

were provided for the care of staff children ... A survey conducted by
the *Bulletin* shows clearly that demand is probably greater than the
committee realised."[10]

In 1974 a ward at Brighton General Hospital was closed due to staff
and nurse shortages. The district mounted a "Back to Nursing" campaign, for married nurses, and set up a "nurse bank" to provide a pool
of nurses "who are unable to work fixed part-time hours but could work
at least four hours weekly."[11]

Brighton schools were also experiencing acute shortages of teachers
and support staff. They expanded efforts to recruit part-time teaching
staff and to extend their catering staffs, and the Borough Council recommended subsidized accommodations and low-interest mortgages to
"married male and female teachers."[12]

Jobs were also relatively easy to find for non-professional women
outside the government sector, although less publicity was directed at
these women and fewer "official" concessions were offered them. Women
to whom I spoke said that factories put on extra evening shifts in the
early 1960s, and several firms began to take on part-time secretarial
staff. One woman told me, "Jobs were so easy to come by then, you just
had to walk in and get hired on the spot, no questions like now. I had
three jobs at one time, for about a year, all cleaning." Another said, "It
would take you a whole morning just to read the 'positions vacant' for
women."

There were also opportunities for home work in a variety of fields,
ranging from making and cleaning clothing to the manufacture of

stuffed toys and artificial flowers and carding buttons. Some firms sent out typing or assembly work to former employees, and women with young children were offered home assembly work. "They even gave you a machine and a big heavy cover to keep it safe from the kids when you weren't sewing," one woman recalled, adding, "Now if you want to start there, if they have any work, you have to buy the machine. No one can afford that."

The reverse side of this somewhat ebullient retrospective picture is "deindustrialization." This is a process which began in Brighton in the 1950s, and affected male workers more severely than it did their wives and daughters. While women were being recruited to do assembly work in the new "modernized" factories in Hollingbury and sent homework by marginal sector factories, traditional industry, especially traditional male manual jobs, were apparently declining. A Trades Council history, written in 1974, notes that "the fifties were a time of great hardship for workers in this area. The boom of the immediate post-war years gave way to a serious recession, which was followed nationally, but not locally, by another period of economic growth."[13] In 1955 the Trades Council reported that the railway workshops were "once again plagued by rumbles of closure" though efforts were being made by the council to guarantee jobs.[14] Two years later the locomotive works were closed. The Trades Council noted in 1958 that "youth prospects of useful employment and proper apprenticeships and trade training in the locality seem to be worsening. We noted that the advent of the 'bulge' in the school leaver groups will call for special care to ensure that youngsters are not exploited in blind alley occupations."[15] In the following year the council reported growing, presumably male unemployment, in the Brighton area caused by "the shortage of industry ... and the wastage of youth who wanted apprenticeships where none were available."[16] This trend continued. In 1971 the Brighton Urban Stucture Plan team referred to declining industrial employment: "The most significant decreases ... due to closures which have occurred ... with the closing of the carriage works and railway workshops."[17] Registered unemployment in Brighton, which, as many women do not register, is primarily a measure of male unemployment, was often above the national average. In 1970 a Trades Council motion condemned the "lack of industry in the area ... this being one of the main factors contributing to the low wages paid generally."[18] Throughout the period there was general discussion of the fact that industrial conditions were deteriorating rapidly.

The stark contrast in the stories of women workers and men workers reflected not only their very different experiences in the labour force in this period,[19] but also a number of fundamental shifts in the nature of wage labour in Brighton in the three decades after the war.

Brighton was not alone in facing deindustrialization. Throughout Britain, between 1960 and 1980, "2.4 million jobs have gone in production industries, while 2.6 million new jobs have been created in service industries ... this trend has created more jobs for women and fewer for men ... In production industries overall, female employment has fallen slightly faster than male employment; but in service industries, 83 per cent of the extra job opportunities since 1961 have been filled by women."[20] The shift toward the numerical dominance of service workers thus led to "a market shift in the balance of men and women at work. In 1961, 31 per cent of the labour force consisted of women, the 1980 figure is 40 per cent. Put another way, for every 100 working men in 1961 there were 45 working women. Today, for every 100 working men there are 67 working women."[21] The expansion of the service sector was thus built upon the "feminization" of the labour force. In Brighton, as in many other urban areas, the jobs explosion was superimposed on the city's deindustrialization.

However the outcome was not, as the bare figures might suggest, an androgynous labour force. As this discussion of the jobs explosion indicates, women's labour was considered to be specific labour. Women workers were assumed to be different than male workers and, even if professionals, as in the case of the doctors noted above, to make up the second string of a two-tier system. Deindustrialization removed opportunities for people called "workers" and "youth." The jobs explosion created opportunities for "married part-time women." The outcome of the simultaneous deindustrialization and jobs explosion was a highly differentiated labour force. Women's entry into this labour force was therefore rarely smooth. In Brighton, as elsewhere, it occurred in a climate of conflict and ambivalence.

In the immediate post-war period, women were actively encouraged to enter the wage-labour force. Restrictions on married women in the civil service and in teaching had been removed in the 1940s.[22] Tax allowances for wives were "substantially increased in order to attract married women into paid employment."[23] In 1956, an International Labour Organization study concluded that "A sound and scientific basis for the employment of women is being increasingly advocated as serving the cause of democracy and as promoting the general welfare."[24] The Economic Survey for 1947 stated that "the need to increase the working population is not temporary, it is a permanent feature of our national life ... women now form the only large reserve of labour left and to them the Government are [sic] accordingly making a special appeal."[25] Such encouragement continued throughout the 1950s and 1960s.[26]

In this period of general economic expansion women entered the labour force in growing numbers, accelerating the trend that had begun in the late 1930s. In 1980 an analyst reported that "around one million extra women have joined Britain's labour force each decade."[27]

This movement took place in spite of society's continued fear regarding maternal deprivation. Such fear, coupled with people's lively recollections of the interwar depressions, led to opposition from some sections of the trade-union movement. In 1947, the same year in which the Economic Survey had made a special appeal for women to enter the labour force, "the TUC Annual Report announced that there was no doubt in the General Council's mind that the home is one of the most important spheres for a woman worker and that it would be doing a grave injury to the life of the nation if women were persuaded or forced to neglect their domestic duties in order to enter industry particularly where there were young children."[28]

Women's dual role was thus another uneasy partner in post-war reconstruction. On one level, supplementing the family wage was necessary to achieve and maintain the level of household consumption which was held to cement the classless consensus. On another level, women in the labour force appeared to contradict the ideal of a home-centred femininity and to pose unknown dangers to the male working class. In the long run, women's activities were to realize both these concerns, although in unexpected ways. In the short term, however, the limits imposed on the form of women's participation in the labour force by their domestic-community role, defused any dangers of women "breaking away" from the family or "stealing jobs from men." These limits ranged from low pay, partly as a result of low rates of unionization, to restricted access to jobs and benefits. But the parameters within which all these diverse disadvantages were contained was women's dual role.

Despite the lip service to childcare and other services, women retained primary responsibility for domestic work and childcare. This was still defined as women's primary role; their wage work "served the cause of democracy" and promoted "the general welfare." Although much of the specific character of women's wage work stemmed from characteristics which could only be attributed to women with major domestic responsibilities, especially dependent children, these characteristics were, in many ways, generalized to all women workers. This is hardly surprising in a labour force which explicitly excluded nurturant and reproductive activities and could not, therefore, recognize their variable character. Women's participation in the labour force in the post-war period was therefore one fraught with both personal and social conflict. An essential component of post-war society became the creation, extension, and eventual "naturalization" of the dual role.

The Creation and Exploitation of the Dual Role.

By 1951 the arrival of the dual role was heralded by some sectors of the women's media. In 1951, *Miracle*, a popular women's magazine, announced: "One thing remains, the wife's ability to do two jobs. Many can do them and find that the stimulation of a job outside the home makes them all the more delightful as wife and mother. The secret lies in a cheerful approach and the ability not to worry over non-essentials with the husband and children lending a hand."[29]

Women's post-war life cycle had taken on an added dimension. Women no longer stopped wage work at marriage, but carried on until the birth of the first child, and later returned to the labour force when the children were older. The dual role of combining wage work and domestic-community work was thus extended, at some time in their lives, to a majority of British women.

By the mid-1950s, many women had come to expect their lives to follow this pattern. A 1955 *Women's Own* questionnaire of thousands of women aged 15–25 found that "few girls today can afford to stay at home and not work. Very few would like such a life! ... Nearly all want to go on working after they are married and until they are expecting their first baby. After the baby is born, more than 80 per cent want to stay at home."[30] *Women's Own* also reported that marriage was the most important ambition of 91 out of every 100 young women who were not already married. However, it was becoming increasingly apparent that the period of "dear housewifeliness" was a short, if absorbing, part of women's lives.

Throughout the late 1950s and early 1960s, a spate of sociological studies investigated women's dual role, largely from the perspective of its effects on the family, and pronounced that women's labour-force participation was an accomplished fact. In 1965 Viola Klein wrote: "The employment of married women in trade and industry, in the public services and the professions has become part of the fabric of Western life. There can be little doubt that it is as characteristic a feature of it as an expanding economy and a rising standard of consumption, and that it is likely to last as long as these continue."[31]

Women in Brighton said that, over the post-war period, the number of women who had "some little job" increased. Almost everyone to whom I spoke also said that, in contrast to the interwar generation, the employment of married women was a "natural" and "expected" thing. "It's just another part of my day"; "It's the normal pattern around here," were frequent comments.

Of the fifty-five women I spoke to, thirty-seven currently had wage work, seven had retired, and eleven were full-time domestic workers.

Table 18
Wage Jobs, Current or Most Recent[1], of 54 Women

Job Description	*Number of Women Holding that Job*		
	Current	*Most Recent*	*Total*
OUTSIDE THE HOME			
Clerical	5	4	9
Cleaner	5	2	7
Waitress (inc. pubs)	6	1	7
Shop assistant	2	3	5
Factory worker	2	2	4
Teacher	3	—	3
School dinner worker	3	—	3
Health professional	2	—	2
Telephone operator	2	—	2
Artist	1	—	1
Nanny	1	—	1
Cook (institution)	1	—	1
Caretaker	1	—	1
"Tea Lady"	—	1	1
Auxiliary nurse	—	1	1
Hairdresser's assistant	—	1	1
Upholsterer	—	1	1
Various[2]	—	2	2
Total	34	18	52
HOMEWORKERS			
Seamstress	2	—	2
Typing	2	—	2
Childminding	2	—	2
Assembly work	1	1	2
Sales	1	—	1
Total[3]	8	1	9

Source: Brighton Community Interviews, 1981

[1] For women who were full-time domestic workers at the time of the interview.

[2] Held two or more jobs, see table 20.

[3] Totals will exceed 54 because some women held more than one job.

All but two of the latter expected to return to wage work when their children were older. Only one of the entire group of women had never had a wage job (due to chronic illness). Most had worked for wages since completing their education, except when their children were young. (See table 18.)

In contrast, only thirty-one of their mothers had had wage jobs. (See table 19.) Of those who had not had wage jobs, twelve had had "too

Table 19
Mothers' Wage Jobs (of 31 Women Whose Mothers
Had Wage Jobs)

Job	Number Who Held Job
Cleaners[1]	6
Family business[2]	6
Laundry[3]	4
Shop assistant	4
Seamstress	2
Factory	1
Other	8
Total	31

Source: Brighton Community Interviews, 1981

[1] Includes 3 domestic cleaners and 3 institutional cleaners.
[2] Includes 3 small shops, 1 printing business, 1 market stall,
1 manufacturer of confectionery.
[3] Includes 2 institutional laundresses and 2 private laundresses.

many children" or "too much work at home," seven had not worked, either because their husbands said no, or "it wasn't done." Five cited other reasons, mainly ill health.

Almost all the women I interviewed expected and, in fact, wanted to continue wage work throughout their adult lives. Almost all said it was "easier" for women to work at wage jobs in their generation, or had been before the recession. Most attributed this to the fact that there was a greater variety of jobs available, that working was socially more acceptable, and that, in fact, it was necessary for women to work for wages. Some women noted it was the smaller families and easier domestic working conditions that made it easier for women to take on wage jobs than before the war. But however available jobs were to women, however their experience of the 1950s, 1960s, and 1970s appeared to contrast with that of their mother's generation, and sometimes that of their male counterparts, the post-war period was not a golden age for women in the labour force.

In Brighton, as in the rest of Britain, women entered the labour force to do specific jobs, and they tended to be segregated within the job market. Most of the women I spoke to, while accepting the inevitability of the fact that they would spend much of their adult lives in the labour force, and often welcoming this, did not see this as their primary job. Many said they had not planned for their future wage jobs when they were in school, nor had their maternal families. Only seventeen of the fifty-five women I interviewed had any post-secondary training. Of

Table 20
Changes in Male/Female Work Force Composition: Greater Brighton
Study Area[1] and Great Britain, 1959–68

| | Rate of Change over the Period | |
	Brighton Study Area	Great Britain
Total employment	1.68	5.70
Female employment	1.35	12.04
Male employment	1.91	2.29
Male share of total employment	−0.20	−2.10

Source: Brighton Urban Structure Plan Team, Survey Report 5 *Employment*

[1] Defined as in note 1, table 17.

these, only twelve were currently using their skills. Those women who possessed recognized marketable skills had acquired them on the job.

Although their jobs exhibited a greater variety than did their mother's jobs (see tables 18 and 19), women were still largely confined to the relatively low-paid "female" sectors.[32] Some women saw this as a problem, although most, especially older women, said they had seen steady progress in jobs opening up to women. One said explictly that some jobs were appropriate to women and "they should stick to them."

Some women had had long-term jobs, up to nineteen years, but the average length of time in the present job was five years. Chequered careers of jobs taken on and dropped due to domestic responsibilities were the norm. Women with post-secondary education had often taken a variety of jobs since their children were born, although generally within their fields. The others had "done everything": unskilled factory work, cleaning, waitressing, shelf filling, shop work, working as nursing aids.

These women often had a wide array of skills and experience in addition to their various home-making skills. Some women were conscious of this: "I can do almost any kind of job that doesn't call for a certificate"; "the women at work have done everything ... if we had to we could run this town." Other women took this knowledge for granted: "Those things aren't really what you call job skills ... all women can do those things." Some saw their range of experience as both a necessity ("You don't have a choice when you have a family, you take what you can") and as an advantage, acknowledging that they were flexible workers ("Women have to chop and change, they can't be like men, get a job and stick to it whatever happens at home"). Others saw this as a problem: "Women don't act like proper employees, they're always quitting or taking time off for their families."

Most women I spoke to did not expect wage work to dominate their lives (although most expected it to dominate their husbands' lives). Their chequered employment careers were a pattern based not on external pressures of wage work processes, but on the rhythms of a human lifecycle and a growing family. These women were creating a more flexible way of working, one which merged the exigencies of human need with the more ephemeral but more rigid demands of formal wage work. While some people saw these patterns as odd or out of synchronization with the wage sector's system of demands and rewards, many women to whom I spoke echoed the childcare activists' assertion that it was the organization of wage work that was out of synchronization with family needs. A woman who had spoken with me quietly, even reticently, for an hour and a half said, with considerable animation, as I was at the door: "Women are stronger than men. They have to be. The men all gave up on their own businesses and on working with their families, but the women, when they go to work, they are still mothers and keep house. They haven't given in. They know what's important ... the children, not making things in a shop. And they don't get any help ... they have to be strong."

Whether one sees women's wage-work patterns as erratic and inconstant, as an accepted necessity, or as an assertion of the fact that "life" is of greater importance than "work," such patterns do have a specific logic. It is a logic derived largely from the domestic-community sphere; it is therefore largely invisible to, or deemed inappropriate to, the wage-work sphere. This logic extends not only into the jobs women take on over their lifetimes, but also into the way they do these jobs.

Time Patterns. For the women to whom I spoke, wage work exhibited very specific time and space patterns. There was a general pattern of women taking on a variety of jobs before their children were born, jobs generally described as "unskilled" or "boring." Of the fifty women with children who currently had or had had jobs, two had become full-time domestic workers on marriage, and forty-two had altered their wage work processes while they had young children. Of the latter group, thirty had become full-time domestic workers, six had taken on homework and six had changed jobs "to be closer to home" or "to have fewer hours." For the thirty women who were or had been full-time domestic workers, the average length of time during which they had been or expected to be in this role was about six years, although some had been full-time domestic workers for periods as short as four months and some for as long as fifteen years. These time variations were attributed to a number of causes: financial need, family crises such as a husband's unemployment, or the death of a child. The most common one was "waiting for the youngest to be in school".[33] On their return to work, most women without "recognized" marketable skills again took on a variety of jobs, described as "what I could get" with hours and location to fit her domestic responsibilities.

Changing jobs or leaving the labour force were thus, in some respects, interruptions to woman's employment career. The subsequent loss of seniority, promotions, and benefits caused women to "lose ground" in their fields. Returning women often found they had to take relative pay cuts.[34]

Women's domestic responsibilities meant that many of them worked part-time. Only five of the thirty-seven women I spoke to who were currently in wage work had full-time jobs of forty or more hours a week. Of these, four had no dependent children and one was a childminder. Of the thirty-two who worked part time (from four to thirty hours a week with an average of sixteen hours), all but four had dependent children. Of these, seventeen had regular shifts, working the same hours and/or days each week, while fifteen had variable hours. These latter included homeworkers, private cleaners, all the teachers and waitresses, and some salespersons. Part-time work may have been a "necessity" for women, but in terms of rewards it imposed tremendous disadvantages. Throughout Britain, part-time workers tended to earn lower hourly wages than full-time workers, and they were less likely to be covered by occupational pension and sick pay schemes. Many were not covered by certain employment protection legislation, nor were they eligible for full National Insurance benefits.[35]

Despite "official" evidence that women did not work shifts as frequently as men did, and certainly did not receive shift differential payments,[36] almost all the women working part-time worked shifts or at least unsocial hours. Two of the waitresses worked split shifts; all the homeworkers and private cleaners, as well as the nanny, varied their hours to accommodate both their employers' and families' needs. Other women worked evenings or weekends so that their husbands or friends could "help" with childcare. This latter group, especially the homeworkers, often had amazing shifts. One homeworker who collated material for a printing firm said: "Sometimes I work for twenty-nine hours at a stretch, without sleeping. My husband and son help some, to get an order out. The whole house is full of the stuff. We eat cold beans out of a can. Sometimes there's nothing to do for days."[37] Women who worked variable or "on-call" hours had similar schedules. One woman with two teenage sons and a husband on short time had recently taken on a second wage job:

I get him [husband] off to work and then wake [her sons] up and get them off and tidy up the house and then go to work [making school dinners] and get home about 3:30 and make their dinners and eat mine and then [her husband] comes home at about 5:30 and I leave for work [waitressing job] at 6:00. I get a break about 9:00 and sometimes [her husband] comes down and we have a drink and chat about the house and the boys and so on. I get off about 11:00. Sometimes [her husband] picks me up. Usually I take the bus. If I miss the last one I have to call and sometimes wake him up. But we manage. It's all right. If it doesn't go on too long.

Of the thirty-seven women holding wage jobs, eight had more than one wage job. Three of these eight women had two wage jobs: waitress/ school dinners, waitress/waitress, waitress/shop assistant; four women had one outside job and home work: school meals/typing, waitress/seamstress, cleaner/seamstress, clerical/childminder; and one woman had three wage jobs: one outside the home and two home work jobs, clerical/ typist/lodgers. The wage-work patterns of all these women included split shifts, as well as variable and unsocial hours.

Attempts to operate within the differing temporal logic of the home and work spheres contributed to a pattern of variable and often "unsocial" wage work hours. Women's attempts to bridge the spaces of their two workplaces also meant that they had specific and often severe spatial constraints.

Space Patterns. The fact that women frequently had to combine their journeys to work with dropping off or picking up children from school or the minder, doing the family shopping, seeing a teacher, or taking the child to the doctor, severely restricted the locations where they were willing and able to do wage work. This was further constrained by the fact that most women worked part-time and felt long journeys to work were not worthwhile. As one women said: "It used to take me two hours, there and back, and then I was only working about three hours. It was a good job, but a waste of time. It took up my whole day and I didn't get paid for that."

Unlike their husbands, most women relied on walking or on public transportation to get to their wage jobs. In the Brighton sample, twelve (or 32 per cent) of the thirty-seven with wage jobs walked to work, as opposed to three of their husbands, and fifteen (or 41 per cent) took the bus, as opposed to ten husbands. Only one woman took her own car while sixteen husbands drove cars or motorcycles. This was a pattern reflected in other areas of Britain.[38] Many women who walked to work said they did not make enough money to justify spending money on bus fares. Those who used public transportation said that their choices of job locations were limited by the fact that buses ran less frequently evenings and weekends and "stopped running too early" in some areas.

Others said fares were prohibitive for long journeys. On the whole, women tended to prefer wage jobs close to home and/or on main bus routes.

In general, the women I spoke to travelled a shorter distance to work than their husbands. They travelled from 5 miles to a few blocks, the average distance being 1.2 miles and an average (return) journey requiring forty-five minutes. Their husbands travelled an average of 2.7 miles to work. The distances women travelled to wage work varied by area. Women in Hanover had the shortest average journeys, less than a mile or about ten minutes travel time; women in Whitehawk had the longest, an average of 2.1 miles and a one hour journey. Women in Hollingbury, a number of whom worked on the nearby industrial estate, travelled an average 1.4 miles, or for about forty minutes. Thus, it was not only the responsibility for the home but its location that structured women's access to wage-work opportunities.

The fact that women's journeys to work were shorter than men's in Brighton as a whole was indicated by the Brighton Urban Structure Plan team, which reported in 1966 that fewer women than men commuted into or out of the study area. The report also noted that industrialists considered women reluctant "to travel far to work ... as many wished to get home quickly to tend to family duties."[39]

Employers were aware of these constraints on women's mobility. In Brighton there had been a shift of population and industry from the central areas, characterized by a skilled, unionized, male labour pool, to suburban industrial estates, characterized by an "unskilled", non-unionized and largely "captive" female labour pool. Throughout Britain, from 1951–71, there was "strong evidence ... that it was shortages of women workers that motivated relocations triggered by labour shortages – the Department of Industry inquiry into locational attitudes during the 1964–67 period, for example, revealed that one firm in nine considered that a shortage of female labour was the 'outstanding' reason for moving; shortages of male labour were rarely mentioned despite the fact that 40 per cent of respondent firms cited labour shortages as a 'major reason'" for investing in new areas.[40] And the Location of Offices Bureau reported in 1977 that "once an office moves to a town it finds a very large hidden supply of potential labour, consisting largely of married women. These are often anxious to work ... near home because of family commitments ... These married women are grateful for the opportunity to work locally and thus become loyal and hard-working employees."[41]

Similarly, service sectors were expanded on the basis of the availability of cheap, flexible female labour – women accustomed to "sacrifice," and unaccustomed to traditional union structures. These women were supposedly working for "pin money." The labour-intensive processes, as well as the wage structures of these sectors, came to reflect this.

The space-time patterns of women with wage jobs thus differed significantly from those of comparable groups of men (co-workers, neighbours, husbands, sons, fathers). This variation, which in most instances took the form of constraints imposed by a different logic, was evident throughout women's lives. Independent women without dependents rarely saw their wage jobs as long term, or as part of a career pattern. This was, by and large, a realistic perspective. For them the constraints of relatively low levels of skill acquisition would be compounded by the constraints which resulted from marriage. After marriage they had "more responsibilities at home," or "husbands fussed if things weren't done"; and the arrival of children imposed even more severe constraints.

The wages earned by the women to whom I spoke were generally low. Of the thirty-seven women with wage work, only twenty-nine could give an accurate estimate of their earnings.[42] For them, wages ranged from 45p to £3.50 an hour, with the average being £1.40, or from £8 to £49 a week take-home pay. These low wages conformed to the general patterns of men's and women's relative earnings in Brighton as a whole. (See tables 14, 15 and 16.)

Most women earned wages that were insufficient to ensure their financial independence. This was true even of the full-time workers and the female-headed households. Of the eight female-headed households, six had incomes of less than £40 a week. Of the seven female-headed households with children still at home, only one woman earned the family income "unassisted." Others survived by various combinations of wages, supplementary benefits, Family Income Supplements, and maintenance payments from husbands and other relatives. In all cases except the one mentioned above, women's wages were seen as a "supplement" to family income.

The Dual Role and the Household

At the same time that the dual role was altering the nature of the wage labour process, it was also creating significant changes in the family and community. The wages women with dependents earned, seen as a supplement to family income, provided a better domestic working environment through the purchase of household equipment, "labour saving" devices, and convenience foods.[43] For many families in Brighton the women's wages had made possible the steady improvement in domestic and working conditions noted above. Women mentioned that their wages had payed for washing machines, hoovers, new cookers, and the redecoration of the lounge. Women frequently said that they had acquired household conveniences or improvements "for themselves," but always added that they had also bought or helped pay for things "for the family," generally recreational equipment and televisions or things for their husbands – cars or equipment, such as carpentry or gardening tools, for his domestic work.

Some women also noted that their patterns and rhythms of domestic work had altered because they had less time and more money. They relied more on convenience foods and labour-saving devices. They used canned soup instead of having a "proper stock pot," which required too much time. They devoted their days off to buying instead of making the children's clothes and bought a clothes washer so husbands and children would help with the laundry. A number of women said their wages also paid for holidays, which they saw as increasingly essential, to get away from the pressure of work both in the home and the workplace, and to the maintenance of family ties. Women said holidays were often the only chance for families with busy and varied schedules, including extended families, to be together.[44] The family lifestyles of most women had become structured around the space-time constraints imposed by the dual role and, concomitantly, had come to depend on the commodities and services and occasional mobility which the supplementary wage allowed.

For many families, primarily those in low income categories, women's "supplementary wage" had always bought essentials; it had always been a necessary and expected part of family budgeting. Low as they were, women's incomes made a significant contribution to family budgets. The group with a second wage earner had a higher percentage in the higher income categories than did the sample as a whole. For seven of the twenty-nine women employed for whom income data was available, their "supplementary" wages lifted the household above the poverty line.

Women's financial contribution to family resources became increasingly crucial as inflation overtook wage rates. Counter Information Services said, of Britain as a whole: "In 1979, 1.3 million men and 4.4 million women grossed less than £60 a week, below the supplementary benefit level for a 'standard family.' If [wage] working wives lose their jobs, the effects on family income are drastic ... However badly women's work is paid ... the loss of this so-called pin money pulls many families below the poverty line. If all employed married women were to lose their jobs, the number of families living below the povery line would treble."[45] For many, at least two wages had become essential to family maintenance. This was true of most women whose mothers had also worked for wages. A number of older women who described themselves as working class said that they and their husbands, before marriage, had planned their future on the basis of two wages for most of their family life. This was also becoming true for more and more middle-class families, for whom a supplementary wage was a phenomenon of the current generation.

So while women, in taking on wage work, had further constrained their space and time, they had also, in gaining more resources for their household work, freed up time and increased mobility in areas such as the purchase of cars and holidays. They had also organized ways of overcoming some of the constraints imposed by the wage sector.

Many women, especially those who called themselves working class, said it was easier for women to find jobs than it was for men. They had no illusions about this, saying it was because women would accept wages and conditions men would not, or because women were seen as "less fussy about things" or "less trouble on the job than men." Several also mentioned having used job-finding and job-sharing networks for women that were said to be less applicable to "proper men's jobs." They worked part-time in shops or as domestic cleaners or waitresses, "sharing" full-time hours with a friend or relative. These arrangements often included reciprocal childcare sharing. Other women had "passed on" their job to a relative or friend when they left. Two women I spoke to had "traded" jobs with friends in order to improve their respective hours or locations. One woman pointed out that such arrangements were easier for women than men "as anyone can do that job, you don't need a skill" and another noted that "women have less to do with stamps and insurance and tax" so it was easier to share and switch jobs. Women who did home work also utilized local networks. Childminders, seamstresses, and typists who worked directly for clients got most of their business through recommendations from friends and former clients rather than through advertising.

Women had therefore organized ways of turning their flexible and "erratic" job patterns to their advantage and making their time constraints more flexible. By the late 1970s and early 1980s, however, jobs were becoming harder for women to find and harder to hold on to. This tended to reinforce existing constraints and create new ones.

Women said they had become more cautious than in the past about quitting a job, unless they had another lined up, even if their families needed more time from them. As one woman said, "It's hard, the family needs the money and they also need me ... but now you have to sacrifice something and with [her husband] on short time ... and rents what they are, it's the time with the children gets sacrificed." Part-time jobs for skilled workers were especially difficult to find. Many women said part-time clerical, health, and education jobs were impossible to find. Two women who worked full-time, but wished to work part-time, said they were "trapped" with their hours as "they're letting all the part-timers go." Many of the casual "little jobs you can pick up here and there" were disappearing. Everyone said there was more competition for vacancies. This meant that for some, shifts and workloads became more irregular. Contract cleaners and waitresses were often "on call" rather than working regular hours; assignments for substitute teachers and private nurses became less frequent: home workers on contract had increasingly variable workloads. The juggling act of housework, childcare, shopping, and wage work became even more precarious, and incomes became less predictable.

For most of the women I spoke to, and for all of those who had come to maturity since the war, wage work was simply a natural and unexamined extension of being a wife and mother – part of the mother's responsibility for ensuring, by whatever means available, the health and relative security of her family. By and large, women expected better domestic working conditions than their mothers' generation had had, and were willing to juggle their time and to take on wage jobs in order to achieve this. In so doing they had accepted, although not passively, a new and pressing burden.

The domestic-community demands on women's time had not diminished with the diminishing flexibility of the job market. If anything, the cuts in support services had placed a greater burden of domestic-community work on women. For most the recession created problems not in terms of redundancy per se, but of adjusting hours, switching jobs, taking on home work, or taking on new jobs. The problem was, in fact, an extension of the conjuring and outwitting of constraints that women had been performing in all aspects of their lives.

THE DUAL ROLE: RECREATING "WOMAN"

The official arrival of women's dual role in the 1940s and 1950s, and its extension in the following decades, demarcated a new adjustment in the relations between work and life, a solution to the problem of a growing need for wage labour, concomitant with a continued need for a family centred around domestic labour. Because of their dual role, all the changes in women's lives became interdependent and mutually reinforcing. And for both the family-community and the wage-labour sector, women's dual role became a self-reinforcing necessity.

In doing two jobs, women reinforced a division between home and workplace at the same time as they effected a balance between them. Most women, especially married women, earned less than the cost of reproducing their own labour power. For the wage sector, they thus represented a cheap, flexible labour force. In the often highly competitive and marginal sectors where many women worked, such as the declining textile and clothing industries and commercial service industries of restaurants and shops, they were necessary to the sustenance of profit levels. In the state sector, women provided services at a minimum cost to taxpayers, that is, to themselves and their families.

At the same time, in their unwaged domestic and community work, women provided alternatives to, and compensated for, inadequacies in public goods and services. They also created and constantly recreated a separate place for rest and recuperation from wage work for their families and themselves. The goods and services their wages helped to pay for further enhanced this "separate place" and potentially lightened their domestic work load. This allowed women to reproduce not only their families' labour but also their own, in the diminished time available to them.

The character of women's wage labour, which derived from the dual role, simultaneously constituted women as a specific sector of the labour force and reinforced their economic dependence on the family. These limitations helped diffuse the threats perceived by "family-defending" social scientists and protectionist trade unionists, and also reproduced the conditions necessary for women's dual role to continue.

Drawn into the labour force to do a waged version of the same type of work they did at home, many thereby provided services for domestic-community workers, including themselves. The type of jobs many women did in the wage sector, which resembled their invisible and devalued domestic work, reinforced the definition of these jobs as "women's work," wherever and however they took place. The assumption that women's wage labour was secondary to their "real" work in the home and community, and therefore that their position in the labour force should be secondary, was reflected and reinforced in post-war education policy, which emphasized "domestic training," especially for working-class girls.[46] The 1948 Newson Report accepted "as unproblematic the fact that the duality of women's social function as wife and mother meets the modern employers' need for labour of a semiskilled variety."[47]

The continuity of content in both aspects of women's dual role thus reinforced the devalued status of women's work. Its status was low because it paid no, or low, wages, and its low status reinforced the low wages paid.

All this reinforced women's dependence on a male wage. Social policy had acceded to, and even reinforced, the idea that women, as a whole, regardless of marital status, should be paid less than men, as a whole, regardless of marital status. This was implicit in the concept of the "family wage" with its assumption of a dependent woman. Equal pay for women had been rejected during the First World War, on the grounds that the "average" male worker had dependents but the "average" female worker did not.[48] This idea was reinforced by the 1946 Royal Commission on Equal Pay, which claimed that "one of the social causes of unequal pay was to secure that motherhood as a vocation is not too unattractive financially compared with work in the professions, industry, or trade."[49]

The assumption that women are financially dependent on men "can thus have disastrous consequences for the woman who has no man to depend upon, yet provisions for state support show a remorseless determination to enforce that expectation wherever possible."[50]

Partly as a consequence of these assumptions, which continued throughout the post-war period, in Britain in 1981 most adult women earned less than the Low Pay Unit's definition of a low-paid worker (about £75 a week).[51] Most married women did not pay full National Insurance contributions and therefore had few or no unemployment or sickness benefits and a reduced pension.[52] As most women outlived their husbands, and as a growing number were divorced or separated, many could look forward to an old age characterized by poverty and insecurity. A number of women I spoke with were either experiencing the beginnings of a widowhood where the loss of a husband was compounded by the realization that "I haven't enough to get by," or were concerned that this would happen to them, despite having had wage jobs throughout most of their lives. One woman, with a recently widowed mother-in-law, an unemployed husband and adult son, and three dependent children at home, asked an unanswerable question, "Why didn't we think about all this before?".

In living out their dual role, therefore, women constantly recreated their own "suitability" for all its aspects. By constantly recreating the conditions and content of work in each area, women reinforced the conditions of their own oppression.

Yet neither this oppression nor the relations which constituted it were static. Nor had women been passive recipients and reproducers of these changes. In struggling for fertility control and better domestic-community working conditions, women had created some of the preconditions for the dual role and laid the basis of its extension. They also created new conflicts and new arenas for struggle in these relations. At the same time, they altered the nature of the wage-labour sphere, not only in forcing concessions such as part-time work, in providing labour to the rapidly growing service sector, and in creating informal job-sharing networks, but also in exerting pressure through more conventional channels, legislative and trade union, although often in unexpected and unconventional ways.

EXTENDING CONTROL OVER THE DUAL ROLE

People often say that women don't get involved in unions. Well with their dual roles, the time constraints of that, they've been prevented. And it's hard to get women to run [for office]. They're not toughened to the political selection process. Women are tougher than men but in a different way. They have the strength that comes from constant family problems and demands. (Margaret Davis, political secretary, Brighton and District Co-op Party and chairman, Southern Regional Council of the Labour Party.)

Women are the most imaginative and active members of this centre [the Unemployed Workers Centre]. They keep the place going and have all the new ideas about how to organize. (Member of the Brighton Unemployed Women's Group.)

At first glance, women's organizations within and around their wage jobs appear to contrast with the complex and energetic networks developed around the "reproductive" aspects of their role. The absence of women's activity in this area is illusory. Women organized around their money-earning work as well as elsewhere. But they did so largely outside of, or even in opposition to, conventional wage-work organizations – the unions, professional associations, and employers' associations. Because they were dealing with a set of problems foreign to, or at least invisible to, conventional wage-work politics, they were developing new networks, new ways of doing things.

Examples were women's job-sharing and swapping networks, homeworkers' networks, and the new jobs in childcare and women's health being created at the interface of the home-community and wage workplace. These women were actively using women's "differences," especially the fact that their lives were structured by the interrelation of work and life, either to develop new ways of working for money or to maintain ways which were apparently vestiges of an earlier era but which were appropriate to their situation.

Other women were acting in more recognizably political ways, attempting to compensate for women's differences through pressure within unions and professional associations, and through using these groups to effect change in wage-labour processes. Many of those who were pressing for change in existing structures might not have seen common cause with those who were "making do" by adapting and altering constraining structures. But both groups were involved in different facets of the active critique and change of wage-work processes, structures, and organizations. Very few of the women to whom I spoke belonged to unions. Of the thirty-seven in wage jobs, six were in unions and another six worked in places where there were unions but they were not members. Of the latter six, the reasons given for non-membership said more about the unions than the inactivity of the women. With the exception of one woman who "didn't approve of unions," these women said that the unions did not "care about" people in their job (casual or part-time workers) or about "women workers."

Most women worked in non-unionized jobs: domestic and casual cleaning, non-union factories, hotels and restaurants. Many felt the idea of a union in their wage workplace was impossible. One woman said, "A union? Not there, not bloody likely." Their jobs were "too scattered" or "unions weren't interested" or, of one factory, "Why do you think they hire women there? Women don't belong to unions or complain or go on strike." For most of these women the structure and reputation of trade unions – seen to be concerned with male, manual workers – placed unions outside their lives, even for those whose husbands were "union men."[53]

Even the women who were trade-union members shared some of these sentiments. Only two of the six members were at all active (one had been a shop steward). The other four gave domestic responsibilities, transportation difficulties, and lack of encouragement by husbands and other unionists as reasons for inactivity. Both of the activists said that taking on "male" union structures was difficult. "It takes courage," the former shop steward said. "At first, I thought they wouldn't take me seriously. And I guess that was true. I had to really prove myself."[54]

Despite the fact that most women were not, and did not foresee them-selves as members of traditional union structures, the "feminization" of the labour force, concomitant with deindustrialization, had increased relative female union membership in the Brighton area. And the greater presence of women was slowly changing the nature of the trade-union movement.

The tendency toward numerical and political dominance of service workers in the Brighton union movement is recorded by the Trades Council. During the war the Trades Council had noted the "addition of several 'white collar' and 'public service' branches."[55] During the 1960s, the "main growth point was the 'white collar unions' while in the early seventies all the major teachers unions affiliated."[56] In its 1966 annual report, the Trades Council had noted with some bemusement:

It is more and more the case that the support, activity, leadership and pressures are coming from our smaller branches, and particularly from our non-manual unions. This does not necessarily blunt the militancy of our attitudes. On the contrary, these unions are in the main extremely active ... Perhaps this reflects a gradual shift in the balance of power on a national scale in the Trade Union movement and certainly we welcome the forces that are emerging: the techni-

cians, the clerks, the shop workers, the draughtsmen, the teachers, and the whole
'white collar' sector which is growing so fast. Yet it would be a pity if this should
correspond with any weakening of interest by those mass unions which, historically, have always provided our main base.[57]

These tendencies were reflected throughout Britain. Despite women's
relatively low rates of unionization, in numerical terms, the majority of
new union members after 1961 were women. This accelerated a trend
towards the numerical dominance of service workers within the trade-
union movement. In Britain as a whole, between 1960–79, there was a
99.5 per cent increase in women members as opposed to a 13.7 per cent
increase in men members.[58]

   This was seen as part of what several people described as the "pro-
letarianization" of white collar workers or, alternatively, the "takeover
of the union movement by 'middle class people.'" Comments regarding
change in the "class character" of the union movement often noted the
fact that the majority of active female members were seen to be in
"middle-class jobs" such as teaching, the health professions, or social
work. This contrasted with the male union leadership which was, or was
perceived to be, from the "manual workers sector."

   Along with this sectoral shift, there was also a growing consciousness
of "women's presence" in the unions. During the war

with women taking an increasing number of industrial jobs the question of
recruitment came to the fore. This was a difficult task. In part the older union
members feared that women would lower the standard of wages, while many
new female operatives replied that they had no desire to join the union since
their jobs were only temporary. In April, 1941, the Trades Council states its
position clearly:

   We urge the Trade Union movement to organize the women now being con-
scripted into industry so that they do not become a source of cheap labour. We
believe that equal wages should be paid for equal work.[59]

In 1948, in the optimism of post-war reconstruction and at the height
of post-war austerity and "making do" a women's advisory committee
was inaugurated by the Brighton Hove and District Trades Council.
The committee visited factories employing women and did "valuable
work on specific cases such as the siting of the food office and other
women's problems."[60] It had subcommittees on youth, food control, and
church liaison, and ran a campaign for immunization against dipth-
eria.[61] But, only five years after its formation, the committee quietly
subsided. Trades Council historians attributed this to the fact that "then,
as now, working women were expected to do two full time jobs, one at
work and another at home, and the combined pressure on them was

too great to enable them to keep up a high level of political activity as well.[62] By 1958, when the TUC affiliation form asked the number of women delegates on committees, Brighton was able to report "very few."[63]

By the 1960s, though most women were not working in traditionally unionized workplaces, they were very evidently in the labour force. The media and social analysts were insisting they had come to stay and so were the women, many of whom were the wives and daughters of trade unionists. In Brighton the issue of women in unions, and of unionizing women, was becoming more and more of a concern. In 1960, at the annual general meeting, the TUC formed a subcommittee to study its report on recruiting women into unions and passed a motion on improving the status of women in industry.[64] Throughout the 1960s and early 1970s, the Brighton Trades Council supported "Equal Rights for Women Trade Unionists" and "Equal Pay for Work of Equal Value."[65] The TUC Working Women's Charter and special meetings to discuss "The Rights of Working Women" were reported in the minutes of this period.

National pressures and the increasing presence and participation of women in local unions and in affiliated community groups had some success in extending union concerns and activities. The Trades Council and its affiliates discussed and sometimes supported campaigns like the FPA contraceptive mobile unit, the Save the Family Planning Clinics campaigns, the campaigns against restricted access to abortion, and the Campaign for Day Care Abortion.

Some women unionists, however, saw this as a very limited victory. Jane Stageman, in her study of women in unions in the Hull area, reported:

It is true that the TUC, under pressure from women inside and outside the movement, has gradually accepted an ever-widening list of aims to end discriminations against women in society. However, these have been treated as "special interest" grievances and have failed, generally, to be pursued as part of the main policy interests of the movement and seen as an integral part of negotiating objectives. Moreover, the passing of egalitarian resolutions at conference level, seems to have made no impact on the continuance of oppressive activities by male trade unionists toward their own wives and daughters in their own homes. The uncritical acceptance of this contradiction has served to perpetuate the present state of affairs – in which greater opportunities for women to develop their potential are still enjoyed by relatively few.[66]

These feelings were echoed by the experience of many of the women I spoke to in Brighton. The formal or national support given to "women's issues" was not, as the activists remarked, reflected at the local level.

When asked about whether women at work ever discussed issues such as childcare, contraception and abortion, and domestic problems, almost all said yes. Advice on these subjects and the sharing of important information were major topics of conversation. But when asked if these were "union issues" the six union members said no. The former shop steward said: "There was a resolution about abortion at the national conference but nobody talks about those things in the local ... I'd never bring them up. It's hard enough to talk about union business."

Given these problems, it is not surprising that women organizers in the Brighton area had the greatest success in organizing separately and in relatively new and less formal structures within the union movement, structures in which their input could be incorporated from the beginning. This was evident in the formation of the childminders' group, which combined service with union concerns, in the 1981 revival of the Trades Council Women's Committee and in the establishment of the Brighton Workers' Centre for the Unemployed in July, 1981.

The Brighton Unemployed Women's Group used the Unemployed Workers' Centre and women formed the majority of its first elected management committee. From within the Trades Council group and the unemployed workers groups, women attempted to provide forums for discussion and action on the diverse and complicated issues affecting both aspects of their dual roles.

The Trades Council Women's Committee was concerned to document and improve the position of women in unions and of unorganized and unemployed women. It went further afield to discuss the nature of women's wage jobs and the effects of new technology on women's wage work and to set up forums to bring women normally outside of union structures – such as homeworkers and full-time domestic workers with young children – into contact with union women. Women within the Unemployed Women's Group and within the Unemployed Workers' Centre as a whole had similar objectives.[67] Trades Union Congress policy on setting up centres for the unemployed had stressed recognition of the importance of women's participation in the centres, and encouraged "making contact with unregistered unemployed women, [and] studying the patterns of women's employment and unemployment." It stated that "wherever possible, crèches should be arranged to coincide with meetings at the centre" and "as far as is practical, activities in the Centres should fit in with arrangements for taking and collecting children from school ... [and] ... men and women should take equal responsibility for organizing this childcare provision".[68] The Brighton Centre opened with a well-equipped crèche room.

The need for such forums, coupled with a desire for more democratic structures and procedures, modelled on the contemporary women's movement, led to separate women's organizations within the union movement. As the Brighton Unemployed Women's Group stated:

The women's group was formed as a result of feelings of alienation from the dominating male influences in the centre generally and in the [Unemployed Workers] Union in particular ... Many of us have been active in the Women's Liberation Movement and so are used to quite different (and we believe better) ways of organizing to those of the U[nemployed] W[orkers'] Union (and trade unions generally) ... [we are convinced] ... that the women's group is where we can find the mutual support which enables us to become active in the centre without becoming honorary men, and also that it is in such a group that we can best get things done. We do not have officers, we do not take votes, we try not to negate each other's contributions: nor do we vie with each other as those dominant in the union do, and we feel that we achieve more as a result ... As unemployed, we welcome the support and co-operation of the employed. As women, we expect the support and co-operation of men, and offer ours in return, but we will not tolerate the dictatorship of anyone.[69]

This perceived "separatism" met with some opposition on the part of male unionists, most of whom said they wanted to serve the "best interests of the union." An activist in the Unemployed Workers' Union stated: "It is clearly important that the women members see themselves as an integral part of the union and play an important part in its organization and campaigns ... Any tendency toward separatism in this respect, either by men or women, is something to be opposed in a friendly way. Insofar as women meet separately to discuss their problems, they should always report back to a general meeting the results of their deliberations and what steps they propose to take to integrate the women in the general working class struggle."[70]

Within the Trades Council, although there was "overwhelming" support for the establishment of a women's committee, there was opposition to the exclusion of men. This opposition on the part of men was based on a concern that a "closed" committee would preclude men discussing "women's issues" and a fear that women would become isolated within the union. According to one committee member, opposition to a closed separate committee was also expressed "by older women in the labour movement ... what they've seen is the Labour Party women's sections at their worst, the real sort of tea and scones gossip centres ... that's what they equate women's committees with ... they have the attitude that if we want equality we can't go around saying we want separate meetings because then we're not equal are we? They tend to think we've got the Equal Pay Act, we've got to work within that."

Women's limited participation in traditional structures, their need to organize separate structures, and the debates surrounding these problems all indicated the lack of fit between the lives and political priorities of most women and traditional union organizations. They also indicated a growing unwillingness among members of traditional wage-work structures to seriously grapple with the question of what kind of organizations might be more fitting to meet the needs of an androgynous labour force.

The implications of all the changes in fertility, childbirth, household form, childcare, and wage work which women had effected since the war have been ambivalent. While increasing women's access to resources these changes imposed new constraints on their space and time. Many of the new resources were both achieved through women's wage work and necessitated by this wage work and the newly extended social roles. Yet while these standards freed women from one kind of space-time constraint – that imposed by long hours of heavy domestic work – the new role imposed a new space-time constraint. Out of it came the call for new arrangements in time and space, and for new resources.

The combination of higher expectations and the new constraints which accompanied them led to a range of new needs, new forms of "making do," and new organizations attempting to extend control over the changing conditions of women's working and living environments.

Smaller families, as noted by several women, were a prerequisite of a lighter, domestic work load, changing domestic work processes, and women's wage work. Extending control over their fertility and the processes of childbirth became an increasingly important and accepted part of balancing space and time. Similarly, the informal neighbourhood support and childcare networks developed by women who spent most of their time in the home and community were no longer as available, nor were they adequate to meet the needs of women whose wage jobs required long periods away from home. Mothers with dual roles needed more formal and reliable childcare facilities. As more and more women looked forward to a lifetime of wage work, and a new generation of women educated in the expanded post-war facilities took on more professional jobs, the assertion of control over the conditions of wage work, and over the resources to balance dual roles became increasingly pressing.

The convergence of these conflicts gave rise to new forms of political consciousness and action. In turn, these were woven into the feminist tradition and became the fabric of the contemporary women's movement.

8 / Organizing Life and Work: The Feminist Tradition

Politics used to be tidier. It was a man's job, stayed in the Labour Party, all for the working man. Now, my goodness, it's everywhere. Everyone is on about politics. (Seventy-three-year-old Hanover woman, long-time Labour supporter.)

The women I spoke to in Brighton in the early 1980s had lost very little of their own social history. They were conscious that society had changed, and was changing, and that their lives meshed into these changes. Some felt swept up by these changes, others felt they had power to create and alter things that were happening. Almost all retained a sense of their ability and their right to intervene, whether this took the form of energetic, collective acts of "swimming against the tide" and creating concrete alternatives, or of quiet, individual decisions to distance themselves from forms of behaviour they felt were wrong, of acting in principled ways in their relations with their children, with Sainsbury's, with the local council.

These women were conscious that they had created new environments, that they had improved the structures, furnishings, and equipment of their homes, or at least that they had survived and done their work with disintegrating structures, inappropriate furnishings, and inadequate equipment. They were aware that their homes were in new places, either because they had relocated or the neighbourhood had changed around them. They knew that their work went on in a variety of sites, that their travel paths were altered, and that there were new places to go, whether these were shopping centres, mother and toddler groups, or women's health centres. Many women knew that the services created by women like themselves – the parent-run or feminist-inspired alternatives – existed because they used them and would continue to exist as long as people used them. Most did not see all this as the creation of a new geography or a new way of human life, but no one was oblivious to the small, essential, and abundant details which had massed together to make a new geography and a new life.

The main argument of this book is that these people had actively altered the quality of their life and work, the nature of their homes and communities, and the activities and characteristics which were attributed to women and men. In changing urban activity and the use of urban resources, they had created new cities. At the same time, through changing their activities, they had created new ways of being women and men, new ways of being human beings.

In their activities and organization, women had always acted from the basis of a contradictory social environment. They had operated primarily through the sphere of "life," a place separated out from "work" and imbued with qualities of dependence, a place regulated by statutory services which were inadequate and based upon obsolete understandings of women's lives and household organization. Because of this, people's actions – their daily work activities as well as their consciously political activities – constantly overstepped the bounds of antiquated environments and derelict gender definitions. By simply living their lives, people had changed the quality and the scope of political life. Politics had spilled out of sectarian and class confines into the households, the family relations, and the bodies and minds which animated the city. It had spilled into concerns about the siting of and access to the bricks, mortar, and moveable resources which surrounded people.

Most people were conscious, as was the woman quoted in the chapter introduction, that politics had changed, that there were new forms of individual and collective organization. For women, these were part of the crucial and idiosyncratic business of reproducing human life and part of the ways this interacted with the more transitory but rigid relations of wage work. None of the individual adjustments women made in this process were inevitable or fully determined in advance. Women had carefully, constantly, and incrementally constructed their lives.

This kaleidoscopic process is an integral part of a feminist tradition. All the actions and feelings and changes discussed in this book can be pulled together, however untidily and temporarily, and seen as a tradition of women organizing to extend the resources available for their lives and work. Changing "woman" and changing cities is both an outcome of this organization and the condition of new forms of organization. This chapter suggests some of the directions in which this feminist tradition might be moving. It looks first at some of the more obvious manifestations – women's networks in Brighton – and then at some broad implications this organization has had for social life, for the city, and for future organization.

THE CHARACTER OF WOMEN'S NETWORKS IN BRIGHTON

The feminist tradition – women organizing to extend the resources available to them – was evident everywhere women's lives took them. Women organized most effectively and easily in those areas which, in very general terms, were "permanent human needs ... health, habitation, family, education."[1] They organized least effectively in those areas which were, historically, provisional and ephemeral: wage labour relations and sectarian politics. It was within the fields of childcare, and to a lesser extent childbirth and fertility control, that organization had been particularly effective, that is, had involved the largest number of women at some time in their lives and had been integrated into, and seen as a constituent part of, their daily activities. As one moved into more "public" areas, especially employment-based organizations, networks became less dense and increasingly problematic both for their participants and for those "outside" them, whether social analysts or political allies and opponents.

This variable density and effectiveness reflected the character of the various fields in which women were working and organizing.

Childcare/Childbirth Networks

Childcare and, to a lesser extent, the ante- and post-natal aspects of childbirth, were activities over which women traditionally had the most control and for which they continued to have the most responsibility. Although, as noted earlier, science and social work established "general standards" in these areas and attempted to formulate universal means for achieving them, the process of caring for young children remained, of all the activities which made up women's lives, the one least susceptible to regulation. The care of children, especially in their pre-school years, was still, *de facto*, ceded largely to mothers, as a "natural" and primarily "private" duty.

Childcare was made up largely of unpredictable and almost wholly immediate demands, the nature and sequence of which were contingent on a variety of factors. The needs of a growing child were varied. They could alter daily, if not hourly. Women caring for young children required daily information about concerns ranging from the price and accessibility of used playpens to a child's behaviour problems. They required daily support to meet needs such as temporary childminding and transportation to shopping centres, as well as reliable and knowledgeable emergency support – experienced medical advice or assistance in carrying on in family crises.

Meeting these needs assumed personal trust. Few mothers would leave their children with a stranger, even for a short time. They also often assumed irregular hours. (If the baby is choking at midnight, it is little comfort to know that the buses will be running by 6:00 AM or that the local Infant Welfare Clinic will be open by 10:00 the next morning.) Childcare needs could best be met through constant and reliable personal contact with local people – people whose knowledge and character could be assessed, verified, and relied on. The need for local support was reinforced by the fact that women with young children often had severe constraints on their mobility and unpredictable and immediate demands on their time. This was also true of those childbirth organizations established to reassert women's control over ante- and post-natal care. Unlike childcare, being pregnant can be treated as a "medical event." But ante- and post-natal care also requires constant, personal support and relies both on informal local networks and on groups such as the National Childbirth Trust (NCT) to supplement "official" medical advice and care.

All the networks for women with young children were based on a dense web of local groups. These networks had been established, were maintained, and grew through personal contact, which itself arose largely out of the similar and pressing needs of women at the child-bearing and early child-rearing stage of their lives. The networks also relied on the making and maintaining of local spaces and times in which to facilitate these contacts. All activists in the organizations had become involved because they needed the facilities provided and had stayed because they had received help from them. Christine Bedford, NCT breast-feeding counsellor, describes her involvement: "I went to one of the first set of classes ... and I hadn't managed to [breast] feed my first child very successfully and that ... concerned me and I met a lady who called herself a breast-feeding counsellor. With her information I managed to feed the one I was then expecting and I decided that quite honestly it was something I could possibly help with. So I contacted the NCT and said 'do you want more counsellors?' and they said 'yes please' and it progressed from there."

The long hours and the constant interruptions to daily life which were part of the jobs of many activists were made possible by the fact that these networks fitted into their daily lives and work processses. Their organizational work provided immediate and necessary support for their work as mothers and housewives. For some, such as childminders and playgroup supervisors, these networks were part of, and supported, their wage work. For many, activists and users alike, the jobs of being a mother and a participant in the group were indistinguishable.

The unity of organizing and being a domestic-community worker with young children often meant that these organizations cut across class lines and across the geographic boundaries in the three neighbourhoods which, for many of the women I interviewed, demarcated class lines. Most of the women who had friendships which cut across these geographic divisions had, as noted above, made them at playgroup or mother and toddler groups and sustained them from a commonality of interest. PreSchool Playgroups Association (PPA) activists said that the majority of participants in courses were working-class women, and that playgroups involved "all kinds of parents," as did the childcare pressure groups and increasingly, the NCT ante-natal and post-natal activities.

These groups were also able to build upon the experience and often the personnel of the interwar feminists and the informal community networks of women in the home. One playgroup supervisor I spoke to often brought her mother – who had run an informal childminding/ playgroup service in her kitchen during the war – into her group to make suggestions or deal with problems. Others regularly consulted with older women in the community.

Parent-run childcare and ante- and post-natal networks, reflecting the work processes from which they arose and this unity of involvement with work and life, were the least susceptible to control by the "expertise" of non-participants. In a very real sense these groups produced their own leadership. "Playgroup moms" became playgroup supervisors and PPA regional delegates; mother and toddler group members started their own groups. The NCT criteria for training and certification as a breast-feeding counsellor or ante-natal teacher – that a woman is a mother and, in the case of breast-feeding counsellors, has breast fed successfully herself – explicitly recognized and attempted to maintain this unity of leader/member, teacher/learner.

Birth Process and Fertility Control Networks

Fertility control and the birth process itself, while defined primarily as women's concerns, had been susceptible to and subjected to a greater degree of external social control than had childcare or pregnancy.

Most women to whom I spoke said birth and fertility control were more male concerns than was childcare. Unlike decisions about what to do with the children once they were there, decisions on the number and timing of children were "family decisions." Almost all women with husbands said they consulted their husbands about beginning birth control or about changing methods (for those who relied on male methods, of course, the partners were active participants), but a much smaller number said that they consulted husbands about child rearing. Without exception, married women who had had abortions said this was a decision made with their husbands. The birthing process itself had also been shared with husbands in some cases, especially by younger women. Birthing and fertility control had also been medicalized to a greater extent than had childcare. Birthing and fertility control could be treated as specific medical procedures with relatively predictable stages and outcomes and appropriate responses. These characteristics thus rendered birthing and contraception amenable to "scientific" prediction and control and to the substitution of commodities or collective services for women's experience or "intuition." In addition both birth and fertility control required medical appliances or drugs, which assumed social production and distribution.

The greater social predictability of fertility control and the birth process was reflected in the different nature of social expertise and popular debates on the "appropriate" size of the population as opposed to its care. Despite the advances in psychological science, most discussions of childhood socialization, of the "kind of people the nation needs" and of the means to achieve this, remained at a moral level, often very general and underlain by unexamined and undisturbed assumptions about gender and class roles. In contrast, fertility could be statistically measured and correlated to other "firm" numerical measures such as resource reserves, density per square mile, and pupil/teacher ratios. Even for debates with a largely "moral" content – to prevent conception or not to prevent conception, to abort or not to abort – the production or non-production of a child was more amenable to hard and fast statements than was the care it would receive. This medical and moral certainty reflected and reinforced the fact that birthing could be seen as a "one-off event" and fertility control as a binary decision.

Given this it was not surprising that the majority of fertility control groups, while still numerically dominated by women, were not organized or run by their users as were the childcare groups. Nor were they as fully integrated into women's lives. The "scientific content" of fertility control rendered the self-help network inadequate, although self-help groups continued as an important supplement, largely in the form of women's health groups and National Abortion Campaign advice centres. The mechanics of birth control and abortion were seen to require a medical "expert." And medical experts, at this time, were, unlike playgroup supervisors and ante-natal teachers, produced outside the system of women's networks. They were therefore largely outside the accountability structures of the women who utilized them.

The two major fertility control groups previously discussed, the Family Planning Association (FPA) and National Abortion Campaign (NAC), were not integral parts of women's lives. While both offered non-medical advice and support by women to women on a local basis, either on a one-time or on a long-term basis, their primary role was as local or national pressure groups. Activists' commitment of time and energy was often as great as those in the childcare/childbirth groups. However these activists experienced a greater discontinuity between their activism and their lives. With the exception of the Brighton FPA's two paid employees, activity for the groups was separated from daily life and wage work.

Wage Work Networks

If childcare and birth were components of domestic-community work, and fertility control was one of its underlying conditions, wage work was, for many women, its opposite. Wage labour has been, of the fields discussed, the one most amenable to social intervention and spatial centralization. The extent to which this happened varied with the nature of the work. The wage jobs most women did occupied either end of the spectrum: from unskilled factory assembly work and automated office processes, which had been most strictly measured and controlled, to the "caring professions" – home helps, childcare workers – where "adequate" performance was difficult to measure. Whatever its content, however, wage work was an activity which had been defined in terms of monetary equivalents, an activity over which people, and women in particular, had a limited amount of control.

Women's organization around employment-based issues had models and experience on which to draw: that of trade unions and professional associations. But unlike the domestic-community based networks, these were models and experience which had evolved, until recently, in the absence of a strong or visible women's presence. Only within the past forty years had there been relatively large numbers of women moving into jobs with recognized skills: professional and, to a lesser extent, manual trades. It was these jobs which had a long tradition of unionization, or which constituted careers around which occupationally-based professional associations were established. Similarly it was within the last two generations that the dual role had become a general phenomenon, and the number of women with dual roles had reached a critical mass which allowed the recognition of these roles in the unions and within professional groups.

In many respects, women were faced with pre-existing traditions, ones which were themselves in transition, but which continued, by and large, to assume and reflect the spatial-temporal separation of "work" and "life" – concerning themselves largely with the former – or which demanded the abstraction of work and life as the content of political activity. Despite the fact that unions were originally inspired by workers' desire for a better home life, as well as better working conditions, many union structures, reflecting the gender-based separation of work from life, had narrowed their concerns to exclude these things. The tension that women experienced in living out dual roles was thus reproduced in union structures. Women were caught between a recognition that domestic-community work *was* work, and a set of structures which denied it status as real work. They were aware that the conditions of domestic-community work structured and constrained their wage-work and union activities, and those of nearly half the labour force. But they found little basis for integrating this into union organizing activity or into the vision which guided such activity. The trade-union movement as a whole was slow to recognize the empirical fact of an androgynous labour force, and even slower to recognize that this meant large sectors of the labour force were also, or primarily, domestic-community workers who required appropriate organizations and visions.

The response to this tension by women had been threefold: non-participation, integration, or "separation." The first had been, as noted above, the most common among the community women to whom I spoke. Among these women, those with dependent children tended to be most organizationally isolated. They were generally the busiest and most likely to be juggling space and time in very complex ways. Their daily lives were the most unpredictable of any group and, in some respects, least under their control. Unlike full-time domestic workers, their space-time constraints and the structural demands of their wage jobs prevented the forms of self-organization which allow an integration of life and work. Unlike wage working women with independent children, these same constraints prevented their identification with or participation in most union or professional structures. The second response – integration – was built on the strategy of interwar employment-based organizations. In Brighton it had largely been the response of older women, primarily those who had relatively "good" wage jobs and relatively independent children. The third response – separation – was largely built upon the experience of younger women within the women's liberation movement; it explicitly recognized the inability of the contemporary trade-union model to meet women's needs. And so these women reacted by setting up structures within, or parallel to, unions or associations that did attempt to meet women's needs. It was this strategy which caused the most bitter debates both within the union movement as a whole and within the women's liberation movement. Many trade unionists, male and female, were both bemused and threatened by separatism and by a philosophy – that of women's liberation – which was unfamiliar and, for many, out of place and/or bourgeois.[2]

Many women who were active in traditional employment-based organizations expressed frustration with their activities. Unlike the networks around childcare, fertility, and childbirth, women in employment-based groups often said they experienced an acute separation between their life and work and their political activity. Some indicated that working in unions or professional organizations had tended to undermine rather than extend their confidence and vision.

However women's attempts to integrate their wage work with the other aspects of their roles were not confined to their presence in, or absence from, traditional union structures. As one moved away from the obvious employment-based organizations, and the obvious frustration experienced by women attempting to integrate or alter these structures, a range of informal networks that had been developed to cope with the apparently fluid demands of the dual role came into view. Some of these have been noted: the arrangements for job sharing or switching and the co-ordination of wage-work hours and childcare hours with other women. Equally important to many women was the development of friendships with women at work, friendships which almost invariably were seen as important sources of information and advice and often as networks for practical help. Lacking an official union tradition, women had thus reproduced, in the wage-work sphere, a form of organization evident in the community.

The comments made by some activists that such networks did not alter wage-work processes directly and may, in fact, have reinforced women's secondary status in the labour force through accommodating the dual role and thus its attendant constraints, are partly true. But only partly. These networks, which were developed quickly and largely invisibly to cope with new sets of problems, can be seen as "emergent" organizations, containing within them examples of new and potential social patterns. It was here that the tensions of pushing and making do, which have appeared in various guises throughout the feminist tradition, were most evident. These informal networks were largely seen as, and functioned as, survival mechanisms. They were characterized by informality and lack of strategic insight. They were also characterized by flexibility and therefore, potentially, by resiliency. Above all, they were characterized by variety. No two arrangements were the same, no two arrangements *could* be the same. Yet here too, tendencies were discernible in the growing discussions of "job sharing" and in the potential reevaluation of wage-work already evident in the childcare field.[3]

Organizing at the Intersection

It is thus evident that women's organization had been most successful in those areas of life "ceded" to them, those areas over which they, as a gender, had maintained the most social control and over which, in capitalist society, the maximum amount of individual control is possible. Women had been most effective in utilizing and in extending the degrees of freedom already available to them. They had been less effective in organizing to consolidate their position and modify situations in those areas which were new, those public spaces they had "invaded" and created within the last two generations – the unionizable and professional sectors of the labour force – and the spaces and adjustments which constituted the dual role.

The fact that women had organized most effectively in areas which were least susceptible to social prediction and control and in which men had the least responsibility is not an indication of any inherent feminine qualities, but an indication that people – female as well as male people – organize best in the environments where they work, the environments which contain and reflect their primary daily activities. Participation and integration appears to be most fully developed through environments where people have some control over space and the resources in it, or have control over the time and the resources to create appropriate spaces, such as the playgroups in community halls or the communal coffee mornings of Working Association of Mothers (WAM) and the NCT in people's living rooms. Organization also appears to be most effective when the networks intersect with people's work spaces and times, when meetings and collective action go on "where I am anyway" and can be fitted in with daily work of childcare, preparing meals, exchanging information.

Neither is the "social location" of women's organizational strength an indication of lack of social effectiveness. Precisely because they have organized most effectively in the places and times where they work and live, and combined work and life in so doing, women have been creative and effective. They have succeeded in altering their households, their communities, and the activities which define "what a woman does." Much of what women have done has been obscured by the fact that it alters the basis of daily life in small incremental ways. Women changed family relations, altered self and social images, created new work patterns and paths in space, lived out new ways of relating to children, to men, to other women. Most of this was not perceived as "political" or even "social" action. While the media and social analysts have proclaimed and sometimes roistered in the transient issues of women's role in the labour force, these "private" changes were largely trivialized or ignored. Yet, the very essence of social change in post-war Brighton lies in these "trivial" and "private" changes.

THE MOVEMENT OF SOCIAL LIFE AND ENVIRONMENT

Any attempt to reduce this complex and imperfectly understood process to a few general statements about "progress" or even "direction" is not only premature, it may obscure the potential importance of still socially invisible or apparently insignificant networks. However the summing up of these changes in the lives of individual women over a forty-year period has indicated some overall changes in the feminist tradition of organization.

All aspects of women's lives and organization appear to have been characterized by a growing social or public content impinging upon and contained within women's decisions and activities. As a consequence of this, the scale and the breadth of concern of women's networks has expanded, and the "issues" articulated in these networks have become more visible and more public. These are changes which are both an outcome of and a response to fundamental alterations in the environments in which women work and organize. During the four decades after the war, women lived and worked in an increasingly complex, specialized, and spatially dispersed city, one in which the physical structure of the homes and neighbourhoods and their internal processes were becoming, increasingly, social matters influenced by statutory agencies and commercial commodities. Within this environment, women's daily lives came to encompass new and more varied roles. These included, for many, growing numbers of contacts: as clients with statutory or commercial organizations in the capacities of parent, patient, welfare recipient; and as consumers of utilities, housing, transportation, margarine, automobiles, and social services. Women's roles often included contact with or participation in a range of local voluntary organizations or "training" as parents by these or statutory groups. For an increasing proportion of women, these new roles also included a wage job, or jobs, with a concomitant set of related contacts.

The implications of this for women have been ambivalent. In opening up new access through their wage-work and general social participation, women also imposed new constraints on themselves. They simultaneously provided themselves with access to new resources and extended their ability to create resources while eliminating some former resources.

Women's expectations about domestic working conditions, about the space, commodities, and services necessary to carry out domestic duties, had enlarged. At the same time, the means through which these necessary resources could be attained and the forms in which they could be provided had become more limited and, in some ways, rigid. The one room household had been, for most people, replaced by a living and working environment with separate places for cooking, sleeping, washing, entertaining, and sleeping. This environment was stocked with a growing range of equipment, machinery, and processed goods. Women had come to rely on commercial firms to provide these goods, and their work was, to some extent, influenced by their geographic and financial access to the means of reproduction – the goods and services used to do domestic-community work – provided by commercial firms.

At the same time, the means of reproduction had become standardized through mass production, advertising, and the exigencies of profit. For many, obtaining these goods and services had become dependent upon holding down a wage job, with all the opportunities and restrictions implied in the dual role. Many older women remarked that the greater ease of contemporary housekeeping attendant upon purchased labour-saving devices had itself been purchased at the cost of decreasing flexibility in domestic-community work. They said that young women were losing the skills of "making do," of substituting, and of household manufacture; "They can't cook real food or sew." One Hanover woman of sixty-four described her daughters as " slaves to Seeboard, Sainsburys, and the ads on television," adding, "What will they do when another depression comes along?"

Similarly, as decisions about fertility, childbirth, and health and family life came more and under social control and specifically under women's control, and as marriage and family life became less inevitable, women took on an increasing "social burden," a burden of making decisions about these matters in terms of a range of external social factors. More and more, the maintenance of the greater control women had over their biological and interpersonal family life called for the collective use of social facilities through which this control was made available. For some women the maintenance of this control became a political priority, necessitating an active defence and simultaneous critique of, for example, fertility and childbirth facilities. For some it also meant creating a growing range of alternative networks to educate themselves and other women in the use, defence, and critique of these facilities. Women were simultaneously defending themselves against medical dangers and inadequacies and providing alternatives which met their widening knowledge and needs. Access to some control called for developing new networks to assure more control and new forms of control.

While most of the women I spoke to were not involved in political action around these issues, almost all community interviewees had opinions on and situated themselves with reference to various aspects of the activists' explicit critiques. For example, most women (forty-seven of fifty-five) identified the need for fertility control. A number saw it as "part of modern life" and expressed annoyance at attempts to curb or restrict access. Most frequently women expressed surprise or frustration at higher user charges for family planning or, in some cases (twenty-three of fifty-five) at repeated attempts to restict access to abortion.

Similarly, in the area of childcare, women's needs were leading towards patterns of more collective organization. The root of this was an ambivalent process. Time and space had, for many women, become more extensive. Women relocated to Hollingbury tended to travel longer distances than before relocation and had to plan activities more carefully than when they lived more centrally. Women who travelled to previously unvisited and distant parts of town to take on wage jobs were more constrained by the need to conform to the hours of these wage jobs, as well as to the hours of public transit. They were also constrained by the hours of collective services, including playgroups and network meetings which, in many cases, had replaced the extended family and neighbourhood groups. As a result of this simultaneous expansion and constraining of space, their needs for childcare became more pressing and more inelastic. A pattern similar to that developing in the fertility control and health networks – a pattern of reliance on social facilities, of critical pressure for their extension and alteration, of creating alternatives – was emerging in the childcare field. This was also evident in employment-based organizations, which, unlike the others, had not traditionally been concerned with women's reproductive roles. While, as noted above, traditional structures were often inimical to the participation and problems of women, here too, both through conventional channels and through alternative committees, women pressed for extension of concerns and for internal procedures to accommodate their diverse needs.

A large number of women to whom I spoke faced, and in many cases explicitly stated themselves to be facing, an increasingly complex working and living environment, one with more, and more varied, social content and with a more explicitly political content. Many older women with grown families said that they were glad they were not bringing up young children at the present time, when there were so many factors "you couldn't control." Younger women also often expressed fears of "uncontrollable happenings," from nuclear war, to losing their jobs, to their children's future unemployment. At the same time many said that women were, on the whole, better informed and educated and, as a result, better able to cope than had been their mother's generation.

The socialization of life in the post-war period was a cumulative process. A growing number of the problems women faced were presented in increasingly "public" forms. Women's organization as a whole, as it dealt more and more with public intervention into formerly "private areas," turned increasingly from the development of alternative arrangements for "making do" in a separate sphere to more visible forms of organization that demanded the extension and change of public facilities, spaces, and services.[4]

Yet while the problems women faced and the tactical responses they made were increasingly manifest in social forms, they were simultaneously defined by and within the private sphere. The public defence of socially provided fertility control facilities was a defence of women's right to control their bodies and contain biological decisions within the household. Women's organization around wage-work issues – especially their suggestions that wage-work processes accommodate human life cycles and nurturing rhythms – reflected their ongoing commitment to the household sphere. In the early 1980s women in Brighton, in their daily routines and in their organization, were responding to and furthering the extension of socialization. Simultaneously they were recreating and politically defending the private. This contemporary feminist tradition was therefore still imbued with the tensions of its predecessors: the tensions between pressuring for change and making do and the tension between defence and integration of the private sphere. This, like all tensions which have permeated women's organization, was not only a limit, it was a source of creativity and a source of change in the feminist tradition.

The development of an identifiable and coherent women's movement from this feminist tradition was both a conscious political creation by women and an expression of change in society as a whole, and therefore in women's basis of organization. The possibility of creating and sustaining a self-conscious political movement of women by women and of defining and naming coherent "women's issues," developed as all apects of women's lives and correspondingly all aspects of women's organization took on increasingly socialized forms.

THE MOVEMENT OF THE FEMINIST TRADITION

The emergence of a popularly recognized and self-conscious women's movment in the late 1960s was not, as has often been presented, a sudden and unaccountable break with a tradition of passive, content, and unorganized women. The "new feminism" of the 1960s and subsequent decades was part of a radical, rooted continuity, a synthesis and articulation of all the conflicts, pressures, and organizations previously discussed.

As this book has indicated, women have always organized to extend the resources available for their work and lives. They have done so from a variety of social environments, environments which, in many ways, they and the previous generation of women created. Thus the home-centred feminism of the interwar period was a response to the pressures, issues, and concerns of women whose work place was the home and community and whose work was finding ways of stretching the male wage to provide adequate resources for family life. These interwar groups both increased the resources available to women in the home and potentially opened up new arenas of access for women. At the same time, they laid the basis for a new set of conflicts which post-war women would confront. The limited vision of interwar feminists and their limited "naming" of women's issues reinforced some existing gender constraints and inadvertently laid the basis for new ones. Just as these were incorporated into the welfare state, and thereby created new problems for women, so they were incorporated, in a slightly altered form, into the "new feminism" of the 1940s and 1950s: the consensus of a home-centred femininity, relieved of drudgery and rendered equal by state services and mechanical aids. This archetypal post-war woman was in turn disintegrated through the extension and institutionalization of women's dual role. As the conflicts women experienced in carrying out these roles coalesced in the 1960s movement, the disintegration of the archetypal women and her reconstitution in a new form became an increasingly deliberate and "public" process.

The feminist tradition has thus been a changeful one. In responding to changing social environments and changing activities of women, it simultaneously and actively altered the parameters of these environments and activities.

This movement of the scope and concerns of the feminist tradition was reflected in the forms of women's collective organization in Brighton. In the early 1980s the feminist tradition in Brighton contained three general groups of organizations.[5] First were the more "traditional" women's organizations, largely extensions of those developed in the interwar period, including the Townswomen's Guilds, the Electrical Association for Women, the Women's Co-op Guild, and the women's sections of the Labour Party. Both their older membership and what, from the perspective of the 1980s, appeared to be a conservative outlook on women's position, reflected their members' concerns with "home-based" women, adjusting and making do. These groups assumed a strong community of women at home.

Second were the networks which had developed around specific, life-cycle based needs of women, especially the needs of those about to have or who had young children. Like those in the first group, these organizations were largely concerned with women's reproductive work. Unlike the earlier organizations, these had developed new spaces and were explicitly attempting to forge new links between home and the wage workplace. They were also attempting to alter the balance of men's and women's work through recognizing and extending the communal nature of childbirth and parenting and through encouraging the involvement of male as well as female parents in these processes. Also unlike the earlier group, these organizations saw themselves as substitutes for extended family and long-time community ties. Included here were the National Childbirth Trust, the Birth Centre, the Family Planning Association, for some of its work, and all of the childcare networks, especially those co-ordinated by parents (playgroups, mother and toddler groups, WAM, childminders' groups). It also included the women's health networks.

Third were those organizations which saw themselves as part of the women's-liberation movement and which were based on a complex and comprehensive social analysis of women's position. As well as providing "safe" spaces for women, they acted to alter traditional organizations along the non-hierarchical lines of the women's movement through emphasizing the importance of personal politics at all levels. These organizations were explicitly concerned to discuss and actively change the nature of family and community: to create alternative family forms, new "communities of women," or feminist influenced social change. Included among them were the National Abortion Campaign, the Brighton Women's Centre, Women's Aid, some members of the Trades Council Women's Committee, and the Brighton Unemployed Women's Group, as well as the Brighton and Hove Women's Liberation Group and its affiliates.

Despite their different analytic and active priorities, these three sets of organizations were united by a radical continuity. All had articulated women's position. All had been concerned to extend the resources women had available to do their work in whatever social environment this work went on. In acting on this concern, all had created new links between the dimensions of women's activities. Each successive wave had built upon the experience of the previous wave and utilized the social spaces and time patterns the previous groups had created.

The first group sought to "educate" women as homemakers and consumers as a means of extending their access to resources, as well as to provide meeting spaces for communal sharing of knowledge. A by-product of these formal meetings was experience in running activities such as crèches and informal playgroups; this experience fed into the more extensive structures of the second group. As one long-time member of the Co-op Guild said, "We did those things [crèches] so we could get on with our committee work. They [parent-run childcare networks] have committee meetings about operating their crèches." In contrast, a young women active in WAM and a "play group mum" said of her mother's involvement in the Women's Institute: "I learned a lot from her, but they were so formal. In their meetings they tried to 'better themselves' and 'reform things' and they never did anything to change their lives. They just met and went home again, to do the same things. She [my mother] never talked to my father about the Institute like I talk to [my husband] about WAM."

The second group of organizations thus extended the social discussion of, and in some cases professionalized, the content of the formerly "natural" functions of childbirth and childcare. If, as the preceding section indicated, women have had most success in organizing in areas least susceptible to social and "expert" control, there may be some grounds for suggesting that, through this extension, women are undermining their own base of strength. There is, however, equal evidence to suggest that women's organization in these areas continued to express the conflicts and strengths of "pressing and making do," and may in fact be extending a "distinctive women's style of handling social problems that will gradually pervade male as well as female society."[6]

Older women were often critical of the "professionalization" of parenting implied by PPA and NCT courses. Some said "women should know these things without going to classes." Others expressed an element of resistance to the threatened erosion of women's control over these activities which they saw as a possible outcome of the "public" discussion of, and writing about, childbirth and childcare. Still others criticized organizations such as the PPA and NCT because their priorities were seen to indicate a lack of concern with broader social issues, "all they can talk about is women's issues." Women in the second group, however, pointed to the necessity for "changing organizations for changing times," arguing that classes and public discussion were means of extending their control over childbirth and childcare, and that "women's issues" *were* broader social issues. This latter argument was most forcefully expressed by the third group, those who identified themselves as activists in, or as actively sympathetic to, the women's-liberation movement.

The "quiet" home-centred feminism of the interwar period expressed the problems women experienced in living and working in a separate, private sphere, with only indirect relations to the productive sphere. The unquiet feminism of the modern period expressed the problems encountered by women working at the intersection of the relations of production and reproduction, women who, as a group, constantly crossed the boundaries of work and life. As the problems of women have changed, so the political priorities of feminists have also altered.

The primary objective of the first set of organizations – extending the resources available to women in a "separate sphere" – has shifted. The second set of organizations was attempting to solve problems located at the boundaries of production and reproduction. They are concerned with the immediate and simultaneously "social" problems of childbirth and childcare in a society where reproductive activities are more socialized, although perhaps less communal, but are only one aspect of women's life time activities. Like the first group, the second were organizing around women's given living and working conditions, around women's "traditional" concerns. Yet its organizations were doing so while consciously professionalizing these concerns and consciously creating concrete and at least semi-permanent times and spaces (playgroups, ante-natal classes) which combined domestic and wage work.

While the second group was not, by and large, attempting to redefine gender or gender activities, it was, in creating networks at the interface of production and reproduction, altering these spheres. The third set of organizations was consciously extending this process, acting to redefine production and reproduction, work and life, and to articulate the ongoing redefinition of "woman."

These changes of focus indicate the ways in which the constitution of the gender category "woman," and consequently the feminist organizational base, have moved. Each set of organizations was retrieving some of the insights and activities of past feminists and assimilating and adapting them into a present set of networks based upon new social conditions and new patterns of adjustment in women's space and time. This process was being articulated and extended by the women's-liberation movement. In the move from the "separate sphere" to the interface of work and life, each set of new networks at once expressed and helped create a new and, it is suggested, more central role for women and for the feminist tradition, in the process of social change.

Contemporary Feminism

In the most general terms, the objective of contemporary feminists is to actively cease reproducing oppressive gender relations and to actively reproduce equal and sustainable ones. To this end, feminism aims to extend control over the processes whereby sex is translated into gender. Underlying much feminist action and analysis is the understanding that gender is historically mutable, that it changes day by day, and that we can either consciously attempt to understand and control this process of change or blindly acquiesce to it. The existence of a self-conscious women's movement is an indication that the former "choice" has been made by some and, as such, the contemporary women's movement can be seen as an exemplar of possible social changes.

Changing gender activity and definitions has always been arduous and demanding, and often controversial. Its outcomes, for the actors and their daughters, have been unpredictable and generally two-edged. In capitalist industrial society, women have usually organized from an environment and around issues which have been defined as "private" and "natural." These environments and issues have been denied the status of "political" or the regularity of science or economy. Qualities of dependence, of non-work, of passive consumption, and of non-logical emotion were seen to form the parameters of women's place. As women moved from this place into "public" places, they were seen as exceptional, as a special-interest group with limited concerns, concerns often deemed peripheral or inappropriate to "real" politics.

The feminist tradition has therefore always actively denied one of the most consistent and foundational dichotomies of capitalist society, the separation out of "life" from the real and measurable business of "work." Women's activities constantly deny that life is separate from work, that life is private, secondary, dependent, or reactive.

The constant balancing and alterations of space and time evident in women's lives is not necessarily conscious in all its aspects. But my discussions with women indicated that most had very clear ideas of the constraints on their space and time and of how, within these constraints, they could best allocate time and energy. Most were certainly aware that they bridged numerous gaps, that they negotiated and synchronized, in one day and over one lifetime, a variety of apparently conflicting roles. Women in Brighton consciously crossed the boundaries of all the dimensions between production and reproduction. They saw the family and community as their workplaces, as places where work and life converged. In discussing problems of getting to the shops; in finding a cheap, nutritious cut of meat which could be prepared in the time available to them; in buying, making, and mending children's clothes so that they would wear well; women actively denied the separation of production from consumption. They were well aware that consumption required productive activity and "a lot of hard work." In discussing marital relations, children's welfare, and their plans and fears for the future, women denied the separation of emotion from logic. They knew that the emotions of love and anger required the constant application of farsighted logic to the business of survival. They knew that, among their networks of female friends, sometimes men were also the "other" – sexually, rationally, productively.

The contrast between what women were doing, and knew themselves to be doing, and the "common sense" which separated out and diminished their activities had given rise to the conscious examination of the relation between work and life by the contemporary women's movement. In attempting to reintegrate the relations of the reproductive sphere into the reconceptualized social whole, and to reintegrate understanding of women's lives as a whole, the contemporary women's movement had analyzed the separate reproductive sphere as a workplace and had seen "life" and "family" as specific parts of the economy, subject to specific influences by market relations.

This process was not one of meshing the two spheres but of understanding and expressing the way they interrelated. As the discussion of childcare indicated, it was a process of creating new spaces which existed

at the intersection of work and life and which concretely articulated the
interrelations. The aim of feminist analysis and action was, more and
more, to understand the processes and to make visible the spaces
through which women changed the relations of these spheres. Feminists
were trying to develop a perspective which, in theoretically generalizing
these processes of change, provided a basis for deliberate action. They
were thus establishing a basis to control change and achieve a greater
sphere of activity for women.

Women's activities, including those of contemporary feminists, had
shifted the boundaries of these spheres in two related ways. On the one
hand, the "political" – those areas of life which were understood as
amenable to principled, strategically situated action – had extended
"inward" from the vague and apparently inaccessible politics of the state,
"the labour-capital relation," the "economy" in general, to the community, the home, the family, and other aspects of interpersonal relations,
and ultimately to the sexual, the most "private" relation of all. These
latter relations were examined with reference to their location and constitution by social relations as a whole and were criticized and changed
in a conscious, collective way. This was most evident in, for example,
the extension of union concerns through conventional and alternative
channels to include fertility control and childcare. It was also evident in
the attempts of national, regional, and local women's groups to be politically sensitive to women's material and emotional needs, such as the
need for crèche facilities or making allowances for women inexperienced
in public meetings and those under stress.

On the other hand, those aspects of life which were personal and
private, and which both social ideology and personal experience suggest
are under some individual control, had extended outward. This was an
articulation of the actions of women discussed above. As biological reproduction, domestic processes, and family relations become more socialized, women's organization, in response, extended the area over
which people felt they had control and choice: from the act of sexuality
to family and household organization and relations, to the neighbourhood, the city, and ultimately to national and international organizations.
This was most evident in the growth of groups such as the FPA and NAC,
Women's Aid and Rape Crisis networks, all of which were (and are)
concerned with the material and political extension of women's control
over their own bodies and which are national networks with international
affiliations. It was also evident in the size and scope of groups concerned
with the "private" issues of childbirth and childcare. Both the PPA and
the National Childbirth Trust have national co-ordinating centres, as
do the British Association for Early Childhood Education and the National Campaign for Nursery Education. Others, such as the Family

Welfare Organization, Dr Barnardo's, Save the Children, the Church of England Children's Society and the Mothers Union, organize specific services for children and for women and also federate on a national and/or international basis.[7]

The conscious shifting of the boundaries of the "political" is a process of attempting to build "new combinations of personal and public forms."[8] It is thus a discursive expression of the inherent tensions in the feminist organizational tradition. This tension now takes the form of prefigurative politics, "of beginning as we mean to go on," "a continuous process of learning what kind of world we want to create as we work for change."[9] Prefigurative politics not only involves presaging and creating the content of a future society, but also presaging and creating the relations through which this content will be appropriated. The emphasis on direct and immediate action has led to the development of a specific organizational form among contemporary feminists – the relatively unstructured, non-hierarchical "small group" for whom ends and means are indistinguishable. This form has grown out of and extends the organizational form of earlier women's organizations.[10] All of the networks discussed in this book have contributed toward producing, and were increasingly articulating "the *nature* of the social order toward which ... transitions are directed."[11]

The frequent charge levelled that most women do not identify with the women's movement is not valid in this context. Only a small minority of the women to whom I spoke identified themselves as activists in the women's movement. Of the community interviewees, five of fifty-five said they were feminists, and one said she "would be if I was younger," while five of the twenty-seven activists interviewed so identified themselves. Yet almost all the women to whom I spoke defined their position with reference to specific actions of the women's movement and with reference to the movement as a whole.[12]

The almost universal expression of opinion (positive and negative) on women's liberation can in part be attributed to the wide publicity given the work of women's movement activists. But it is also in part attributable to the nature of the movement itself. While only a minority of women are consciously involved in the process of the active reconstitution of gender, all women are affected by and contribute to effecting the processes whereby gender is constituted and changed. Most women I met in Brighton had taken advantage of improved fertility control, childbirth, and health facilities and would be unlikely to accept, as their biological duty, the bearing and burying of an uncontrolled number of children. For most women who had become mothers in the post-war period, pregnancy and childbirth was a planned or at least comprehensible event, not a female fate. Most women did not expect that their lives would be bounded by household manufacture or service which would take up most of their waking hours and all the years of their adulthood. Their childrearing practices were imbued with concerns for their children's psychological well-being and future economic security. Many women spoke of their daughter's future jobs and the training necessary to these as a given part of planning in the family. A majority saw their own wage-work as a standard means of contributing to family resources. Women's wages were a complement to the activities of substituting, mending, and "stretching" which constitute "making do" in the household. And it was precisely the understanding and altering of these processes – the constituents of gender – which concerned the women's movement.

Women in post-war Brighton had created new space and time and altered the nature of that which they had. It is easy to be over-optimistic about the effectiveness of women's organization, especially from the sometimes heady perspective of a feminist rediscovery of women's history and effectivity. It is perhaps even easier, especially given the difficulty of balancing feminism under attack, to assume women are in a "steady state," or even pedalling backwards. What this latter view forgets is the simple profound lesson of social history: the gas heat, the regulated pregnancy, the washing machine and the private bedroom; the possibility, however limited, of satisfying work, of companionate sexual relations, and of "keeping the kids on your own." It forgets the extent to which women themselves have created these situations and these resources.

Women did this as part of constructing a particular kind of woman living in a particular kind of city, through social and individual patterns of actions made up of being a mother, a sexual being, a domestic-community worker, a citizen, and a wage earner. These patterns were constructed carefully, often painfully, sometimes consciously, always actively. All of these activities which all these women carried out have become part of the feminist tradition and thus part of the social environment and of the nature of human beings: the constituents of the movement of social change.

> Looking back now, I wonder sometimes why we ever put up with some of the old ways, things my daughters would never do ... I suppose it just seemed natural to us, we just did what we had to do. But all that has changed. We do so many things differently now. (Sixty-two-year-old woman in Whitehawk.)

Appendix

The author used the following questionnaires during her interviews in Brighton. These interviews tended to be conversations rather than rigid question-and-answer sessions.

SCHEDULE A

Questionnaires destined to the various activist groups were chosen from Schedule A. Interviewees were given the general section and then the section appropriate to the group they represented. The inteviews varied in length, from forty-five minutes to six hours; in many cases they involved repeat visits and attendance at group functions.

HISTORY AND CAMPAIGNS IN BRIGHTON
1 History of the organization
When was the Brighton group formed?
By whom?
Why was it formed?
Why are you involved? For how long?
Who are most of the members?
2 Priorities
What are your major priorities in Brighton?
Do these conform to national priorities?
What is your relationship to the national organization?
Do you feel that Brighton has special problems?
Is it easier or more difficult to organize here?
3 Organization
How do you organize?
How are you funded?
4 Campaigns
What are your current campaign issues?
How about the past?
What are your plans for the future?

BIRTH CONTROL/CHILDBIRTH SERVICES AS A WHOLE
1 Do you feel generally that the demand for birth control/abortion/better maternity/childbirth services is growing in Brighton? Why?

2 What kind of general direction do you think it should take? What kinds of facilities and forms or organization would you like to see?

3 Do you think provision will expand/change in this way? Why/Why not?

4 Have government expenditure cuts put any pressure on your centre/organization recently? If so, how?

Do you think these cuts are making it more difficult for women to get adequate services?

5 In general, are there problems in provision you have encountered/are encountering now/foresee in the future?

6 Many groups are suggesting that there have been major changes in women's patterns of sexual activity in the last thirty to forty years. Do you agree? In what way? Has it had an effect on the demand for services? Some are suggesting that many women are choosing to have children independently or are forced into a single-parent situation. Is this increasing? Is it influential?

7 Are women in general becoming more aware, informed, and critical about provision? Demanding better services? Why do you think this is happening?

What kinds of demands or complaints are people making?

Are men becoming more involved, concerned? Why?

8 Do you think ways of organizing around the demand for provision is changing, i.e., are there more pressure groups? are they organized differently?

9 Do you think feminism/women's liberation has influenced the demands, awareness, ways of organizing?

RELATIONS TO OTHER GROUPS CONCERNED WITH BIRTH CONTROL / CHILD BIRTH

1 What kind of co-operation do you have with the:

Area Health Authority

Community Health Council

Education Department

Local Authority Social Services

Unions/Trade Council?

2 Has there been a changing emphasis on birth control/abortion/childbirth/maternity services by:

Local Area Health Authority

Central government

East Sussex County Council?

3 The 1974 reorganization of the NHS was supposed to provide better connection between hospital and domiciliary care. How did it propose to do this? Was it successful? What was the effect on service provision?

4 Has there generally been more of a move from hospital/central provision to community/domiciliary provision? From the NHS to private provision?

5 Co-operation with voluntary bodies?

Family Planning Association

Pregnancy Advisory Service
British Pregnancy Advisory Service (Wistons)
Brook Advisory Centres
National Abortion Campaign
National Childbirth Trust
National Association for Maternal and Child Welfare
Association of Radical Midwives
Society to Support Home Confinements
Association for Improvement in Maternity Services
Maternity Alliance

6 Have you ever been involved in the "Save the Family Clinic" campaign? Do you know anything about it?

7 Have you ever been involved in anti-cuts campaigns generally?

ABORTION

A Facilities

1 What facilities are provided in Brighton?
2 How many people use each? Is this changing? Why?
3 What are the relative advantages and disadvantages of each?
4 What other services do each provide?
5 What percentage of terminations are on NHS in Brighton? Is this increasing or decreasing? Why?

B. Organization

1 What is the current legal status of abortion?
2 Do you foresee future changes?
3 Is the NHS service adequate?
4 In Brighton, what is the incidence of coincident sterilization or pressure for it?
   Is there any use of menstrual regulation?
   How about day-care abortions?
5 NAC sees a woman's right to choose as fundamental to women's equality. What do you understand by a woman's right to choose?
   Do you agree that abortion is a feminist issue?
   Do you agree with abortion on demand?

BIRTH CONTROL

1 What facilities are provided?
2 How many people use each type of provision?
3 What are the relative advantages and disadvantages of each?
4 What other services do each of the following provide?
   FPA Clinics
   BPAS

GP's surgeries

Hospital clinics

5 What is the legal status of birth control provision under the NHS? What is provided free? How many people use the free provisions? Is this expanding? Why? Why not?

6 Recently there have been controversies about the provision of birth-control advice and materials to people under sixteen. Do you agree that this should be freely available to under sixteens?

Why do you think this has become an issue recently?

CHILDCARE/EDUCATION AS A WHOLE

1 Do you feel generally that the need for childcare/education is growing in Brighton? If so, why?

2 What kind of general direction do you think it should take?

3 Do you feel childcare/education will expand? Why or why not?

4 What pressures have been put on your department/organization recently?

Government expenditure cuts: are they having an effect? What kind of effect?

Are you getting pressure from the council?

Do you have associations with pressure groups? How?

Are parents complaining? What do they want?

Are you being pressured by the unions, trade councils?

What are your plans for the future?

5 In general, what kinds of problems are you encountering in provision?

6 In general, what kinds of complaints, response by other groups are you aware of?

7 In general, do you think that ways of organizing around daycare/education are changing? Why?

8 Have you had anything to do with "Save Brighton's Nursery Schools" campaign?

9 In general what would you say are the major priorities and problems of childcare/education for under fives?

10 Do you think these have changed over the years? Why?

11 The National Childcare Campaign, at its founding convention, said that childcare is a major political issue. Do you agree? Why/why not?

12 The campaign also said that comprehensive childcare is fundamental to women's equality. Do you agree? How?

RELATIONS TO OTHER GROUPS CONCERNED WITH CHILDCARE/EDUCATION

1 The Under Fives Liaison Committee

2 Is there a similar committee for older children's care needs?

3 What kind of co-operation do you have with statutory bodies?

Local Education Authority

Area Health Authority

Local Authority Social Services
Family Consultative Centre
Brighton Council
Central government departments
Is there a changing emphasis, direction on childcare/education by the:
Council
Central government
Local authority
4 How about co-operation with voluntary bodies?
PPA
Church of England Children's Society
British Association for Early Childhood Education
National Society for the Prevention of Cruelty to Children
National Childcare Campaign
National Campaign for Nursery Education
Gingerbread
Parents Without Partners
Working Association of Mothers
National Childbirth Trust
National Consumers Council
Volunteer Bureau
Citizens Advice Bureaus
Dr Barnardo's
Save the Children
Fair Play for Children
National Association for Maternal and Child Welfare
British Association of Settlements and Social Action Centres
5 One of the major issues in the discussions about childcare education just now seems to be the relation between parent participation/voluntary work and professionals. How do you feel about this? Do you think parent-run schemes are becoming more popular? Why? Why not?
6 Some groups are suggesting that fragmentation among groups concerned with childcare/education is a problem. There are suggestions that a statutory body be formed to co-ordinate all aspects of childcare for under fives. Do you agree? Who would you include? In what capacity?

NURSERY SCHOOLS
1 How many places are provided?
Has this service expanded over the years?
Is there a growing demand for nursery schools? Why?
2 What are the main objectives of nursery schools?
When were they first set up? Under what legislation?
Do they adequately fulfill this function?
3 What are the fees/costs?

4 What are the hours? Has this changed?

5 Who uses them on the whole? Has this changed? Why?

> How do people enrol their children for nursery school?
>
> How do people find out about them?
>
> Is there a waiting list? Is it increasing or decreasing?

6 Who runs them?

> What kind of training do they have?
>
> Has the type of training changed over the years?
>
> Is it going to change in the future, do you think?
>
> Are pay and conditions for nursery-school teachers an issue?
>
> Are these teachers unionized?
>
> What are your plans for the future?

(Similar questionnaires were used for nursery classes, day nurseries, private nurseries, childminders, playgroups, mother and toddler groups, after school schemes and holiday play schemes.)

CONSUMERS ORGANIZATION AS A WHOLE

1 Do you think that consumers generally are more informed than they were in the past, say, forty years ago? In the last ten years or so?

2 Is there generally more organization around consumption issues than there was, say, forty years ago? Or ten years ago?

> Why/why not?
>
> Have the issues changed ? Why/why not?

3 Many groups in the community are suggesting that retail provision is becoming more centralized. Do you think this is true?

> Do you think bigger retail chains, the disappearance of independent traders, operated to the advantage or disadvantage of the consumer? Why?
>
> How about the shift from state services to private i.e. Health, Education?
>
> Do you think this is happening? Why?
>
> What are the implications?

4 Many groups also suggest that purchased goods and state services are becoming increasingly important in the way people live their lives. Do you agree?

5 Has there been a tendency toward greater consumer protection legislation? If so, why?

6 Do women tend to have specific concerns in consumer organizations and in consumer issues? What concerns? Why?

> Has this changed over the last forty years? Ten years? Have women become more involved in consumer organization? Have the issues changed?
>
> Are men becoming more involved in household consumption issues?
>
> Do you think feminism has had an influence on women as consumers?

7 Are people generally more critical of advertising claims and standards? Have women become more active in objecting to 'sexist' advertising?

8 Have government expenditure cuts put more pressure on consumers? On women as consumers specifically? How?
Have they shifted the emphasis in consumer issues?
9 In general what direction do you see the consumer movement taking in the future?

RELATIONS WITH OTHER GROUPS CONCERNED WITH CONSUMPTION
1 What kinds of co-operation do you have with
    Statutory bodies: Local Authority Social Services, schools
    Trading Standards Department
    Local Council
    Union Trade Council?
2 Is there a changing emphasis on consumer issues and education by statutory bodies at the local level? National level?
3 Co-operation with other bodies?
    Electrical Association for Women
    Electricity Consumers Council
    Women's Gas Federation and Young Homemakers Club
    Gas Consumers Council
    Domestic Coal Consumers Council
    Post Office Users Action Committee
    Union Trade Council
    Citizen's Advice Bureau
    Community Health Council
    National Consumers Council
    Mutual Aid Centres
    Cooperative Union
    Women's Co-operative Guild
    Credit Unions
    Good Housekeeping Institute and Magazine
    Other women's magazines
    British Standards Institute
    Advertising Association
    Advertising Standards Association
    Health Education Council
    National Association for Patient Participation in General Practice
    Patients Association
4 What other groups have organized around or been concerned with consumer issues in Brighton?

SCHOOLS
1 How many students are there in the school?
    What is the catchment area?

Do all local children attend this school? If not why not?

Do they mostly go on to local secondary shool?

Do you have a high turnover of pupils or are most children here throughout their school career?

2 Do you run any after-school-hours schemes for students at the school?

Do you know of any such schemes in this area?

Who organizes them?

3 Holiday schemes

Do you run any schemes for students in school holidays?

Do you know of any such schemes in the area?

Do you think the demand/need for after-school-hours and school-holiday
schemes is expanding? Why?

4 How do you feel about the suggestion of some groups that school facilities
should be used by other groups outside school hours, i.e., youth clubs, playgroups?

5 Do you have a Parent/Teacher Group or Friends of the School group here?
If so what do they do?

Other than this, what channels exist for contact with parents? Do you
think generally that parents are becoming more involved in the schools,
more concerned about children's education?

6 Do you have any associations with community associations in this area?

7 Do you have any associations with voluntary groups in general?

8 Do you have any associations with statutory bodies other than the Department
of Education?

9 Have government expenditure cuts affected the school in any way?

Do you think, or see any evidence that they are affecting conditions in
general?

10 Are there a lot of wage-working mothers in the area?

Has this increased or decreased in the last ten years?

How about single parents?

11 Can you tell me a bit about general problems in the area?

ADDITIONAL QUESTIONS FOR HIGH SCHOOLS

1 Do you have a career-guidance service in the school?

What do most of the students want to do in life generally?

Does this differ significantly between boys and girls?

Is it getting more difficult to place students in apprenticeships or jobs?

2 Have you had any association with the Youth Opportunities Program?

How many students have you placed with them?

In what kinds of jobs?

Do you think it is a good program?

3 What percentage of the students, generally, do "O" levels? "A" levels? CSE?
Leave with no qualification?

COMMUNITY CENTRES

1 What goes on in this centre?
2 Who uses the centre?
3 How are you funded?
   How do you publicize events?
4 When and how was the centre founded? By whom? Original funding?
5 Have the government expenditure cuts affected your work here at all? How?
   Have they affected the work of groups using the centre?
6 Is this area, in general, changing? What kinds of new problems are emerging?
7 Do you think that women as a whole are becoming more active in community
   work and activities? In what capacities?
8 Have ways of organizing in the community changed in the last ten years? Last
   few years?

PLAYGROUP QUESTIONNAIRE

Name of Playgroup:
Address of Playgroup:

1 When was your group started?
2 Was it started by parents in the area? If not, by whom?
3 Did you have any outside advice or help in setting up the group? If yes, from
   whom?
4 Do you have a playgroup leader? If yes, how many hours a week does she
   work? Is she paid? How much? Has she attended any courses on playgroups
   or on care of under fives? If yes, which courses?
5 Do you have a parents' rota for helping in the group?
6 Do parents stay with their children at the group?
7 Do parents help with fund raising? If yes, how?
8 Do you get any grants for toys, rent, milk, or other costs? If yes, from whom?
9 What are your other sources of funds (other than parents' fund raising and
   grants)?
10 Is there a mother and toddler group associated with your playgroup?
11 Do any childminders use your playgroup?
12 What have been your major successes in the playgroup?
13 What are your major problems?
14 Why do you think playgroups have become so popular in the last ten years?

SCHEDULE B

The following questionnaire was used to interview women in the community.
These interviews tended to be animated conversations that varied in length from
thirty minutes to over four hours. I was often invited back for another conversation (and sometimes a meal).

A   TO ALL

1 Do you housekeep for anyone besides yourself here?
    self
    adults
    children
  If children: How many ＿＿＿＿ girls ＿＿＿＿ boys?
               What are their ages?

2 Are there any elderly people or invalids that you look after to any extent, living here or elsewhere?
  If yes: Do you have help in caring for them?
         Do you use any public services?
         Are these adequate?
  If no: What changes would you like to see?

3 Do you at present have a paid job? No/Yes
  If yes: How many hours do you work every week?
                        Part   Full
        What exactly is your job?

(If yes to paid job: Part B.   If no: Part D.)

B   PAID WORK

1 Journey to work:
      Where is your paid job?
      How do you usually get to work?
      How long does it take you to get to work?
      Do you find the travelling a problem?
      Why did you choose that job?
      Would you take a job further away from home?

2 Working conditions:
      How long have you worked there?
      Is your job secure or is there a danger of redundancy?
      Do you like your job? What do you like or dislike about it?
      What would you say are the main reasons why you go out to work?
      Is there a union at work?
        Which?
        Are you in it?
        Is it a good union?
        Do you have equal pay?
        Are there a lot of other women working where you work?
        Are there a lot of women in the union?
        Does the union ever bring up issues like crèches at work? Equal pay or opportunities for women? Abortion or birth control? Women in the union and on the union executive?

Do you ever discuss these things with the people you work with?
   Childcare (would the women like a crèche at work?)
   Equal pay
   Abortion or birth control
   Maternity services
   Women in the union?
If full-time: Would you prefer to work part-time?
                Why? Why not?
                If yes: Why haven't you got a part-time job?
If part-time: What are your main reasons for working part-time?
                Would you rather work full-time if you could?
If you were unemployed would you sign on?
If yes: Would you get the full unemployment benefit?
If no: Would you qualify for a supplementary benefit?
         If no: Why not?
Do you think women have a harder time than men holding down paid
jobs? Do you think they get better or worse jobs?

If children: Part C.   If no children: Part E.

C   CHILDCARE
1 Arrangements:
   Who looks after the children while you are at work?
   How far away is that?
   How do you take them and collect them?
   Are you satisfied with these arrangements?
      If not: What changes would you like to see?
2 If not user of a Nursery
   Do you know whether there are any nurseries in this area?
   Would you use a nursery if there were one?
      If yes: What kind would you prefer; state or private? Why?
      If no: Why not?
3 Facilities for School-age Children
   Do you know of any facilities for school-age children in this area? After
   school hours? During school holidays?
   Would you make use of after-school facilities if they were available? Of
   school-holiday facilities?
      If yes: What type would you prefer and where?
      If no: Why not?
4 If your children were ill, would your employer allow you time off work, should
   you need it?
5 What do your children think about your going out to work?

(Go on to E)

D   NO PAID JOB

1 Do you ever feel you would like a paid job? Why? Why not?

> If yes: Part-time or full-time? What would you like to do?
>
> Why would you prefer part/full-time?
>
> What would you look on as your main reasons for wanting a job?

2 What would you say are the main reasons why you haven't a job at present?

(Go on to E)

E   PREVIOUS JOBS

1 Have you had any (other) paid jobs in the last ten years?

> If yes: What did you do?
>
> When was that?
>
> Was it full or part-time?
>
> Where was it?
>
> Why did you leave?
>
> Did you sign on when you left?

F   DOMESTIC WORKING CONDITIONS

1 Home

> How long have you lived in this house/flat?   Why did you move here?
>
> Do you own or rent the house?
>
> If rent: Do you rent from the council or privately?
>
> Do you like the house/flat?
>
> What do you like/dislike about it?

2 Amenities

> Do you have a garden or play area where you can see the children?
>
> How many bedrooms do you have?
>
> Do you have a phone? central heating? central hot water?
>
> Do you have a refrigerator? separate freezer? washing machine? vacuum cleaner? radio? TV? car/use of car?
>
> Do you get any help with the household duties from anyone in the household or from someone outside?

3 Neighbourhood

> How long have you lived in this neighbourhood?
>
> Where did you live before?
>
> What do you like about the neighbourhood?
>
> What do you dislike about it?

4 Shopping

> Where do you usually shop?
>
> Which post office do you use?
>
> Do you have any difficulty getting your shopping done? Getting to the post office? Getting to the bank?

If difficulties: What kind of shopping do you have most difficulties with? Why?

Do you know of any consumer organizations or women's clubs concerned with consumer issues?

If yes: Which? Have you ever been a member?

Do you prefer supermarkets or small shops? Why?

Do you think consumer products are improving?

Do you think there is a growing need for consumer protection?

5 Mobility

Do you go downtown often? Why do you usually go? How do you usually go?

In general, do you have any difficulty getting around to do the things you have to do?

If yes: What do you have the most difficulty with?

6 Organizations

If children: Do your children go to any playgroups or nursery classes?

If yes: Where? Who runs it? Do you help?

Do you or did you belong to any groups or clubs? Mother and toddlers, voluntary organizations, community associations?

Do you know of a community association in this area?

Do you use the community centre?

If no: Why not?

If yes: What for?

Do you know your neighbours?

Are most of your friends in the neighbourhood?

If children: Part G

If no children: Part H

G CHILDBIRTH

1 Maternity

Did you have any of your children in Brighton? Where? Were you satisfied with your treatment there?

Did you attend any ante-natal clinics? Were you satisfied with your treatment? Did you have any problems getting to the clinic?

Did you attend any mothercraft or childbirth classes? Where? Did you find them useful?

Did you attend any post-natal clinics? Where? How old were you when your first child was born?

How old were you when your last child was born?

2 If has or had paid job:

Have you ever had a child while working at a paid job?

If yes: Did you get maternity pay? Was your job kept open for you?

3 Would you like more children? Why or why not?

4 Would you like to have or have you had a home confinement?

    Would you/did you prefer that to hospital delivery? Why/why not?

5 Did you breast-feed any of your children?

6 Have you ever used the Family Planning Clinic or got family planning advice from a doctor?

H   OPINIONS

1 For women with children, what do you think are the attractions of going out to work?

    What do you think are the drawbacks?

    Did your mother go out to work when you were a child?

     If yes: What did she do?

2 Do you think, on the whole, that it is easier for our/your generation to do paid work than for our/your mothers' generation?

    How about housework?

    How about life generally?

    What do you think are the major problems facing people in this country today?

    Any problems of specific concern to women?

3 Do you think, on the whole, that women get a better or worse deal out of marriage than men?

4 A lot of people I've talked to have suggested that parents in general are under more pressure than they were ten years ago.

    Do you agree?   Why or why not?

5 Do you think there are ways in which women are treated unfairly in this country at the moment?

6 Do you think public spending cuts are making it harder for women to get jobs?

    Do you think they are making it harder for women in other ways?

7 What do you think of the women's liberation movement?

I   INFORMATION

1 Are you single/married/divorced/widowed/separated

    If M/W/D: How long?

    If M/W: What was/is your husband's occupation?

2 Where were you born?

3 How long have you lived in Brighton?

4 Are your parents living? Where?

5 Could you show me from this [card] the group which includes your weekly household income from all sources?

    Under £40

    Between £40 and £80

    Between £81 and £120

Between £121 and £160
Between £161 and £200
Between £201 and £250
More than £250.
If you have any paid job, how much do you earn?

6 Could you tell me the sources of your income?
Wages
Supplementary benefits
Pension
Other
Unemployment Insurance
Family allowance
Other benefits

7 Have you done any further training of any kind since high school?

8 What class would you say you are in?

9 Do you read any magazines or newspapers? Which ones? How often?

Notes

CHAPTER ONE

1 Myrdal and Klein, *Women's Two Roles*, 20.

2 Counter Information Services, *Women Under Attack*, 8.

3 Analysts have argued, in retrospect, that "it is now a commonplace that the period 1976 to 1981 saw mounting changes in the structure and levels of manufacturing employment which have no precedent in post-war Britain" (Townsend and Peck, "An Approach to the Analysis of Redundancies," 69), while industrial restructuring in the "post-1979 recession" created qualitative as well as quantitative changes in the labour force (Lloyd and Shutt, "Recession and Restructuring").

4 Initially women's greater entry into "public life," especially in the labour force, gave rise to a liberal feminism which focused on legal and political attempts to give women "equal rights" within the confines of given social relations. This work is exemplified in Betty Frieden's pathbreaking *Feminine Mystique* and underlies many academic studies of women. Socialist feminists and radical feminists analyzed gender in terms of overall social and psychological relations. For discussion, see Beechey, "Some Notes on Female Wage Labour"; Connell, *Gender and Power*; Segal, *Is the Future Female?*.

5 These include Bebel, *Women Under Socialism* (originally published 1883); Engels, "The Origin of the Family" (originally published 1891); Gilman, *Women and Economics* (originally published 1898). This rediscovery is discussed by Elizabeth Wilson (*Only Half Way to Paradise*, 195).

6 Sexuality and sex categories are also socially constructed to some extent. See deBeauvoir, *The Second Sex*, 1–128, 249–400; Fransella and Frost, *On Being a Woman*, 55–77; Greer, *The Female Eunuch*, 25–47; Wilson, *Only Half Way to Paradise*, 81–111. The social definition of sexuality is especially evident in the legal and social construction of lesbianism. See Birke, "From Zero to Infinity"; Brackx, "Prejudice and Pride"; Whiting, "Female Sexuality"; Wilson, *Only Half Way to Paradise*, 101–4.

7 One of the fullest discussions of breaking the link between sex and gender is found in Marge Piercy's *Woman on the Edge of Time*.

8 Kuhn and Wolpe, "Feminism and Materialism," 7.

9 Engels, "The Origin of the Family," 447.

10 Ibid.

11 See Beard, *Women as a Force in History*; Clark, *Working Life of Women*; Ehrenreich and English, *For Her Own Good*; Pahl, *Divisions of Labour*.

12 For a fuller discussion of pre-capitalist relations of production and reproduction and the transition to capitalism, see Mackenzie, "Building Women, Building Cities"; Mackenzie and Rose, "Industrial Change"; Tilly and Scott, *Women, Work and Family*.

13 See deBeauvoir, *The Second Sex*; Ehrenreich and English, *For Her Own Good*.

14 Wallsgrove, "The Masculine Face of Science," 236–7.

15 Alison, "Strolling across Sussex."

16 Fothergill and Gudgin, *Unequal Growth*; Lloyd and Shutt, "Recession and Restructuring"; Massey and Meegan, "Industrial Restructuring".

17 Farrant, "The Early Growth of the Seaside Resorts," 212–3. Some of the sense of early history in Sussex resort towns is captured in Jane Austen's unfinished *Sanditon*.

18 Farrant, "The Early Growth of the Seaside Resorts," 213; Lowerson, "Resorts, Ports and 'Sleepy Hollows,'" 232. For discussion of conditions in the neighbouring town of Hastings in the early twentieth century, see Robert Tressell's *The Ragged Trousered Philanthropists* and in Brighton in the interwar period, Graham Greene's *Brighton Rock*.

19 Gray, "Housing in Sussex," 253.

20 Ibid., 254.

21 Ibid., 256–7; Fielding and Dunford, "Population and Employment"; chapter 7 this volume.

22 Gray, "Housing in Sussex"; Lowerson, "Resorts, Ports and 'Sleepy hollows,'" 232. On housing provision, see chapter 4 this volume and on social services see chapters 5 and 6 this volume.

23 Gray, "Housing in Sussex," 254.

24 In many respects, this could be seen as a "locality study." See Cooke, *Global Restructuring*; Murgatroyd et. al., *Localities, Class and Gender*.

25 There are specific feminine and masculine words for many of the activities discussed here, apart from the modification of "worker" by the addition of "woman". For example, the activities involved in mothering and fathering make up the content of the newly popularized word for the activity of "parenting." This book talks about mothers, as well as parents, but looks at parenting primarily from the perspective of mothers – just as it looks at the labour force from the perspective of those participants who are women, and usually wives and mothers, as well as wage earners.

26 Some of the concepts underlying these ideas are more fully discussed in Bhaskar, "On the Possibility of Social Scientific Knowledge"; Giddens, *Central Problems in Social Theory* and *A Contemporary Critique of Historical Materialism*.

CHAPTER TWO

1 Beechey, "Some Notes on Female Wage Labour," 55; Branson and Heinemann, *Britain in the Nineteen Thirties*, 32; Land, "The family wage," 62;
Oakley, *Women's Work*, 57–8; White, *Women's Magazines*, 99. For independent women, although their numbers in the labour force also declined,
there was a growing range of jobs open, especially in clerical and tertiary
fields, and a shift away from domestic service (Gittens, "Married Life and
Birth Control," 55).

2 Spring Rice, *Working Class Wives*, 105.

3 Brittain, *Testament of Youth*, 575. Also see Spring Rice, *Working Class Wives*,
131–49; Women's Group on Public Welfare, *Our Towns*, 90–7.

4 Spring Rice, *Working Class Wives*, 94.

5 Women's Group on Public Welfare, *Our Towns*, xv.

6 Spring Rice, *Working Class Wives*, 155. A number of other studies have
been conducted which revealed grossly inadequate resources and nutrition
among large sectors of the population (Branson and Heinemann, *Britain
in the Nineteen Thirties*, 223–5).

7 Branson and Heinemann, *Britain in the Nineteen Thirties*, 245; Spring Rice,
Working Class Wives, xi and 29–30.

8 Women's Group on Public Welfare, *Our Towns*, 33.

9 Oren, "The Welfare of Women in Labouring Families," 235–7; Spring
Rice, *Working Class Wives*, 29–30 and 106–57 and 210–12.

10 Branson and Heinemann, *Britain in the Nineteen Thirties*, 224 and 258–9;
Good Housekeeping Institute, Correspondence, mimeographed information; White, *Women's Magazines*, 102.

11 Land, "The family wage," 63; Oren, "The Welfare of Women in Labouring Families," 235–6.

12 National Association of Women's Clubs, *Annual Report*.

13 Electrical Association for Women, Correspondence, mimeographed information, 2.

14 Tilly and Scott, *Women, Work and Family*, 207.

15 Sharp, *Buyers and Builders*, 8.

16 Ibid., 13.

17 Family Welfare Association, *Annual Report*; National Association for Maternal and Child Welfare, *Brief History*.

18 Women's Group on Public Welfare, *Our Towns*; Spring Rice, *Working Class
Wives*.

19 Women's Group on Public Welfare, *Our Towns*, vii.

20 Barret and McIntosh, "The Family Wage," 57; Branson and Heinemann,
Britain in the Nineteen Thirties, 183 and 235; Land, "The Family Wage," 63–
71; Spring Rice, *Working Class Wives*, 192–3.

21 Brittain, *Testament of Youth*, 610.

22 Brittain, *Lady Into Woman*, 52–3, also 74; and Brittain, *Testament of Youth*, 582–3.

23 Leathard, *The Fight for Family Planning*, 4; Titmuss and Titmuss, *Parents' Revolt*, 66.

24 Family Planning Association Working Party, *Family Planning in the Sixties*, 4(5); Leathard, *The Fight for Family Planning*, 44.

25 Leathard, *The Fight for Family Planning*, 216.

26 Branson and Heinemann, *Britain in the Nineteen Thirties*, 182; Leathard, *The Fight for Family Planning*, 29.

27 Leathard, *The Fight for Family Planning*, 215.

28 Gittens, "Married Life and Birth Control," 58; Spring Rice, *Working Class Wives*, xi.

29 Gittens, "Married Life and Birth Control," 58; Political and Economic Planning, *Population Policy*, Note 52.

30 Leathard, *The Fight for Family Planning*, 24.

31 Abrams, *The Population of Great Britain*, 32; Beveridge, *Changes in Family Life*, 112–17; Branson and Heinemann, *Britain in the Nineteen Thirties*, 182–3; Eugenics Society, Correspondence, leaflets; George, *Social Security*, 188; Leathard, *The Fight for Family Planning*, 24; Political and Economic Planning, *Population Policy*, 138–50; Reddaway, *The Economics of Declining Population* , 60–9 and 107–19; Schenk and Parkes, *The Activities of the Eugenics Society*.

32 Abrams, *The Population of Great Britain*, 35; Reddaway, *The Economics of Declining Population*, 243–5.

33 White, *Women's Magazines*, 101.

34 *Women's Fair*, February 1938 quoted in White, *Women's Magazines*, 109.

35 Abrams, *The Population of Great Britain*, 36–40; Beveridge, *Changes in Family Life*, 78–9; Reddaway, *The Economics of Declining Population*, 238–43; Titmuss and Titmuss, *Parents' Revolt*, 39. Demands were also made for the expansion of services and income to the increasing proportion of elderly people who would be dependent on a dwindling proportion of younger productive workers (Branson and Heinemann, *Britain in the Nineteen Thirties*, 248–55; Moroney, *The Family and the State*, 34–6; Titmuss, *Poverty and Population*, 29–33).

36 Markusen, "City Spatial Structure," 31.

37 Harris, "Comment on Willmott," 59.

38 Wilson, *Only Half Way to Paradise*, 160.

39 Douie, *The Lesser Half*; Ferguson and Fitzgerald, *Social Services*, 22–5; Brighton community interviews.

40 Riley, "War in the Nursery," 106. Also Brittain, *Lady Into Woman*, 53; Women's Group on Public Welfare, *Our Towns*, 107.

41 London Women's Parliament, *Woman Power*, 15–16. Married and independent women, in war time as well as later, worked both to assist the war effort and because they badly needed the money. This was especially true

of those whose husbands were on army pay (Ferguson and Fitzgerald, *Social Services*, 22; London Women's Parliament, *Woman Power*, 2–3).

42 Ferguson and Fitzgerald, *Social Services*, 9–13 and 30–9 and 154–7 and 181 and 303–28; London Women's Parliament, *Woman Power*, 11; Riley, "War in the Nursery," 84–5.

43 Women's Group on Public Welfare, *Our Towns*, xiii. Also Douie, *The Lesser Half*, 83; Women's Committee for Peace and Democracy, *Will Your Child Be Safe?*.

44 Women's Committee for Peace and Democracy, *Will Your Child Be Safe?*, 15–16.

45 Ferguson and Fitzgerald, *Social Services*, 13.

46 Ibid., 211. Emphasis in original. Also Myrdal and Klein, *Women's Two Roles*, 53–4; Thirkell, *Peace Breaks Out*; White, *Women's Magazines*, 130–45.

47 Douie, *The Lesser Half*, 91.

48 Ibid.

49 Barrett and McIntosh, "The Family Wage," 55.

50 Spring Rice, *Working Class Wives*, 96.

51 Women's Group on Public Welfare, *Our Towns*, 94.

52 Williams, *Politics and Letters*, 432.

53 Ibid, 429.

54 Most pre-feminist analysts and many feminists dismiss or ignore women's groups of this period and their contemporary counterparts. This dismissal is informed by the convention that real politics is in the workplace and by an acceptance of the political militant as "without ties, bereft of domestic emotions ... hard, erect, self-contained, controlled, without the time or ability to express loving passion, who cannot pause to nurture, and for whom friendship is a diversion." (Rowbotham, "The Women's Movement," 68). As Rowbotham points out, these superhuman, or subhuman, prerequisites pretty much exclude women from "real politics" (ibid., 67–6 and 78–82) and also exclude the majority of human activity and creativity. The rediscovery of the feminist tradition in the context of the contemporary women's movement should elicit some more sensitive and inclusive treatments.

55 Beveridge, quoted in Land, "The Family Wage," 72.

56 Great Britain, His Majesty's Government, *Report On The Social Insurance*, 49.

57 This demand for labour also led to recruiting of immigrants, primarily from "New Commonwealth" countries (Brooks, *This Crowded Kingdom*, 127; Friend and Metcalf, *Slump City*, 57–9).

CHAPTER THREE

1 Quoted in Gilbert, *The New Dragon Enclosed*, 25.

2 Gilbert, *Brighton*, 187–95.

3 Brighton Hove and District Joint Town Planning Advisory Committee, *Preliminary Report*, 10.

4 1951 Outline Development Plan, summarized by Gilbert, *Brighton*, 235.

5 See for example, Ambrose, "Who Plans the Brighton Area Housing Crisis?"; Brighton Corporation, Planning, *Old Town Scheme*; Brighton Corporation, *Town Council Agenda and Proceedings*, Planning Committee, 8 December 1970, 20 January 1972, 19 January 1973, Corporation Estates Committee, 1 June 1972, 8 March 1972, Highways and Transport Committee, 1 September 1979, 15 February 1971; Brighton and Hove *Official Guide Books*; Brighton and Hove Gazette *Year Books* and *Guides*. There have been continued protests against these developments, some successful. See Brighton Marina Ad Hoc Campaign, *The Brighton Marina Outrage*; Save Brighton Station Campaign, *The Brighton Station Scandal* and the *Brighton Voice*.

6 East Sussex County Council, *Urban Programme*, 1. The report goes on to say that Brighton was "consistently grouped with towns such as Birmingham, Bolton, Bradford, Doncaster, Gateshead, Leeds, Rotherham, Salford, St. Helen's, Sunderland, North and South Tyneside for incidence of 8 out of 10 of the need indicators used by the D[epartment] of E[nvironment] in the process of designating local authorities under the Inner Urban Areas Act, 1978."

7 Ibid., 3–5.

8 Brighton Corporation, Medical Officer of Health, *Annual Report*, 1972.

9 Ibid.

10 Brighton Corporation, Borough Treasurer's Department, *Brighton's Finances*, 1970–1 to 1979–80.

11 Rowbotham, "The Women's Movement," 43–4.

12 Wilson, *Only Half Way to Paradise*, 195.

13 These included the records of the Town Council, the minutes and annual reports of the various municipal committees and departments, the Medical Officer of Health's *Annual Reports* and, where appropriate, the records of various departments of the East Sussex County Council. I was given unpublished material from, and spoke with people in, the Brighton Housing Advisory Centre, the Community Health Services, the Social Services and Education departments, as well as their county counterparts in Lewes. In all cases, people working in these invariably busy agencies were co-operative and often went to great lengths to supply me with answers to what was often a long list of disparate and unusual questions. This was especially true of the staff of the Brighton Reference Library, with whom I spent most of my waking hours over a two-month period. I also corresponded with and obtained information from 119 national "women's organizations" and social service organizations.

14 Oakley, "Interviewing Women," 58.

15 Although such ideas are becoming more widespread throughout social sciences as a whole (see, for example, Sayer, "Defensible Values in Geography" and articles in Massey and Meegan, *Politics and Method*; Murgatroyd et. al., *Localities, Class and Gender*), they have been pursued most immediately, personally, and specifically in the growing literature on feminist methodology. See Harding, *Feminism and Methodology*; McRobbie, "The Politics of Feminist Research"; Roberts, *Doing Feminist Research*; Stanley and Wise, *Breaking Out*.

16 I have never seen a textbook admonish against peeling vegetables, but a great many do admonish against "responding to the interviewee." One can only assume that the former, like female homosexuality to the Victorian British, was so unthinkable as to require no forbidding.

17 Oakley, "Interviewing Women," 50; also noted by Rubin, *Worlds of Pain*, 15–22.

18 The discrepancies in the number of people interviewed in each area were largely due to logistical considerations. However, as the object of the interviews was to build up a perspective on women's subjective and active response to changes in their lives, not to establish a representative sample of anything, neither this discrepancy nor the relatively small sample presents problems. Similar sample sizes are the rule in research which, in Hannah Gavron's words is aiming to "build up a picture of the lives of the women studied" (Gavron, *The Captive Wife*, 147), or from Ann Oakley's more explicit feminist perspective, work which makes "possible the articulation and recorded commentary of women on the very personal business of being female in a patriarchal capitalist society" (Oakley, "Interviewing Women," 48–9).

CHAPTER FOUR

1 Birmingham Feminist History Group, "Feminism as Femininity," 48.

2 Wilson, *Only Half Way to Paradise*, 12.

3 Brighton was planned on numerous occasions: the 1928 plan of the Brighton, Hove and District Joint Town Planning Advisory Committee under the Town Planning Act of 1925; the 1937 Central Area Plan; the 1951 Outline Development Plan under the Town and Country Planning Act of 1947; the Brighton Town Centre Report and the series of structure plans and the Old Town Scheme which emerged in the early 1970s in conjunction with local government reorganization. Two themes unite these: first a growth in the amount of intervention recommended and the powers available to intervene, and second an increasing concern with traffic and transportation.

4 Gilbert, *Brighton*, 210–15 and 223.

5 Ibid., 223; Lowerson, "Resorts, Ports and 'Sleepy Hollows,'" 232.

6 And both sides involve a process of environmentally coercing and "uplifting" the working class out of its "slum habits." These processes were compontents of national housing policies.

7 Brighton, Hove and District Joint Planning Advisory Committee, *Preliminary Report*, 50–1.

8 Brighton Corporation, Housing Manager, *Annual Report*, 1955, 14–15.

9 Ibid.

10 Weston, "Brighton Housing Estates," 82. The same reports also noted with pride that raised verges and deep margins at the kerbs would "prevent prams being wheeled upon the grass" Presumably the estate was to be looked at, not lived in. Forty-five years and two generations later, women are still hauling and bouncing prams and pushchairs onto the inhospitable and overgrown verges.

11 Gilbert, *Brighton*, 224.

12 Gilbert, *The New Dragon Enclosed*, 50.

13 Great Britain, Office of Population and Census Surveys, Census Occupation Tables, 1931.

14 Brighton Corporation, Planning Committee, *Planning Central Areas*, 15.

15 Brighton Corporation, Housing Manager, *Annual Report*, 1951 and 1954; Brighton Corporation, Medical Officer of Health, *Annual Report*, 1956, 36 and 1961, 58.

16 Brighton Corporation, Housing Manager, *Annual Report*, 1948, 5.

17 Brighton Corporation, Planning Committee, *Brief Report*, 7.

18 Brighton Corporation, Housing Manager, *Annual Report*, 1954, 6.

19 Ibid., 1956, 8.

20 Ibid., 1953, 7.

21 Ibid., 1952, 5.

22 Brighton Urban Structure Plan Team, *Brighton Urban Structure Plan Survey Reports*, Survey Report 8, Industry and Commerce, 7.

23 Brighton Corporation, Planning Department, 1951, 8–9. There were objections by local industrial groups, including the Trades Council, to "inadequate allocation of land for industrial use" in the early plans and pressures to speed the development of those sites which had been established (Brighton, Hove and District Trades Council History Sub-Committee, *A History of Brighton Trades Council*, 68).

24 Brighton Urban Structure Plan Team, *Brighton Urban Structure Plan Survey Reports*, Survey Report 8, Industry and Commerce, 8.

25 Brighton Corporation, Planning Committee, *Reports of Survey Amendments*, Survey Amendment 6. For further discussion of industrial relocation and restructuring, see Brighton Urban Structure Plan Team, *Brighton Urban Stucture Plan Survey Reports*, Survey Report 8, Industry and Commerce; Conference of Socialist Economists, Brighton Labour Process Group, *A Case Study of Creeds*.

26 Brighton Corporation, Housing Manager, *Annual Report*, 1952, 5.

27 Brighton Corporation, Medical Officer of Health, *Annual Report*, 1964, 33.

28 In the period 1949–54, an average of 35 Home Nursing staff members made 115,904 visits; in 1970–3 the staff had grown to 52 and the number of visits was 171,774. The Domestic Help Scheme employed 22 staff in 1951 and 238 in 1970. In 1970, 89 per cent of their visits were to the elderly (calculated from Brighton Corporation, Medical Officer of Health, *Annual Reports*).

29 See Ambrose, "Who Plans the Brighton Area Housing Crisis?"; Bennett, *Housing in Brighton*; Brighton, Hove and District Trades Council, History Sub-committee, *A History of Brighton Trades Council*, 61.

30 This is increasingly evident in town plans, for example, Brighton, Hove and District Joint Town Planning Advisory Committee, *Report of the Regional Planning Scheme*, 71; Brighton Urban Structure Plan Team, *Brighton Urban Structure Plan Survey Reports*, Survey Report 12, Transportation; East Sussex County Council, County Engineer's Department, *Brighton Area Traffic Mangement Study*; Great Britain, Department of the Environment, *Brighton Area East West Trunk Road*; Wilson and Womersley, *Brighton Town Centre Interim Report*.

31 *Brighton Voice*, 7, 1974.

32 *Brighton Voice*, 11, 1979; 2, 1980; 4, 1980.

33 P. Gilbert has competently documented developments in Moulescoombe (Gilbert, *The New Dragon Enclosed*).

34 Quoted in Gilbert, *The New Dragon Enclosed*, 54.

35 Radwan, *Whitehawk*, 1.

36 Barrow, *Report on Whitehawk*, 4.

37 Brighton, Hove and District Trades Council, *Minutes*, 20 February 1963; Moss, *Live and Learn*, 75–7; Radwan, *Whitehawk*; Interviews.

38 Brighton Corporation, *Town Council Agenda and Proceedings*, Education Committee, 9 February 1971; Highways and Transportation Committee, 29 June 1970, 4 January 1971, 28 June 1971, 16 April 1971, 30 October 1972; Housing Committee, 3 March 1971, 28 June 1972, 28 March 1973; Parks Committee, 3 January 1973; Interviews.

39 Brighton Corporation, Medical Officer of Health, *Annual Report*, 1959, 45.

40 Brighton Corporation, Housing Manager, *Annual Report*, 1953, 6.

41 Ibid., 1949.

42 Brighton Corporation, Medical Officer of Health, *Annual Report*, 1959, 46.

43 Ibid.

44 Brighton Corporation, Housing Manager, *Annual Report*, 1957, 6–7.

45 Brighton Corporation, Medical Officer of Health, *Annual Report* 1958.

46 For example, in 1952, total advertising expenditure in Great Britain was £123 million while in 1979 it was £2,129 million. Even accounting for inflation, this is a rise from .94 per cent of gross national product in 1952 to

1.34 per cent in 1979, and from 1.23 per cent of total consumer expenditure in 1952 to 1.90 per cent in 1979 (Advertising Association, "Advertising expenditure"). Also see Advertising Association, *Find Out About Advertising*; Good Housekeeping Institute, Correspondence, mimeographed information; White, *Women's Magazines*; Wilson, *Only Half Way to Paradise*, 12–14; Young and Willmott, *The Symmetrical Family*, 28–31.

47 For example, between 1956 and 1967, the percentage of households with washing machines rose from 19 to 61 per cent, with refrigerators from 7 to 46 per cent, with vacuum cleaners from 51 to 81 per cent (Young and Wilmott, *The Symmetrical Family*, 23). Also see Friend and Metcalf, *Slump City*, 111–13; Myrdal and Klein, *Women's Two Roles*, xi-xiii.

48 Brighton Urban Structure Plan Team, *Brighton Urban Structure Plan Survey Reports*, Survey Report 9, Shopping, 29.

49 The National Consumer Congress Directory for 1981 lists 121 national organizations concerned wholly or partly with consumer affairs.

50 Horrocks, "The Work of the Consumer Standards Advisory Committee," 183.

51 Ibid., 184–5.

52 Electrical Association for Women, *55th Annual Report*.

53 Co-operative Women's Guild, *Rules*.

54 Brighton Corporation, Medical Officer of Health, *Annual Report*, 1964, 63. They were, although not precisely in the way he may have envisaged. Also, by this time, most working-class married women were in wage work, earning the money to pay for improved domestic working conditions.

55 Quoted in Riley, "War in the Nursery," 104; also see Wilson, *Only Half Way to Paradise*, 19.

CHAPTER FIVE

1 National Abortion Campaign, *Statement of Principles*.

2 Rich, *Of Woman Born*, 182.

3 For discussion of the population "bomb" see Brooks, *This Crowded Kingdom*; Ehrlich, *The Population Bomb*. Groups established in this period include the Conservation Society, Friends of the Earth, Population Stabilization, and Doctors and Population. Whether or not these groups and the media celebration of the bomb had any direct effect on most people's lives, they did create a new social atmosphere, one apparently more sympathetic to the discussion of and action around fertility-control policy and facilities.

4 Quoted in Wandor, "Introduction," 2.

5 Brighton Corporation Medical Officer of Health, *Annual Report*, 1951, 13.

6 Family Planning Association Working Party, *Family Planning in the Sixties*, 3(2), 4(10), and 5(5). Also Leathard, *The Fight for Family Planning*, 102

and 125; Population Investigation Committee, *Towards a Population Policy*, 19–20.

7 Family Planning Association Working Party, *Family Planning in the Sixties*, 2(3) and 2(9); Brighton Corporation, Medical Officer of Health, *Annual Reports*.

8 Family Planning Information Service, *Inform* 9; Brook Advisory Centres, *Annual Report*, 1980, 2; Brighton Corporation Medical Officer of Health, *Annual Reports*; Great Britain, Department of Health and Social Services, *Community Health Service Statistics for Brighton Health District*.

9 Leathard, *The Fight for Family Planning*, 222–3.

10 Ibid., 102–8 and 223. It has been argued that doctors' attitudes had long delayed the development of oral contraception, for which the chemical technology was available as early as 1938 (Walsh, "Contraception," 182–3).

11 Wilson, *Only Half Way to Paradise*, 98–9 and 109.

12 Campaign Against Depo Provera, Correspondence, mimeographed information; Leathard, *The Fight for Family Planning*, 111–2; Pill Victims Action Group, Correspondence, mimeographed information; Walsh, "Contraception," 202–5.

13 Brooks, *This Crowded Kingdom*, 102–22.

14 Brighton Corporation Medical Officer of Health, *Annual Reports*, 1970 and 1971.

15 Leathard, *The Fight for Family Planning*, 187.

16 Ibid., 212.

17 Campaign for Common Sense on Abortion, *Abortion Black Spots*.

18 Lafitte, *The Abortion Hurdle Race*, i.

19 *Guardian*, 13 June 1981.

20 Brighton Campaign for Day Care Abortion, *Working Party Report*, 10.

21 Brighton Campaign for Day Care Abortion, *Working Party Report*; Brighton Health District, Community Health Council, *Annual Report*, 1978–9; *Brighton Voice*, 1.1978; Brighton Hove and District Trades Council, *Bulletin* 2 December 1978; Trades Council Minutes, 21 February 1977.

22 Smith, "A Brief Outline." Also see Pregnancy Advisory Service, Correspondence and leaflets; Birth Control Trust, *Abortion*.

23 Brighton Campaign for Day Care Abortion, *Working Party Report*, 4.

24 Co-ord, Correspondence.

25 Himmelweit, "Abortion," 68.

26 Most of the historical attempts to collectivize these decisions, to develop the social mechanisms, and to regulate individual decisions have been fragmentary, clumsy, and repressive. There have been two extreme scenerios for collective regulation envisioned in novels: Zoe Fairbains' horror story in *Benefits* and Margaret Atwood's dystopia in the *Handmaid's Tale*. These contrast with Marge Piercy's utopia in *Woman on the Edge of Time*.

27 Great Britain, Office of Population Censuses and Surveys, *Census*, 1971;

Population Trends; General Household Survey Unit, "The Changing Circumstances of Women,"; Registrar General, *Statistical Review*, 1970: Wrigley, *Population and History*.

28 Great Britain, Office of Population Censuses and Surveys, *Social Trends*.

29 Brighton Corporation, Medical Officer of Health, *Annual Report*; East Sussex Area Health Authority, Information Services Department, *Child Health Statistics*.

30 Brighton Corporation, Medical Officer of Health, *Annual Report*, 1951, 10.

31 Between 1945 and 1970, the number of municipal and private midwives dropped from 17 to 10 and the number of hospital midwives rose from 21 to 46. In 1945 municipal and private midwives cared for 652 cases and by 1970 they cared for only 58; over the some period hospital cases had risen from 2,159 to 2,983. In 1981 however, there were 17 municipal midwives and only 36 employed in hospitals (ibid.; Royal Sussex County Hospital Records).

32 Brighton Women and Science Group, "Technology in the Lying in Room," 171.

33 Ibid., 170.

34 Of the 49 women who had at least one of their children in hospital, 16 expressed only criticisms of the delivery process, 15 were fully satisfied, and 18 were critical of some aspects, primarily "interference" and lack of information and support. The majority (37) felt that the service was becoming more humane and especially appreciated having "companions" (generally fathers) at the birth. Most also praised the care staff members took, when they had the time. But almost all (44) said the service was understaffed and underfunded.

   With respect to ante-natal care, staff members were aware of problems, especially the fact that the ante-natal clinic was too small; they encouraged shared care with a GP and ante-natal staff, an option most women said they far preferred.

35 Association of Radical Midwives, Correspondence, leaflets; Maternity Alliance, *Conclusions and Recommendations*; Society to Support Home Confinements, Correspondence, mimeographed information.

36 National Childbirth Trust, Correspondence, leaflets.

37 Summary of suggestions by National Childbirth Trust, Brighton and Hove Branch *Newsletter*, April-May, 1981, 3–5.

CHAPTER SIX

1 Mitchell, *Psycho-analysis and Feminism*, 231.

2 After John Bowlby, who emphasized the dangerous effects of maternal deprivation. But in the immediate post-war period, the foremost theorists were Melanie Klein and her followers – Isaacs and Winnicott. The construction of motherhood was also influenced by Anna Freud and Dorothy

Burlington (Bowlby, *Childcare*; Mitchell, *Psycho-analysis and Feminism*, 228–31; Myrdal and Klein, *Women's Two Roles*, 124–7; Nava, "The Family," 37–9; Riley, "War in the Nursery," 94–9).

3 Brighton Corporation, Medical Officer of Health, *Annual Report*, 1951, 11.

4 Ibid., 1961, 24; 1967, 29; 1968, 34.

5 Brighton Corporation, Children's Department, *Annual Report*, 1954, 7.

6 Ibid, 1959, 8.

7 Wilson, *Only Half Way to Paradise*, 72–7.

8 Brophy and Smart, "From Disregard to Disrepute," 13. Also see Jane Ursel's illuminating discussion of this process in an earlier period in Canada (Ursel, "The State and the Maintenance of Patriarchy"). Both her discussion and other historical investigations indicate that socialization was a cumulative process over the period of capitalist development. See Mackenzie, *Women and the Reproduction of Labour Power*; Mackenzie and Rose, "Industrial Change."

9 Brighton Corporation, Medical Officer of Health, *Annual Report*, 1951, 1.

10 Brighton Corporation, Housing Manager, *Annual Report*, 1953.

11 Brighton Corporation, Medical Officer of Health, *Annual Report*, 1954, 17.

12 Ibid. The numbers rose from 39,306 in 1941 to 3,035,988 in 1971. Since the late 1970s there has been a gradual decrease.

13 Brighton Corporation, School Medical Officer, *Annual Report*, 1952.

14 Ibid., 1954.

15 Ibid., 1963, 24.

16 The Social Service Department is responsible for administration of the day nursery, for supervision of private nurseries, playgroups, mother and toddler groups, and childminders; the Department of Education is responsible for nursery schools and classes. Two committees, the Brighton Liaison Group for Under Fives, set up in 1979, and The Under Fives (TUF), set up in 1981, have been attempting to co-ordinate services. The extent to which such co-ordination is possible or even desirable has been a matter of some controversy among activists and statutory workers.

17 Quoted in National Childcare Campaign, *Nurseries*, 15.

18 Ibid., 7.

19 Throughout the post-war period, Brighton had one day nursery, usually with places for fewer than fifty children. Brighton Corporation, Medical Officer of Health, *Annual Reports*; Interview with Pre-School Care Officer, Brighton Social Service Department.

20 Social-service workers say that these rumours are exaggerated. This is likely true, but the fact that they exist makes the service even less accessible to those who need it. See also Jackson and Jackson, *Childminder*, 43–8 and 66–9 for discussion of day nursery care in other areas in Britain.

21 Brighton Corporation, Medical Officer of Health, *Annual Reports*; East Sussex County Council, Social Service Department, *Report of the Departmental Working Group* and *Preschool Groups*.

22 National Campaign for Nursery Education, *Questions on Nursery Education*, 2. In fact, the 1944 act did not permit, it required the authorities to provide education.

23 East Sussex Area Health Authority, Information Services Department, *Child Health Statistics* Two of these, Moulsecoomb and Whitehawk, are educational priority areas and have two classes each.

24 Ibid.

25 National Campaign for Nursery Education, *Statement of Principle*.

26 *Women's Fightback*, 1.1981.

27 National Childcare Campaign, *Nurseries*.

28 *Brighton Voice*, 11.1977

29 *Guardian*, 21 April, 1981.

30 Counter Information Service, *Women in the 1980s*, 14; Jackson and Jackson, *Childminder*, 174–83.

31 This permission was never widely used in Brighton and, with the growing cuts in the social-service budget in the late 1970s and early 1980s, its use was becoming less frequent and confined to children in exceptional cases (Interviews; East Sussex County Council, Social Services Department, *Report of the Departmental Working Group*, 23–4).

32 Jackson and Jackson, *Childminder*, 76.

33 Brighton Corporation, Medical Officer of Health, *Annual Reports*.

34 Molly Evans, the pre-school care officer for the Brighton Social Services Department, provided most of the official support to childminders. However, while I was doing this research, this aspect of her job was "terminated," leaving little in the way of statutory services for childminders.

35 The National Childbirth Trust, Brighton and Hove Branch *Newsletter* (April-May, 1981) reported that an area women was told she was "disgusting" and "immoral" and threatened with the police when she breast-fed her baby in a local community centre.

36 National Equal Opportunities Committee, *Women and the Cuts*, 2–3.

37 Jackson and Jackson, *Childminder*, 174–82.

38 The former group includes the statutory childcare professionals who themselves need full-time care for their children. In Brighton, the groups supporting full-time professional care included NCNE, NCCC, and "Save Brighton's Nursery Schools" campaign. Parent-run groups included the PPA, mother and toddler groups, and groups such as WAM. Although, on the whole, the two sets of groups maintain mutual respect, there is, in the words of one activist, some "rubbing up against each other."

39 PreSchool Playgroups Association, *Report on Parental Involvement*, 35.

40 National Childminding Association, *Who Cares?*, Spring, 1979, 3.

41 Brighton Liaison Group for Under Fives, *Minutes*; National Childcare Campaign, *Nurseries*; Working Party on Integrated Training for Under Fives Workers, *Working Party Report*.

42 National Childminding Association, *National Childminding Association*.

43 Its formation was influenced by the "action research" initiated by Jackson and Jackson and others (Jackson and Jackson, *Childminder*, 241–57).

44 East Sussex County Council, Social Services Department, *Report of the Departmental Working Group*, 9.

45 Brighton Liaison Group for Under Fives, *Minutes*; East Sussex PreSchool Playgroups Association, *Summary of Survey*; PreSchool Playgroups Association, *Membership Form*; Steering Committee of the Under Fives Group, TUF *Group*; Working Association of Mothers, *East WAM News*.

46 PreSchool Playgroups Association, PPA *Coming of Age*, 14.

47 National Childcare Campaign, *Nurseries*, 11.

48 Nursery school and nursery class workers are National Union of Teacher members; day nursery workers, who are less likely to be unionized, are National Union of Public Employees members.

49 Jackson and Jackson, *Childminder*, 252; National Campaign for Nursery Education, *Nursery Education Under Attack*; National Childcare Campaign, *Newsletter*, June, 1981; Trades Union Congress, TUC *Charter on Facilities for the Under Fives* and *Women Workers*.

50 Job Sharing Project, Correspondence, newsletters; National Childcare Campaign, *Nurseries*; PreSchool Playgroups Association, PPA *Coming of Age*, 14; Rowe, *Nursery Education*.

CHAPTER SEVEN

1 Myrdal and Klein, *Women's Two Roles*, xi.

2 Bennett, *Situations Vacant*, 11–12; Brighton Corporation, Medical Officer of Health, *Annual Reports*; Brighton Hove and District Trades Council, *Minutes* and *Annual Reports*; Brighton Hove and District Trades Council, History Sub-committee, *A History of Brighton Trades Council*, 69; Gray, "Housing in Sussex."

   The Institute of Municipal Treasurers and Accountants' *Yearly Housing Statistics* indicate that council house rents in Brighton in the late 1970s and early 80s were among the highest in the country. Protests about council rents have been a consistent feature of local politics (Brighton Hove and District Trades Council, *Minutes*, 18 August 1948, 18 May 1949, 20 December 1967; *Annual Reports*, 1957, 1967, 1970; Gilbert, *The New Dragon Enclosed*, 55; Moss, *Live and Learn*, 75–6), as have protests about the general cost of living by the Trades Council, the Women's Co-op Guild, and local consumers' groups (Brighton Hove and District Trades Council, *Minutes* 18 February 1948, 20 July 1966; *Annual Reports*, 1952, 1955, 1971; Interviews).

3 East Sussex County Council, *Urban Programme*, 3–4.

4 Klein, *Britain's Married Women Workers*, 140–1; Myrdal and Klein, *Women's Two Roles*, x; Rosenbaum, "Social Services manpower," 6.

5 Brighton Corporation, Medical Officer of Health, *Annual Report*, 1966, 4.

6 Ibid., 1966, 37.

7 Ibid., 1970, 41.

8 East Sussex County Council, Social Services Department, *Report of the Departmental Working Group*, 18.

9 *Brighton Hospitals Bulletin*, 50, 2.

10 Ibid., 51, 1. Although a crèche was eventually established at Newhaven, one of the smaller hospitals, the same never materialized in Brighton. In 1981 the Brighton area Association of Scientific, Technical and Medical Staff organizer attempted to revive this project; she met with similar enthusiasm from staff and similar "cost conscious" reservations on the part of management.

11 *Brighton Hospitals Bulletin*, 3, 1974; also 9, 1974.

12 Brighton Corporation, Town Council, *Agenda and Proceedings*, Estates Committee, 20 October 1972.

13 Brighton Hove and District Trades Council, History Sub-committee, *A History of Brighton Trades Council*, 70.

14 Brighton Hove and District Trades Council, *Annual Report*, 1955.

15 Ibid, 1958.

16 Brighton Hove and District Trades Council, *Minutes*, 27 May 1959.

17 Brighton Urban Structure Plan Team, *Brighton Urban Structure Plan Survey Reports*, Survey Report 5, Employment, 8. Also see Fielding and Dunford, "Population and Employment."

18 Brighton Hove and District Trades Council, *Minutes*, 15 October 1970.

19 Not all men in Brighton were losing their jobs. In fact the rate of increase in female employment over the 1950s and 1960s was slower than that of male employment. Although the male share of employment fell very marginally, this decrease was less severe than for Britain as a whole (see table 20).

20 Kellner, "The Working Woman," 26–7.

21 Ibid.

22 Women's Group on Public Welfare, *Our Towns*, 107. In the case of teaching, the group urged this not only to help fill a need, but also so that the teachers might communicate better with mothers and thus strengthen the bond between home and school.

23 Land, "The Family Wage," 7.

24 International Labour Organization, *The War and Women's Employment: The Experience of the UK and US* quoted in Wilson, *Only Half Way to Paradise*, 4.

25 Great Britain, *Economic Survey*, 1947, quoted in Wilson, *Women and the Welfare State*, 156.

26 Klein, *Britain's Married Women Workers*, 140–1; Myrdal and Klein, *Women's Two Roles*, 194–5; Wilson, *Only Half Way to Paradise*, 43–4.

27 Kellner, "The Working Woman," 26.

28 Coote, "The Long Fight," 8.

29 White, *Women's Magazines*, 141.

30 Ibid., 152–3.

31 Klein, *Britain's Married Women Workers*, 21.

32 On the average, women's earnings are lower than those of men. In 1971 in Britain as a whole, women in manual jobs earned 51.1 per cent of average male wages, a decline from 54 per cent in 1948, while women in non-manual jobs earned 54 per cent of average male wages (calculated from Great Britain, Department of Employment, *Women and Work*). This was largely a function of the fact that women are both horizontally and vertically segregated in the job market (McIntosh, "Women at Work," 1143). Women are concentrated into the new "female" sectors of the economy, sectors characterized by low pay, low rates of unionization, and labour-intensive work processes. Three-quarters of all women wage-workers are in service industries, doing a waged version of the same types of work they do in the home (Counter Information Services, *Women in the 1980s*, 8). Women also tend to be vertically segregated into the less skilled and lower-paid jobs in any job category (McIntosh, "Women at Work," 1144; Great Britain, Department of Employment, *Women and Work*).

33 Throughout Britain, many women interrupt their wage-work in their twenties to become mothers; they then either take on homework or jobs with fewer hours, or work full-time as domestic workers. While for men, participation rates in the labour force are highest for the 25–34 age group, for women this age group has the lowest participation rate. Women also have the lowest relative rate of unionization (Kellner, "The Working Woman," 30).

34 For Britain as a whole, returnee women, aged 40–49, had the lowest rate of wages relative to men's (calculated from Equal Opportunities Commission, *Annual Report*, 1981).

35 Counter Information Services, *Women in the 1980s*, 10; Hurstfield, *The Part-time Trap*, 40–4; McIntosh, "Women at Work." The low wages and poor benefits are reinforced by the fact that part-time workers have particularly low rates of unionization (Coote and Kellner, "What Employers Do," 9; Hurstfield, *The Part-time Trap*, 69–71).

Part-time workers tend to be used as a flexible, easily expendable labour force and to be concentrated in the lowest skilled, most unpleasant jobs, with few prospects (Hurstfield, *The Part-time Trap*, 51–2, 20–1). Young and Willmott note that "employers ... have found that women, with their thoughts elsewhere, can be put onto jobs so monotonous that few men would stand them" (Young and Willmott, *The Symmetrical Family*, 274).

36 Coote and Kellner, "What Employers Do," 43. A 1979–80 survey found that 41.7 per cent of men and 12.1 per cent of women received overtime pay while 15.9 per cent of men as contrasted to 9.2 per cent of women received shift payments (McIntosh, "Women at Work," 1145).

37 When I visited her the living room, dining room, and hall were overflowing with "stuff." We sat crosslegged on the floor and drank tea off the bundles.

38 For Britain as a whole, see National Equal Opportunities Committee, *Women and the Cuts*, 4.

39 Brighton Urban Structure Plan Team, *Brighton Urban Structure Plan Survey Reports*, Survey Report 5, Employment, 21.

40 Friend and Metcalf, *Slump City*, 96.

41 Ibid., 108.

42 The others had such variable wages as to make accurate assessment impossible or, in two cases, did not know household income, only "what he gives me for housekeeping" and their own wages. The former group includes the nurses and teachers who, although they received a standard rate when employed, had variable hours and were unable to give an estimate. The average is therefore biased toward the low side, but does include all the full-time workers.

43 For Britain as a whole, see Jephcott, Seear, and Smith, *Married Women Working*, 116–24; Myrdal and Klein, *Women's Two Roles*, 83–5.

44 Holidays, which frequently meant a stay with relatives or self-catering arrangements, were not, for most women, a rest from domestic work. But they often provided opportunities to do this work communally, with friends or members of extended families, and in a different setting.

45 Counter Information Services, *Women in the 1980s*, 3–4.

46 Wilson, *Women and the Welfare State*, 81–3.

47 John Newson, *The Education of Girls* quoted in Birmingham Feminist History Group, "Feminism as Femininity," 52.

48 Barrett and McIntosh, "The Family Wage," 52; Land, "The Family Wage," 71–2; Wilson, *Only Half Way to Paradise*, 45–7.

49 Quoted in Land, "The Family Wage," 72.

50 Barrett and McIntosh, "The Family Wage," 60.

51 Pond and Bennett, *Low Pay*.

52 Counter Information Services, *Women in the 1980s*, 4; Lister and Wilson, *The Unequal Breadwinner*, 11–13. Although married women's reduced rate was being phased out from April 1977, these reduced benefits applied to the majority of married women in the early 1980s. This insecurity is exacerbated by the relatively low number of women who, as noted above, enjoyed occupational pensions or sickness benefits.

53 Throughout Britain relatively few women, especially those in service sectors, are in unions (Hurstfield, *The Part-time Trap*, 70; Kellner, "The Working Woman," 28–30). In 1977 only 38 per cent of women in wage jobs in the UK were unionized, as opposed to 62 per cent of men (*Social Trends*, 10).

54 Throughout Britain women's domestic responsibilities often preclude the

time and the energy to form unions, or to push for recognition of their specific needs within existing union structures (Coote, "Powerlessness," 8–12; Hakim, "Homeworking," 1108; Stageman, "A Study of Trade Union Branches").

55 Brighton Hove and District Trades Council, History Sub-committee, *A History of Brighton Trades Council*, 58.

56 Ibid.

57 Brighton Hove and District Trades Council, *Annual Report*, 1966.

58 Calculated from Equal Opportunities Commission, *Annual Reports*; Great Britain, Office of Population Censuses and Surveys, *Social Trends*.

59 Brighton Hove and District Trades Council, History Sub-committee, *A History of Brighton Trades Council*, 56.

The position of women in the labour force has always caused bewilderment among trade unions. Internationally, women's entry into the labour force was associated with "deskilling" and "dilution," in the manufacturing sector during both wars (Beechey, "Some Notes on Female Wage Labour," 55–6; Douie, *The Lesser Half*, 89), and in both manufacturing and service throughout the post-war period (Braverman, *Labour and Monopoly Capital*, 273–4; Hurstfield, *The Part-time Trap*; 21–2; Poulantzas, *Classes in Contemporary Capitalism*, 322–7; West, "Women, Sex and Class," 236–45). Coupled with the fact that the low-status, low-paid sectors occupied by most wage-earning women expanded concomitant with "deindustrialization," women's labour-force participation elicited a protectionist response on the part of many male trade unionists and often discouraged the organization of women.

60 Brighton Hove and District Trades Council, *Annual Report*, 1948.

61 Ibid., 1950, 18. The 1950 publication discusses this committee under the subheading "The Human Touch." One can only hope that this is not meant to imply that men are other than human.

62 Brighton Hove and District Trades Council, History Sub-committee, *A History of Brighton Trades Council*, 67. However, as indicated above, women's struggles over the issues which had concerned this committee did not subside. They merely moved into the community networks where their progress (one would speculate on the basis of current experience) was easier and swifter but was not, apparently, seen by male trade unionists as "political."

63 Brighton Hove and District Trades Council, *Annual Report*, 1958.

64 Brighton Hove and District Trades Council, *Minutes*, 16 March 1960.

65 One such motion adds that the council "reject the proposition ... that [equal pay] ... must come at the expense of the male wage" (Brighton Hove and District Trades Council, *Minutes*, 18 February 1970).

66 Stageman, "A Study of Trade Union Branches," 57.

67 Brighton Hove and District Trades Council, Women's Committee, *Minutes*.

68. Trades Union Congress, *Unemployed Workers' Centres*, Annex B.

These innovative measures were not welcomed by all centre users, nor was the presence of children in other areas of the centre. Unlike most women, some male trade unionists appear to have developed their political *modus operandi* in the absence of the concrete manifestations of the future working class. On finding a baby peacefully asleep in an open and otherwise empty filing cabinet drawer, a visiting union official had to be reassured that the child had as much right to the filing cabinet as any other member of the working class.

69 Brighton Unemployed Women's Group, *Thoughts on the Structure of the Centre*.

70 Edwards, *Unemployed Workers' Union*.

CHAPTER EIGHT

1 Williams, *Politics and Letters*, 150–1.

2 The debate between radical and socialist feminists which is evident within the women's liberation movement as a whole is, in some respects, reproduced within the union movement. Many radical feminists see the need for separate organization as virtually universal and as permanent. Socialist feminists, in contrast, while defending the need for some separate organization as a basis for formulating strategy and providing support for the more democratic procedures of feminist organizing, see such separate organizing as temporary. It is, in effect, a tactical response, necessary to establish the analysis, confidence, and procedural means with which to eliminate the gender oppression which makes such separate organizing necessary.

3 For a fuller discussion of "emergent" political forms see Williams, *Marxism and Literature*. For discussion of some of the social possibilities of women's informal networks, see Klodawsky and Mackenzie, "Gender Sensitive Theory"; Mackenzie, "Women's Responses" and "Neglected Spaces."

4 Raymond Williams analyses this tendency in political life generally in terms of a transition from "alternative" to "oppositional" forms of culture and politics (Williams, *Marxism and Literature*, 125–6).

5 These forms were not mutually exclusive, nor did they encompass the variety of the active networks. But participants themselves, in describing their activities, their priorities, and their relations to other groups, delimited the following typology.

6 Wekerle, Peterson and Morley, "Introduction," 26.

7 It is interesting to note that the 1980 PPA Annual General Meeting held in Brighton was larger than the TUC, also held in Brighton that year. It is also interesting to note that the local daily paper, the *Argus*, did not mention the PPA meeting until urged to do so by the organizers, and then reported it under the headline "2000 women get together for a chat."

8 Rowbotham, "The Women's Movement," 22.
9 Hartsock, "Feminist Theory," 73.
10 For discussions of this organizational form, see Hartsock, "Feminist Theory"; London Women's Liberation Workshop, "Organising Ourselves"; Rowbotham, "Women's Liberation," "The Beginnings of Women's Liberation," and "The Women's Movement"; Segal, *Is the Future Female?*; Wainwright, "Introduction"; Wandor, "The Small Group."
11 Williams, *Politics and Letters*, 430. Emphasis in original.
12 The interview contained the specific question "What do you think of the women's liberation movement?" All but two of the community interviewees and all of the activists expressed opinions. The majority of the former (37 of 53) had generally positive opinions; they felt it was "necessary" and justified their answers with reference to issues raised by other questions. Almost all were critical of some specific actions of women in the "movement," largely on the grounds that women's liberation activists were "too aggresive," "too noisy," "did not consider women with children," or "did not consider working-class women." Activists who did not identify themselves with the women's liberation movement tended to be more specific and often criticized specific organizational strategies which differed from those employed by "less militant" groups.

Interviewees frequently volunteered their opinions on the women's movement in the course of conversation on other issues, especially birth control and wage labour. It is likely that some identified me, as an independent woman, an academic, and someone doing "research on women," as a feminist and thus expressed these opinions more readily, comfortably, or forcefully than they might have to other guests. However, in most cases, the opinions expressed were evidently the result of previous thought and discussion. Many women said explicitly that they discussed these issues with family, friends, and husbands, as well as read about them in the newspaper or watched related things on television.

Bibliography

Abrams, Mark. *The Population of Great Britain: Current Trends and Future Prospects.* London: George, Allen and Unwin 1945.

Advertising Association. *Find Out About Advertising.* London: Advertising Association 1979.

– "Advertising Expenditure." *Forecast of Advertising Expenditure.* London: Advertising Association 1980.

Alison, L. "Strolling across Sussex." *New Society* (10 July 1980): 78–80.

Ambrose, Peter. *Who plans the Brighton area housing crisis? A study of the relationship between structure and housing scarcity with case study material from the Brighton area.* Brighton: unpublished paper 1976.

Atwood, Margaret. *The Handmaid's Tale.* Toronto: McClelland and Stewart 1985.

Association of Radical Midwives. Correspondence, Leaflets. London: Association of Radical Midwives 1981.

Barrett, Michele, and McIntosh, Mary. "'The Family Wage': Some Problems for Socialists and Feminists." *Capital and Class* 11 (1980): 51–72.

Barrow, Ruby. *Report on Whitehawk Youth and Community Work.* Brighton: Whitehawk Community Centre 1975.

– *Report on Whitehawk and Marine Area.* Brighton: Whitehawk Community Centre 1978.

Baxter, R.G., and Howe, D.J. "Municipal Activities in Brighton during the Past Twelve Years: A Record of the Engineering and Allied Work 1924–1936." *Institute of Municipal and County Engineers Journal* (7 July 1936): 31–76.

Beard, Mary. *Women As a Force in History: A Study in Traditions and Realities.* New York: Collier 1962.

Bebel, August. *Women Under Socialism.* New York: Schocken Books 1971.

Beechey, Veronica. "Some Notes on Female Wage Labour in Capitalist Production." *Capital and Class* 3 (1977): 45–66.

Bennett, Mathew, ed. *Situations Vacant: Unemployment in Our Area: A Discussion Paper.* Brighton: University of Sussex Centre for Continuing Education 1976.

– Housing in Brighton, *Occasional Paper* 7. Centre for Continuing Education, University of Sussex, Brighton 1977.

Beveridge, William et. al. *Changes in Family Life.* London: George Allen and Unwin 1932.

Bhaskar, Roy. "On the Possibility of Social Scientific Knowledge and the Limists of Naturalism." *Journal for the Theory of Social Behaviour* 8, no. 1 (1978): 1–28.

Birke, Lynda. "From Zero to Infinity: Scientific Views of Lesbians." In Brighton Women and Science Group, *Alice Through the Microscope: The Power of Science over Women's Lives*, 108–23. London: Virago 1980.

Birmingham Feminist History Group. "Feminism as Femininity in the Nineteen Fifties?" *Feminist Review* 3 (1979): 48–65.

Birth Control Trust. *Abortion: the NHS and the Charities*. London: Birth Control Trust 1977.

Bowlby, John. *Childcare and the Growth of Love*. Harmondsworth: Penguin 1963.

Bowlby, Sophie, Foord, Jo, and Mackenzie, Suzanne. "Feminism in Geography." *Area* 13, no. 4 (1981): 19–25.

Brackx, Anny. "Prejudice and Pride." In Feminist Anthology Collective, eds., *No Turning Back: Writing from the Women's Liberation Movement, 1975–1980*, 162–71. London: Stage 1 1981.

Branson, Noreen, and Heineman, Margot. *Britain in the Nineteen Thirties*. St. Albans: Panther 1973.

Braverman, Harry. *Labour and Monopoly Capital: The Degradation of Work in the Twentieth Century*. New York: Monthly Review Press 1974.

Brighton Campaign for Day Care Abortion. *Working Party Report*. Brighton: Brighton National Abortion Campaign 1979.

Brighton Co-operative Society. Leaflets. Brighton: Co-operative Society 1981.

Brighton Corporation. *Brighton and Hove Official Guides*. 1953–69.

– *Financial Statistics*. 1949–68.

– Borough Treasurer's Department. *Brighton's Finances*. 1969–80.

– Children's Department. *Annual Reports*. 1953–4, 1958–9.

– Housing Department. *Council Housing in Brighton*. 1967.

– Housing Department. *Housing Allocation Scheme* 1970.

– Housing Manager. *Annual Reports*. 1949–64, 1965–7.

– Medical Officer of Health. *Annual Reports*. 1950–73.

– Planning Commmittee. *Planning Central Areas, Report and Development Plan*. 1937.

– Planning Committee. *Brief Report on Outline Development Plan for the Borough*. 1951.

– Planning Committee. *Development Plan, 1953*. 1953.

– Planning Committee. *Town and Country Planning Act 1962 Development Plan*. 1962.

– Planning Committee. *Reports of Survey Amendments and Comprehensive Development Areas*. Number 6 Hollingbury Industrial Estate. 1966.

– Planning Department. *Old Town Scheme*. 1974.

– School Medical Officer. *Annual Reports*. 1940–73.

– *Town Council Agenda and Proceedings*. 1949–81.

Brighton Evening Argus. 1949–81.

Brighton Health District, Community Health Council *Annual Reports*. 1974–81.

Brighton Hospitals Bulletin 1971–4. Continues as *Brighton Health Bulletin* 5. 1974–6. 1981.

Brighton Hove and District Joint Town Planning Advisory Committee. *Preliminary Report.* 1928.

– *Report of the Regional Planning Scheme.* 1932.

Brighton Hove and District Trades Council, *Annual Reports.* 1949, 1961, 1963–4, 1966–81.

– *Bulletin.* 1978–9.

– *Minutes.* 1919–50, 1958–60, 1963–72, 1974–81.

– *Executive Committee Minutes.* 1951–3, 1958–60, 1963–81.

– *Women's Committee Minutes.* 1981.

– *Brighton Trades Council: 1890–1950.* Brighton: Trades Council 1950.

– History Sub-committee. *A History of Brighton Trades Council and Labour Movement, 1890–1970.* Brighton: Trades Council 1974.

Brighton and Hove Gazette. *Year Book and Guide.* 1950–3, 1977–80.

Brighton and Hove Mothercraft Training Society. *Annual Report.* Brighton: Brighton and Hove Mothercraft Training Society 1981.

Brighton Liaison Group for Under Fives. *Minutes.* 1979–81.

Brighton Marina Ad-Hoc Campaign. *The Brighton Marina Outrage.* Brighton: Brighton Voice 1974.

– *Marina Campaign Newsletters* and *Factsheets.* Brighton: Marina Campaign 1974.

Brighton Nursery Schools Joint Action Committee. *Save Brighton's Nursery Schools.* Brighton: Brighton Nursery Schools Joint Action Committee 1981.

Brighton Social Services Department. *Day Care Services for Children Under Five in Brighton.* Brighton: Social Services Department 1980.

– *Childminders Newsletter.* Brighton: Social Services Department 1980–1.

Brighton Unemployed Women's Group. *Thoughts on the Structure of the Centre from the Unemployed Women's Group.* Mimeo, Brighton: Workers Centre for the Unemployed 1981.

Brighton Urban Structure Plan Team. *Brighton Urban Structure Plan Survey Reports.* Brighton: Urban Structure Plan Team 1971.

– *Greater Brighton Urban Structure Plan Draft Written Statement.* Brighton: Urban Structure Plan Team 1971.

Brighton Voice. 1973–81.

Brighton Women and Science Group 1980. "Technology in the Lying in Room." In Brighton Women and Science Group, *Alice Through the Microscope: The Power of Science over Women's Lives,* 165–81. London: Virago 1980.

Brighton Workers' Centre for the Unemployed. *Information Bulletins.* Mimeos, Brighton: Workers' Centre for the Unemployed 1981.

Brittain, Vera. *Lady into Woman.* London: Andrew Dakers 1953.

– *Testament of Youth: An Autobiographical Study the Years 1900–1925.* London: Fontana/Virago 1979.

Brook Advisory Centres. *Annual Report, 1979/80.* London: Brook Advisory Centre 1981.

– Mimeographed information, correspondence. London: Brook Advisory Centre 1981.

Brooks, Edwin. *This Crowded Kingdom: An Essay on Population Pressure in Great Britain.* London: Charles Knight 1973.

Brophy, Julia, and Smart, Carol. "From Disregard to Disrepute: The Position Of Women in Family Law." *Feminist Review* 9 (1981): 3–16.

Campaign Against DepoProvera. Mimeographed information, correspondence. London: Campaign Against DepoProvera 1981.

Campaign for Common Sense on Abortion. *Abortion Black Spots.* London: Campaign for Common Sense on Abortion 1981.

Clark, Alice. *Working Life of Women in the Seventeenth Century.* London: Frank Cass 1968.

Conference of Socialist Economists, Brighton Labour Process Group. *A Case Study of Creeds.* Mimeo. Brighton: Conference of Socialist Economists 1976.

Connell, Robert. *Gender and Power.* Cambridge: Polity Press 1987.

Cooke, Philip, ed. *Global Restructuring, Local Response.* London: Economic and Social Research Council 1986.

Co-operative Women's Guild. *Rules.* London: Co-operative Women's Guild 1966.

Co-ord. Correspondence, leaflets. London: Co-ord 1981.

Coote, Anna. "The Long Fight Out of Silence." In Anne Coote and Peter Kellner, eds., *Hear This Brother: Women Workers and Union Power*, 7–9. London: New Statesman 1980.

– "Powerlessness and How to Fight It." In Anna Coote and Peter Kellner, eds., *Hear this Brother: Women Workers and Union Power*, 10–24. London: New Statesman 1980.

Coote, Anna, and Kellner, Peter. "What Employers Do and Say." In Anna Coote and Peter Kellner, eds., *Hear This Brother: Women Workers and Union Power*, 41–5. London: New Statesman 1980.

Counter Information Service. *Women Under Attack.* CIS Anti Report 15, London: Counter Information Services 1976.

– *Women in the 1980s.* London: Counter Information Services 1981.

deBeauvoir, Simone. *The Second Sex.* New York: Bantam 1961.

Douie, Vera. *The Lesser Half: A Survey of the Laws, Regulations and Practices Introduced During the Present War Which Embody Discrimination Against Women.* London: Women's Publicity Planning Association circa 1945.

Dubinsky, Karen. "Lament for a Patriarchy Lost?: Anti-feminism, Anti-abortion and REAL Women in Canada." In *Feminist Perspectives* 1. Ottawa: Canadian Research Institute for the Advancement of Women/Insitut Canadien de Recherches sur les Femmes 1985.

Dworkin, Andrea. *Right Wing Women.* New York: G.P. Putnam Sons 1983.

East Sussex Area Health Authority. *Brighton Health District Community Health Services Statistics.* Lewes: East Sussex Area Health Authority 1975–80.

– Information Services Department. *Child Health Statistics.* Lewes: East Sussex Area Health Authority 1976–80.

– Information Services Department. *Health Statistics*. Lewes: East Sussex Area Health Authority 1976–80.

East Sussex County Council. *Urban Programme: Evidence of Social Need*. Lewes: East Sussex County Council 1978.

– *Resource Allocation Statement and Departmental Information Gazette*. Lewes: East Sussex County Council 1979/80.

– County Engineer's Department. *Brighton Area Traffic Management Study*. Lewes: East Sussex County Council 1973.

– Social Services Department. *Report of the Departmental Working Group on the Under Fives*. Lewes: East Sussex County Council 1976.

– Social Services Department. *Preschool Groups, Nurseries and Childminders Regulations Act, 1948 and Health and Services and Public Health Act, 1968*. Lewes: East Sussex County Council 1979.

East Sussex Preschool Playgroups Association. *Summary of Survey*. Brighton: Preschool Playgroup Association 1980.

Edwards, Dudley. *Unemployed Workers Union: A Few Ideas*. Mimeo. Brighton: Workers Centre for the Unemployed 1981.

Edwards, S. *St. George's Infants 1880 – Queen's Park First, 1980*. Brighton: Queen's Park School 1980.

Ehrenreich, Barbara, and English, Dierdre. *For Her Own Good: 150 Years of the Expert's Advice to Women*. London: Pluto Press 1979.

Ehrlich, Paul. *The Population Bomb*. London: Ballantine/Friends of the Earth 1971.

Eichler, Margrit. "The Pro-family Movement: Are They For or Against Families?" In *Feminist Perspectives* 4a. Ottawa: Canadian Research Institute for the Advancement of Women/Institut Canadien de Recherches sur les Femmes 1985.

Electrical Association for Women. *55th Annual Report 1979/80*. London: Electrical Association for Women 1980.

– Correspondence, mimeographed information. London: Electrical Association for Women 1981.

Engels, Frederick. "The Origin of the Family, Private Property and the State." In Karl Marx and Frederick Engels, *Selected Works*, 449–583. Moscow: Progress 1970.

Equal Opportunities Commission. *Annual Reports*. Manchester: Equal Opportunities Commission 1977–80.

– *Equality Between the Sexes in Industry: How Far Have We Come?* Manchester: Equal Opportunities Commission 1981.

Eugenics Society. Correspondence and leaflets. London: Eugenics Society 1981.

Fairbains, Zoe. *Benefits*. London: Virago 1979.

Family Planning Association Working Party. *Family Planning in the Sixties*. London: Family Planning Association 1963.

Family Planning Information Services. *Inform*. London: Family Planning Information Services 1974–80.

– *Fact Sheets*. London: Family Planning Information Services 1977–81.

Family Welfare Association. *Annual Report 1979/80*. London: Family Welfare Association 1981.

– Leaflets, correspondence. London: Family Welfare Association 1981.

Farrant, Sue. "The Early Growth of the Seaside Resorts c.1750 to 1840." In The Geography Editorial Committee, eds., *Sussex: Environment, Landscape and Society*, 208–20. Gloucester: Alan Sutton 1983.

Ferguson, Sheila, and Fitzgerald, Hilda. *Social Services, U.K. History of the Second World War*. London: HMSO 1954.

Fielding, Anthony, and Dunford, Mike. "Population and Employment in Sussex 1950–80." In The Geography Editorial Committee, eds., *Sussex: Environment, Landscape and Society*, 270–92. Gloucester: Alan Sutton 1983.

Fothergill, S., and Gudgin, G. *Unequal Growth*. London: Heinemann 1982.

Fransella, Fran, and Frost, Kay. *On Being a Women: A Review of Research on How Women See Themselves*. London: Tavistock 1977.

Friedan, Betty. *The Feminine Mystique*. New York: Dell 1963.

Friend, Andrew, and Metcalf, Andy. *Slump City: the Politics of Mass Unemployment*. London: Pluto 1981.

The Guardian. 1979–81.

Gavron, Hannah. *The Captive Wife: Conflicts of House Bound Mothers*. Harmondsworth: Penguin 1966.

George, Victor. *Social Security: Beveridge and After*. London: Routledge and Kegan Paul 1968.

Giddens, Anthony. *Central Problems in Social Theory: Action Structure and Contradiction in Social Analysis*. London: Macmillan 1979.

– *A Contemporary Critique of Historical Materialism*. Vol. 1, *Power, Property and the State*. Berkeley: University of California 1981.

Gilbert, Edmund. *Brighton, Old Ocean's Bauble*. Hassocks: Flare 1975.

Gilbert, Peter. *The New Dragon Enclosed: A History of Three Brighton Council Estates*. Masters Thesis, University of Sussex, Brighton 1977.

Gill, Colin. *Work, Unemployment and the New Technology*. London: Polity 1985.

Gilman, Charlotte. *Women and Economics*. New York: Harper and Row 1966.

Gittens, Diana. "Married Life and Birth Control between the Wars." *Oral History* 3 no. 2 (1975): 53–64.

Good Housekeeping Institute. *Short History*. London: Good Housekeeping Institute 1980.

– Correspondence, mimeographed information. London: Good Housekeeping Institute 1981.

Gray, Fred. "Housing in Sussex: Affluence and Poverty." In The Geography Editorial Committee, eds., *Sussex: Environment, Landscape and Society*, 250–69. Gloucester: Alan Sutton 1983.

Great Britain, Department of Employment. *Women and Work: A Statistical Survey.* Manpower Paper 9. London: HMSO 1974.

– Department of Environment. *Brighton Area East West Trunk Road.* London: HMSO 1973.

– Department of Health and Social Security.

Community Health Service Statistics for Brighton Health District. London: HMSO 1975–80.

– His Majesty's Government. *Report on the Social Insurance and Allied Services.* Cmnd 6404. London: HMSO 1942.

– Office of Population Censuses and Surveys. *Census.* 1921–81. London: HMSO.

– Office of Population Censuses and Surveys. *Population Trends.* London: HMSO.

– Office of Population Censuses and Surveys. *Social Trends.* London: HMSO.

– Office of Population Censuses and Surveys, General Household Survey Unit. "The Changing Circumstances of Women, 1971–1976." *Population Trends* 13 (1978): London: HMSO.

– Registrar General. *Statistical Review.* London: HMSO 1951–73.

Greene, Graham. *Brighton Rock.* Harmondsworth: Penguin 1970.

Greer, Germaine. *The Female Eunuch.* London: Paladin 1975.

Hakim, Katharine. "Homeworking: Some New Evidence." *Employment Gazette* (October, 1980): 1105–10.

Harding, Sandra, ed., *Feminism and Methodology: Social Science Issues.* Bloomington, Indiana: Indiana University Press and Milton Keynes: Open University Press 1987.

Harris, C. "Comment on Willmott." In M. Buxton and E. Craven, eds., *The Uncertain Future: Demographic Change and Social Policy.* London: Centre for Studies in Social Policy 1976.

Hartsock, Nancy. "Feminist Theory and the Development of Revolutionary Strategy." In Zilla Eisenstein, ed., *Capitalist Patriarchy and the Case for Socialist Feminism*, 56–77. New York: Monthly Review 1979.

Himmelweit, Susan. "Abortion: Individual Choice and Social Control." *Feminist Review* 5 (1980): 65–8.

Horrocks, Joan. "The Work of the Consumer Standards Advisory Committee." *Journal of Consumer Studies and Home Economics*, 1 (1977): 183–91.

Hurstfield, Jennifer. *The Part-time Trap: Part-time Workers in Britain Today.* Low Pay Pamphlet 9, London: Low Pay Unit 1978.

Huws, Ursula. *Your Job in the Eighties: A Woman's Guide to the New Technology.* London: Pluto 1982.

Institute of Municipal Treasurers and Accountants. *Housing Statistics.* London: Institute of Municipal Treasurers and Accountants 1950–68.

Jackson, Brian, and Jackson, Sonia. *Childminder: A Study in Action Research.* Harmondsworth: Penguin 1979.

Jephcott, Pearl, Seear, Nancy, and Smith, John. *Married Women Working.* London: Allen and Unwin 1962.

Job Sharing Project. Correspondence, leaflets, newsletters. London: Job Sharing Project 1981.

Kellner, Peter. "The Working Woman: Her Job, Her Politics and Her Union." In Anna Coote and Peter Kellner, eds., *Hear This Brother: Women Workers and Union Power*, 25–39. London: New Statesman 1980.

Klein, Viola. *Britain's Married Women Workers*. London: Routledge and Kegan Paul 1965.

Klodawsky, Fran, and Mackenzie, Suzanne. Gender Sensitive Theory and the Housing Needs of Mother-led Families: Some Concepts and Some Buildings. In *Feminist Perspectives* 8. Ottawa: Canadian Research Institute for the Advancement of Women/Institut Canadien de Recherches sur les Femmes 1987.

Kuhn, Annette, and Wolpe, Ann-Marie. "Feminism and Materialism." In Annette Kuhn and Ann-Marie Wolpe, eds. *Feminism and Materialism: Women and Modes of Production*, 1–10. London: Routledge and Kegan Paul 1978.

Land, Hilary. "The Family Wage." *Feminist Review* 6 (1980): 55–78.

Lafitte, Francois. *The Abortion Hurdle Race: The Role of the Doctor as a Taker of Abortion Decisions*. London: British Pregnancy Advisory Service 1975.

Leathard, Audrey. *The Fight for Family Planning: The Development of Family Planning Services in Britain, 1921–74*. London: Macmillan 1980.

Lister, Ruth, and Wilson, Leo. *The Unequal Breadwinner: A New Perspective on Woman and Social Security*. London: National Council for Civil Liberties 1976.

Lloyd, Peter, and Shutt, John. "Recession and Restructuring in the North-West Region, 1974–1982: The Implications of Recent Events." In Doreen Massey and Richard Meegan, eds., *Politics and Method: Contrasting Studies in Industrial Geography*, 16–60. London: Methuen 1985.

London Women's Liberation Workshop, Tuffnell Park Group. "Organizing Ourselves." In Michelene Wandor, ed., *The Body Politic: Women's Liberation in Britain, 1968–1972*, 103–7. London: Stage 1 1972.

London Women's Parliament. *Woman Power*. London: London Women's Parliament n.d. circa 1941.

Lowerson, John. "Resorts, Ports and 'Sleepy Hollows': Sussex Towns 1840–1940." In The Geography Editorial Committee, eds., *Sussex: Environment, Landscape and Society*, 221–34. Gloucester: Alan Sutton 1983.

Mackenzie, Suzanne. *Women and the Reproduction of Labour Power in the Industrial City: A Case Study*. University of Sussex Urban and Regional Studies Working Paper 23. Brighton: University of Sussex 1980.

– "Editorial Introduction." *Antipode* 16(3) (1984): 3–10.

– "Women's Responses to Economic Restructuring: Changing Gender, Changing Space." In Roberta Hamilton and Michele Barrett, eds., *The Politics of Diversity: Feminism, Marxism and Nationalism*, 81–100. London: Verso 1986.

– "Neglected Spaces in Peripheral Places: Homeworkers and the Creation of a New Economic Centre." *Cahiers de Geographie du Quebec* 83 (1987): 247–60.

– "Building Women, Building Cities: Toward Gender-Sensitive Theory in the

Environmental Disciplines." In Caroline Andrew and Beth Moore-Milroy, eds., *Life Spaces: Gender, Household, Employment*, 13–30. Vancouver: University of British Columbia Press 1988.

Mackenzie, Suzanne, and Rose, Damaris. "Industrial Change, the Domestic Economy and Home Life." In Jim Anderson, Simon Duncan and Ray Hudson, eds., *Redundant Spaces in Cities and Regions? Social Geography and Industrial Change*, 155–99. London: Academic 1983.

McIntosh, Andrew. "Women at Work: A Survey of Employers." *Employment Gazette*. (November, 1980): 1142–9.

McRobbie, Angela. "The Politics of Feminist Research: Between Talk, Text and Action." *Feminist Review* 12 (1982): 46–57.

Markusen, Ann. "City Spatial Structure, Women's Household Work, and National Urban Policy." In Catharine Stimpson et. al., eds., *Women and the American City*, 20–41. Chicago: University of Chicago Press 1980.

Massey, Doreen, and Meegan, Richard. "Industrial Restructuring Versus the Cities." *Urban Studies* 15 (1978): 273–88.

– eds. *Politics and Method: Contrasting Studies in Industrial Geography*. London: Methuen 1985.

Maternity Alliance. *Conclusions and Recommendations of Perinatal and Neonatal Mortality: The Report of the Social Services Committee, 1980*. London: Health Education Council 1981.

Mitchell, Juliet. *Psycho-analysis and Feminism*. New York: Vintage 1975.

Moroney, Robert. *The Family and the State: Considerations for Social Policy*. London: Longmans 1976.

Moss, Les. *Live and Learn: a Life and Struggle for Progress*. Brighton: QueenSpark Books 1979.

Murgatroyd, Linda, Savage, Mike, Shapiro, Dan, Urry, John, Walby, Sylvia, Warde, Alan, with Mark-Lawson, Jane. *Localities, Class and Gender*. London: Pion 1985.

Myrdal, Alva, and Klein, Viola. *Women's Two Roles: Home and Work*. London: Routledge and Kegan Paul 1968.

National Abortion Campaign. *Statement of Principles*. Mimeo. London: National Abortion Campaign 1980.

National Association for Maternal and Child Welfare. *Brief History*. London: National Association for Maternal and Child Welfare 1981.

– *Annual Report*. London: National Association for Maternal and Child Welfare 1981.

National Association of Women's Clubs. *Annual Report*. London: National Association of Women's Clubs 1981.

National Campaign for Nursery Education. *Questions on Nursery Education for Use During General and Local Elections*. London: National Campaign for Nursery Education 1978.

– *Statement of Principle*. London: National Campaign for Nursery Education 1980.

– *Nursery Education Under Attack.* London: National Campaign for Nursery Education 1981.

National Childbirth Trust. Correspondence, leaflets. London: National Childbirth Trust 1980.

– Brighton and Hove Branch. *Newsletters.* Brighton: National Childbirth Trust 1981.

National Childcare Campaign. *Newsletters.* London: National Childcare Campaign 1980–1.

– *Nurseries: How and Why to Fight for Them.* London: National Childcare Campaign 1981.

National Childminding Association. *Who Cares? The Newsletter of the National Childminding Association.* London: National Childminders Association 1979–83.

– *National Childminding Association.* London: National Childminding Association 1981.

National Consumer Congress. *Directory.* London: National Consumer Congress 1981.

National Equal Opportunities Committee. *Women and the Cuts.* Mimeo. Manchester: National Equal Opportunities Committee 1980.

Nava, Michaela. "The Family: A Critique of Certain Features." In Michelene Wandor, ed., *The Body Politic: Women's Liberation in Britain 1969–1972*, 36–44. London: Stage 1 1972.

Oakley, Ann. *Woman's Work: The Housewife Past and Present.* New York: Vintage 1976.

– "Interviewing Women: A Contradiction in Terms." In Helen Roberts, ed., *Doing Feminist Research*, 30–61. London: Routledge and Kegan Paul 1981.

Oren, Laura. "The Welfare of Women in Labouring Families: England, 1860–1950." In Mary Hartman and Lois Banner, eds., *Clio's Consciousness Raised: New Perspectives on the History of Women*, 226–44. New York: Harper and Row 1974.

Pahl, Ray. *Divisions of Labour.* Oxford: Basil Blackwell 1984.

Piercy, Marge. *Woman on the Edge of Time.* New York: Fawcett Crest 1976.

Pill Victims Action Group. Correspondence and mimeographed information. London: Pill Victim's Action Group 1981.

Political and Economic Planning. *Population Policy in Great Britain.* London: Political and Economic Planning 1948.

Pond, Chris, and Bennett, Fran. *Low Pay – 1980s Style.* Low Pay Review 4. London: Low Pay Unit 1981.

Population Investigation Committee. *Towards a Population Policy for the United Kingdom.* Supplement to Population Studies. London: Population Investigation Committee 1970.

Poulantzas, Nicos. *Classes in Contemporary Capitalism.* London: New Left Review 1975.

Pregnancy Advisory Service. Correspondence and leaflets. London: Pregnancy Advisory Service 1981.

PreSchool Playgroups Association. *Report on Parental Involvement in Playgroups.* London: PreSchool Playgroups Association 1978.

– *Membership Form.* London: PreSchool Playgroups Association 1979–80.

– PPA *Coming Of Age in the Eighties: Thoughts of the President and Vice-Presidents.* London: PreSchool Playgroups Association 1980.

Queen'spark. 1979–81. Brighton.

Radwan, Eva. *Whitehawk: The Awakening of a Community.* Brighton: Sussex Association of Youth Clubs 1970.

Reddaway, William. *The Economics of Declining Population.* London: Allen and Unwin 1939.

Rich, Adrienne. *Of Woman Born: Motherhood as Experience and Institution.* Toronto: Bantam 1977.

Riley, Denise. "War in the Nursery." *Feminist Review* 2 (1979): 82–108.

Roberts, Helen, ed. *Doing Feminist Research.* London: Routledge and Kegan Paul 1981.

Rosembaum, S. "Social Services Manpower." *Social Trends* 2 (1981): 2–8.

Rowbotham, Sheila. "Women's Liberation and the New Politics." In Michelene Wandor, ed. *The Body Politic: Women's Liberation in Britain, 1969–1972,* 3–20. London: Stage 1 1972.

– "The Beginnings of Women's Liberation in Britain." In Michelene Wandor, ed., *The Body Politic: Women's Liberation in Britain, 1969–1972,* 91–102. London: Stage 1 1972.

– "The Women's Movement and Organising for Socialism." In Sheila Rowbotham, Lynn Segal and Hilary Wainwright, eds., *Beyond the Fragments: Feminism and the Making of Socialism,* 21–157. London: Merlin 1979.

Rowe, Kay. *Nursery Education and Equal Opportunities for Women.* National Campaign for Nursery Education 1977.

Rubin, Lillian. *Worlds of Pain: Life in the Working Class Family.* New York: Basic 1976.

Save Brighton's Station Campaign. *The Brighton Station Scandal.* Brighton: Save Brighton Station Campaign 1974.

Sayer, Andrew. "Defensible Values in Geography: Can Values be Science Free?" In David Herbert and Ron Johnston, eds., *Geography and the Urban Environment,* 29–56. London: John Wiley 1981.

Schenk, Faith, and Parkes, A. *The Activities of the Eugenics Society.* London: Eugenics Society 1969.

Segal, Lynn. *Is the Future Female? Troubled Thoughts on Contemporary Feminism.* London: Virago 1987.

Sharp, Evelyn. *Buyers and Builders: The Jubilee Sketch of the Women's Co-operative Guild, 1882–1933.* London: Women's Co-operative Guild 1933.

Smith, Nan. "A Brief Outline of the Background to and the Development of the BPAS" London: British Pregnancy Advisory Service 1977.

Society to Support Home Confinements. Correspondence, mimeographed information. London: Society to Support Home Confinements 1981.

Spring Rice, Margery. *Working Class Wives: Their Health and Conditions*. London: Virago 1981.

Stageman, Jane. "A Study of Trade Union Branches in the Hull Area." In Anna Coote and Peter Kellner, eds., *Hear This Brother: Women Workers and Union Power*, 49–62. London: New Statesman 1980.

Stanley, Liz, and Wise, Sue. *Breaking Out: Feminist Consciousness and Feminist Research*. London: Routledge and Kegan Paul 1983.

Steering Committee on the Under Fives Group. *TUF Group*. Brighton: Steering Committee of the Under Fives Group 1981.

Thirkell, Angela. *Peace Breaks Out*. London: Hamish Hamilton 1946.

Tilly, Louise, and Scott, Joan. *Women, Work and Family*. New York: Holt, Rinehart and Winston 1978.

Titmuss, Richard. *Poverty and Population*. London: Macmillan 1938.

– *Essays on the Welfare State*. London: Allen and Unwin 1958.

Titmuss, Richard, and Titmuss, K. *Parents' Revolt: A Study of the Declining Birth Rate in Acquisative Society*. London: Secker and Warberg 1942.

Townsend, Alan and Peck, Francis. "An Approach to the Analysis of Redundancies in the UK (post-1976): Some Methodological Problems and Policy Implications." In Doreen Massey and Richard Meegan, eds., *Politics and Method: Contrasting Studies in Industrial Geography*, 64–91. London: Methuen 1985.

Trades Union Congress. *The Under Fives: Report of a TUC Working Party*. London: Trades Union Congress 1978.

– *TUC Charter on Facilities for the Under Fives*. London: Trades Union Congress 1979.

– *Women Workers: 1980: Report for 1979–1980 of the TUC Women's Advisory Committee and Report of the 50th TUC Women's Conference*. London: Trade Union Congress 1980.

– *Unemployed Workers' Centres: TUC Action Program*. Circular 205. London: Trades Union Congress 1981.

Tressell, Robert. *The Ragged Trousered Philanthropists*. London: Granada 1965.

Ursel, Jane. "The State and the Maintenance of Patriarchy: A Case study of Family, Labour and Welfare Legislation in Canada." In James Dickinson and Bob Russell, eds., *Family, Economy and State: The Social Reproduction Process Under Capitalism*, 150–91. Toronto: Garamond 1986.

Wainwright, Hilary. "Introduction." In Sheila Rowbotham, Lynn Segal and Hilary Wainwright, eds., *Beyond the Fragments: Feminism and the Making of Socialism*, 211–53. London: Merlin 1979.

Wallsgrove, Ruth. "The Masculine Face of Science." In Brighton Women and Science Group, *Alice Through the Microscope: The Power of Science Over Women's Lives*, 228–40. London: Virago 1980.

Walsh, Vivian. "Contraception: The Growth of a Technology." In Brighton

Women and Science Group, *Alice Through the Microscope: The Power of Science Over Women's Lives*, 182–207. London: Virago 1980.

Wandor, Michelene. "Introduction." In Michelene Wandor, ed., *The Body Politic: Women's Liberation in Britain, 1968–1972*, 1–5. London: Stage 1 1972.

– "The Small Group." In Michelene Wandor, ed., *The Body Politic: Women's Liberation in Britain, 1968–1972*, 107–16. London: Stage 1 1972.

Wekerle, Gerda, Peterson, Rebecca, and Morley, David. "Introduction." In Gerda Wekerle, Rebecca Peterson, and David Morley, eds., *New Space for Women*, 1–34. Boulder, Colorado: Westview 1980.

West, Jackie. "Women, Sex and Class." In Annette Kuhn and Ann-Marie Wolpe, eds., *Feminism and Materialism: Women and Modes of Production*, 220–53. London: Routledge and Kegan Paul 1978.

Weston, J. "Brighton Housing Estates and Rural Development." *Institute of Municipal and County Engineers Journal* (7 July, 1936): 81–4.

White, Cynthia. *Women's Magazines, 1963–1968*. London: Michael Joseph 1970.

Whiting, Pat. "Female Sexuality: Its Political Implications." In Michelene Wandor, ed., *The Body Politic: Women's Liberation in Britain, 1968–1972*, 189–213. London: Stage 1 1972.

Williams, Raymond. *Marxism and Literature*. Oxford: Oxford University Press 1977.

– *Politics and Letters: Interviews with New Left Review*. London: New Left Review 1979.

Wilson, Elizabeth. *Women and the Welfare State*. London: Tavistock 1977.

– *Only Half Way to Paradise: Women in Post War Britain, 1945–1968*. London: Tavistock 1980.

Wilson, H.N., and Womersley, L. *Brighton Town Centre Interim Report*. Brighton: Brighton Corporation 1968.

Women's Committee for Peace and Democracy. *Will Your Child be Safe?* London: Women's Committee on Peace and Democracy 1939.

Women's Fightback 1980–3. London.

Women's Group on Public Welfare. *Our Towns: A Close Up*. London: Oxford University Press 1943.

Working Association of Mothers. *East WAM News*. Brighton: Working Association of Mothers 1981.

Working Party on Integrated Training for Under Fives Workers. *Working Party Report*. London: Working Party circa 1980.

Young, Michael, and Willmott, Peter. *The Symmetrical Family*. London: Routledge and Kegan Paul 1973.

Index